FROM CLASSROOM TO COURTROOM

Michael Craig Hillmann

authorHOUSE®

AuthorHouse™
1663 Liberty Drive, Suite 200
Bloomington, IN 47403
www.authorhouse.com
Phone: 1-800-839-8640

*This book is a work of non-fiction. Unless otherwise noted, the author
and the publisher make no explicit guarantees as to the accuracy
of the information contained in this book. In some cases, names of
people and places have been altered to protect their privacy.*

First published by AuthorHouse 1/9/2008

ISBN: 978-1-4343-5062-6 (sc)
ISBN: 978-1-4343-5064-0 (hc)

Library of Congress Control Number: 2007908734

Printed in the United States of America
Bloomington, Indiana

This book is printed on acid-free paper.

All inquiries should be directed to:
Michael Craig Hillmann
P.O. Box 8016, Austin, TX 78713, USA
512–653–5152 (tel), 512–458–2924 (tel/fax), mchillmann@aol.com

In memory of
Ralph J. Hillmann
(1892–1980)

TABLE OF CONTENTS

Chapter 1

A Court Deposition

"Question and answer is not a civilized form of conversation."
Patrick O'Brian

*"It takes two to speak the truth,
—one to speak, and another to hear."*
Henry David Thoreau

*"Je voudrais bien savoir si la grande règle
des toutes les règles n'est pas de plaire."*
Molière

*"If you're not annoying somebody,
you're not really alive."*
Margaret Atwood

The Clements Office Building on the northwest corner of Guadalupe and West 15th Streets in downtown Austin houses the Office of the Attorney General of the State of Texas. There, on September 9, 2002, I submitted to a court deposition, under subpoena by the Defendants, in a court case called "Aman Attieh vs. The University of Texas at Austin" [= UT].

My deposition, and seven or eight others before and after mine, came at the end of eight years of strife in UT's Department of Middle Eastern Languages and Cultures. The strife began when a Dean of the College of Liberal Arts named a Palestinian Christian Arab to serve as Chair of that department of fifteen faculty colleagues in Arabic, Hebrew, Persian, and Turkish. There followed almost constant complaints and allegations of favoritism, intimidation, abuse, harassment, and racism. On the heels of the later naming of an American-born Orthodox Jewish rabbi to the same position came charges of prevarication and dishonesty, harassment, ethnic, religious, and gender discrimination, initiation of three faculty grievance procedures, contested promotions cases, and allegations of plotting, wrongdoing, immorality, plagiarism,

1

and ghost writing of faculty research writing. In addition, there were charges "so serious" they were never revealed to the departmental faculty at large, along with an even larger number of student complaints, the wholesale exodus of graduate students from the department, and graduate student petitions to transfer supervision of their dissertations out of the department. Five or six UT faculty careers ended in the process, most dramatically and publicly among them that of a Lebanese Shi'ite Muslim Arab woman who had taught Arabic in the department for sixteen years. A Dean of the College of Liberal Arts threatened the first department Chair with dismissal from the faculty and dismissed the second from his Chair position.

I sat at the head of the long conference table in the 11th floor conference room of the General Litigation Division of the Attorney General's offices. A video camera stared at me from the other end of the table. The Shi'ite Muslim Arab woman's attorney sat halfway down the table to my left. Assistant Attorney General Judith Horowitz, representing UT, sat on the right side of the table. A room-length, floor-to-ceiling window behind her framed the landmark, 307–foot high University of Texas Tower.

As I was being sworn in, the thought crossed my mind that the fact of a court deposition made me much farther away from The Tower than the physical distance of eight blocks. Or maybe not. Under the Tower in the "Main Building" are UT's Office of Legal Affairs, which had initiated investigations of faculty in my department, including me, and the Office of the Provost, where our departmental faculty affairs underwent special review for years and where decisions which brought me the subpoena took place.

The deposition began as follows.

The Videographer: This is the video deposition of Michael Craig Hillmann held in Austin, Texas. The time is now 9:30 a.m. We are now on the record.
Horowitz (Q): Are you taking any medication that would impair your ability to give truthful answers today?
Hillmann (A): No, I'm not.
Q. I'm showing you what has been marked as Exhibit 1. Can you identify that for the record.
A. This is a mid-1990s curriculum vitae.
Q. Okay. I apologize. It's the most recent I could find.

Q. Looking at your CV on page 1 under "Professional Positions," you indicate "President, Perspepolis Enterprises." Can you tell me what that is?

A. Persepolis Enterprises [now Persepolis Institute, Inc.] is an ad hoc group of Persian and Arabic specialists who, since 1977, have been providing non-academic language training, test development, textbook writing, expert testimony in court proceedings, and other activities for business and government.

Q. So any royalties from textbooks go to you?

A. I don't write textbooks for royalties. I write textbooks for fees [paid upon manuscript completion]. If I wrote textbooks for royalties, then I would be in an [ethically] ambiguous position when I recommended adoption of the textbooks [in UT Persian courses].

Q. Did you offer Arabic [in a Persepolis program] last summer?

A. Yes.

Q. Did Dr. Aman Attieh [plaintiff in "Attieh v. UT"] teach Arabic at your summer program?

A. Yes.

Q. So she was here in Austin this summer teaching at your Arabic program?

A. Yes.

Q. Was there. . .another Arabic instructor this summer who worked for you?

A. Yes.

Q. Who was that?

A. Walid Hamarneh, who is Assistant Professor of Arabic and Comparative Literature at The University of Western Ontario; and Chaouki Moussa, who is a Ph.D. student in Arabic Studies at The University of Texas at Austin [and] a former Assistant Instructor of Arabic there.

Q. Walid Hamarneh was up for tenure at UT and was not granted tenure. Is that right?

A. That's correct.

Later in the deposition, this exchange took place.

Q. As of February 8, 2000, had you had any meetings with any student groups with respect to the status of the search [for a new Arabic language teaching position in the Department of Middle Eastern Languages and Cultures]?

A. That's a good question for an important reason. Throughout all of this [controversy in MELC over Attieh's position and a faculty search for someone to replace her], Professor [Robert] Stofberg [, 1998–2002 MELC Chair, assumed]—and the Dean also assumes—that I was involved with the students [protesting treatment of Attieh and] in fact writes to a student saying that I must have told the student something. Refuting a negative [characterization] is tough.

Q. Yes, it is, Dr. Hillmann. It's very tough.

A. I am on. . .under oath, right?

Q. Yes, you are.

A. I had no contact at any time with any students except at announced meetings of students and faculty and on one or two occasions when a student came to my office to ask questions [and] had nothing to do with any of the public relations, any of the activities of the SAAUT student group, and didn't know the names of people in the group until later. . .I understand why people have his notion [that I colluded with or influenced students], because I was perceived to be on Aman Attieh's side or Peter Abboud's side. But Sarmeena Karmally, Jack Tannous, Mark Sullivan, Alexa Firat, all the people in SAAUT will gladly, if someone pays their way, testify that I had no input in anything. In fact, what appealed to me most about this student movement was not that they were right or wrong, but that they knew how to do it on their own. I can't get a meeting with the president of The University of Texas at Austin. They had no trouble [meeting with him]. So whatever I've written, that's what I did.

Q. Okay.

A. In other words. . .the Dean is just plain wrong here.

The deposition then turned to a controversial appointment in Arabic in the spring of 2000.

Q. Is it your belief that the majority of the [MELC Executive Committee] faculty who voted for Dr. Mohammad Mohammad [to join MELC in 2000 as Associate Professor of Arabic] did not have a sincere belief that he was the better candidate?

A. They didn't have any grounds for such a conclusion, there being no discussion of his file at any meetings I attended and no discussion of his file and no written representation of his file at the meetings where we voted. . .As far as I could tell, I was the only person who had read his [book] manuscripts.

Q. His file was available for members of the Executive Committee to read, correct?

A. That's correct.

Q. And the members of the [Arabic] Search Committee all read all of the files, didn't they?

A. I doubt it, but it's possible.

Q. Well, you weren't on the Search Committee, so.

A. Why would you ask me the question then?

Q. Your answer implies. . .

A. It implies nothing. I have the doubt.

Q. [In your Equal Employment Opportunity Commission affidavit, it] "says that the people that made a decision didn't have a basis for making it because they lacked information," and in order for you to make that statement, Dr. Hillmann, you would have to know that they had not reviewed his file, correct?

A. No, of course not. That just doesn't make sense in terms of logic. I can have doubts about things to which I am not privy. Statement of doubt is a doubt.

Q. Well, let's go about it this way. Do you know whether Dr. Stofberg reviewed Dr. Mohammad's file?
A. I doubt it. . .Oh, no. No, I don't know.
Q. Do you know whether Peter Abboud reviewed Dr. Mohammad Mohammad's file?
A. Yes.
Q. Because he told you he did?
A. He later talked about it in such a way that could only have derived from his reading the same manuscripts I read.
Q. Okay. All right. And you read his file?
A. Yes.
Q. Did Dr. Zilkha read his file?
A. I doubt it. . .My doubts come from this. . .The procedure in our department at such meetings is for files to be put on the table, and then we watch faculty kind of grab for the files to look at them for the first time, and. . .two people at most have notes in front of them [showing] that they have actually read the files.
Q. Off the record [for a lunch break].

Before leaving the conference room for lunch, I asked Ms. Horowitz how much of the afternoon the deposition would likely use up. She hazarded a guess that it would continue until late in the day. So, after lunch in the building's first floor cafeteria, I called Sorayya from the foyer outside of the deposition room to tell her to pick me up after six. As I was talking to Sorayya, Assistant Attorney General Horowitz passed by and smiled.

The deposition resumed minutes later as follows.

The Videographer: We're back on record.
Q. Dr. Hillmann, did you have occasion to speak with anybody during the lunch break?
A. Yes.
Q. Did you speak with Peter Abboud?
A. No.
Q. Did you speak with Dr. Attieh?
A. No. I haven't spoken to Peter Abboud since July 15. I have said hello to Aman Attieh since then once and saw her socially once. . .[And] I've made it a point not to talk to them about any of this business.
Q. Well, regardless of whether you talked to them about this business, have you talked to them at all?
A. Yes [months ago]. That's what I've just said. [In any case] they don't know—my [telephone] conversation at lunch was in Persian. Neither one of them knows Persian.
Q. Okay.

Horowitz's questions momentarily caught me off guard. Then it dawned on me that people in cahoots naturally think other people are in cahoots. That realization led to a spontaneous decision right then and there to write *From Classroom to Courtroom*, to tell its story through an unadorned paper trail of complaints, grievances, reports, letters, memos, and depositions, without knowing how the story would turn out or what, if any, light it would shine on our Middle Eastern Studies enterprise. At that moment, I supposed that the story would high-light cultural conflicts and differences, American, Israeli, Arab, Jewish, Muslim, and Iranian(-American), which had brought a small depart-ment of Middle Eastern language faculty to the brink of a court trial.

Q. You've had her [Attieh] in your home?
A. Yes.
Q. You've been to her home?
A. Yes.
Q. On how many occasions have you been to dinner with her or in her home or she in your home where Dr. Abboud was not also there?
A. A little bit less than half the time.
Q. So the majority of the time Dr. Abboud is there?
A. Yes–well my wife invites nine or ten people and certainly wouldn't in-vite one Arabic colleague without the other.
Q. On how many occasions have you been out with Dr. Attieh and Dr. Abboud just as two couples?
A. Never.
Q. You've never been out with just them?
A. Oh, yes, but they're not a couple.
Q. Dr. Hillmann, isn't it true that while you and Sorayya were staying in Paris you invited Dr. Abboud and Dr. Attieh to come spend the holi-days with you?
A. That's possible. I don't recall that, but that's possible. We invited my brother to come. We invited lots of people to come. We were showing off. I invited them to come visit us when we were away in New York.
Q. Did they come?
A. Yes.
Q. Together?
A. Yes, on the same plane.
Q. Where did they stay?
A. At our house.
Q. In how many rooms, Dr. Hillmann?
A. One stayed in one bedroom, the other stayed in another bedroom. Gosh!
Q. Isn't it fair–isn't it true, Dr. Hillmann, that you extended an invitation to the two of them as a couple to come and stay with you in Paris?
A. Not by your definition of couple. . .the most important meaning for this gathering [deposition] is the word "coupling," the way Eliot used it in *Four Quartets*. Is that where we're getting to?

The University of Texas was presumably thinking that if it could establish that long-time widower Abboud and long-time single parent Attieh were having sex, they could argue that Attieh didn't deserve to keep her job as Senior Lecturer of Arabic or didn't deserve serious consideration for the new Associate Professor position in Arabic. The University of Texas, which prided itself on its non-Western programs, apparently had no idea about, or attached no importance to, the effects such an allegation could have psychologically on a middle-aged Muslim Arab woman academic in the context of her culture.

Q. [In an Equal Employment Opportunity Commission affidavit, you write under Item 6–] Her entire work history came under attack: "Since the fall of 1998, I have heard and read attacks on Aman Attieh's teaching, teaching methods, and teaching materials by MELC and DMES faculty unfamiliar with her textbooks and in-class methods. . ." Well, so what you're saying is that her entire work history did come under attack?
A. Yes.
Q. . . .by colleagues, correct? You're saying they were misguided.
A. No. I'm saying they didn't know Arabic or [language] teaching.
Q. But they did criticize her?
A. Yes. Oh, yes.
Q. You just disagree with the propriety of the criticism?
A. Not the propriety. The accuracy.
Q. Accuracy. All right. And you disagree with the propriety of Dr. Stofberg [MELC Chair, 1998–2002].
A. . . .I question the propriety of his penalizing her on the basis of her personality as an Arab Muslim woman.
Q. Well, and that's a phrase you keep using over and over and over again.
A. Because my only issue in all of this, that has me all these streets down from the University is February 16 [2000].
Q. And that's when she wasn't given an interview [for the new Arabic position]?
A. That's my only issue.
Q. Okay.
A. . . .everything else smacks to me of discrimination [in]. . .the behavior of MELC management. But the gun with the bullet coming out of it before the smoke even starts, for me, is that.
Q. Notwithstanding that if she had had the interview, there would have been no difference in outcome?
A. And do you not have trials where everybody knows what the outcome is going to be?
Q. Well, I'm not going to debate you, Dr. Hillmann. I think the record will speak for itself.
A. If that were true, we wouldn't be having this meeting.

Throughout the day, the Assistant Attorney General behaved as an official representative of The University of Texas at Austin in such fashion as to imply that people like me did not more essentially represent the same university. She had it reversed. I represented The University of Texas and its values as a university while she represented a slew of categorical, black and white, non-intellectual views inconsonant with much of university life. Her view, deriving in part from her employment responsibility to hold that view, that nothing positive existed on the plaintiff's side of a case, reminded me how far apart attorneys can cause classrooms and courtrooms to be. In the classroom I use texts to get students to realize that things aren't black and white, while Assistant Attorneys General in courtrooms use texts to get judges and juries to think that things are black and white.

The Assistant Attorney General also seemed not to appreciate how humanist academics like me think. When I told her that academics like me refuse and avoid administrative assignments and positions, she seemed not to believe me, as if a Persianist teacher-scholar should seek validation of academic competence by becoming director of a Center for Middle Eastern Studies or chairman of a Department of Middle Eastern Studies or dean of a College of Liberal Arts. For this humanist academic at Texas, my life of reflecting on texts and writing down my reflections makes for the best shot at a Pyrrhic triumph over transience. For this humanist academic, administrative chores would only decrease any chances of that and, before that, of living with and in discourse and dealing sanguinely and exuberantly with life's heady, steady march to its end.

That evening over dinner, I regaled Sorayya with an embellished deposition report in the conspiratorially dim lighting at nearby Mars Restaurant. When I told her of my plan to turn the experience into a book, she sighed, but acquiesced, perhaps kidding herself momentarily that a Howard Zin bestseller would come of it. I disabused her of such a hope by describing how I envisioned the book. It would present and characterize in chronological order documents which got my department from its classrooms to a courtroom, peppered with entries from personal journals from 1994 onward. To what end, I couldn't tell Sorayya, who shook her head as if to say—and she later said it when she read the book's first draft—no one would want to read such a story told in such a way. I thought, no matter, my story would mean that the audience for whom I would write the book would read it and would learn the facts of the case, who really said and did exactly what, even if the case was low stakes (except for one person). Moreover, my readers would easily fill in blanks and connect dots and get points. Finally, as the middle volume between *From Durham to Tehran* and *To and from a Village in Maine*, *From Classroom to Courtroom* would advance an autobiographical adventure.

Reza Abbasian (Sorayya's brother), Peter Abboud, Aman Attieh, and Sorayya on a PATH train from Jersey City to the World Trade Center. Winter 1994.

Chapter 2

1970–1993

"...that oldest human longing–self revelation."
Zora Neale Hurston

"Better to write twaddle, anything, than nothing at all."
Katherine Mansfield

When I back my car out of our garage and driveway weekday mornings and start down Perry Lane hill, I see the UT Tower in the southeast distance four miles away. Fifteen minutes later, walking with scores of other people across Guadalupe Street toward UT's West Mall, The Texas Union to my left and my West Mall Office Building destination a little farther along to the right, my thoughts turn to my world of language and literature. A review quiz in Second-year Persian that needs photocopying. Isn't there a better word in Persian for "sophisticated" than *bafarháng* or *farhikhté*? A lecture on Achebe's *Things Fall Apart*, which needs copies of Yeats's "The Second Coming" for discussion of its title. A revision of manuscript pages from *Sounds That Remain: Essays on Persian Poetry* which need printing.

If I don't remember to thank my lucky star for my kind of weekday life on the way to West Mall Office Building, I'll likely do so more than once later during the day, washing my hands in front of the mirror in the office men's room, the moment the bell rings to begin or end a class, or when I look up from my desk and see that it's dark outside, my absorption in reading or writing having stolen a couple of hours, purloining I never complain about.

The Tower sits in the middle of many University of Texas things. East, South, and West Malls fan out symmetrically from it. On the West Mall, students engage in what they think of as free speech on many days, with suited Dean of Students representatives in sun glasses listening from the porch of the Academic Center. On Wednesdays, clubs and service organizations set up tables on the West Mall to get their words out or to attract new members. When the University Tajik Association occasionally has a table, I join the group for an hour or so. From the South Mall extends an unobstructed view to the Texas State Capitol seven blocks south, with a life-size statue of Jefferson Davis almost presiding over part of the view, statues of Robert E. Lee, Albert Sidney Johnston, and John H. Reagan not far away. The Tower itself also reminds me almost every day of the August day in 1966, when Charles Whitman wounded a score of people and killed fourteen from atop it, among the latter a Peace Corps trainee preparing for two years in Iran where I was about to begin my second Peace Corps year as an Instructor of English at Mashhad University. Under the Tower in the Main Building are the President's Office, Office of the Provost, Instructional Technology Services, and Office of Legal Affairs. To the northeast of the Tower lies Gebauer Hall, UT's oldest building and home to the College of Liberal Arts where most of the complaints by and about Middle Eastern Languages faculty got aired and where a series of fateful pronouncements originated. Just east of the Tower lies the Flawn Academic Center, which houses the Equal Employment Opportunity Office where several Middle Eastern Languages faculty members filed complaints.

The West Mall Office Building, across from the Academic Center, is home to my department of fifteen or sixteen colleagues, a group of people of whom most students at one of America's biggest universities are unaware, even if everyone knows the West Mall Office Building because the University Station of the U.S. Postal Service occupies most of its basement floor. For years, until the move to the Gebauer Building in 1999, the College of Liberal Arts had its offices on WMB's fourth floor.

Offices for Middle Eastern Languages faculty occupy the back or south parts of the fifth and sixth floors of the West Mall Office Building. On the 5th floor—I take the stairs up and down instead of the elevator—one walks from the north front of the building past the busy and famous Center for Mexican and Mexican American Studies to reach a cluster of six windowless Middle Eastern Languages offices and five offices with windows. My office is at the south end of the corridor around the corner to the left next to the back stairs. In the mid-1990s, at a height of seven feet at the end of the main corridor a 4"x7" plastic plaque with "Michael Hillmann 5.146" on it jutted out from the wall. One day during the 1998–1999 academic year, a colleague broke the plaque off its bracket. The rationale for the action he presented with this rhetorical question in a later court deposition: "Why should only Michael Hillmann have a plaque on the wall announcing the location of his office?"

When the College of Liberal Arts decided in 1994 that the Department of Oriental and African Languages and Literatures would split into two departments, a Department of Middle Eastern Languages and Cultures (MELC) and a Department of Asian Studies, The Center for Middle Eastern Studies director of the day negotiated space for MELC on the 5th and 6th floors of the West Mall Office Building. The negotiation did not end well for MELC, both in the number of rooms allotted to it and the number of windowless rooms assigned to its faculty.

Upon hearing that more than half of our new offices would not have windows, I refrained from window shopping, ready to take any office assigned me. Of course, I knew that my books would get me an office with a window, which it did. In the case of two monographless associate professors, a flip of a coin decided which of them would get an office with a window and who wouldn't. Losing the coin toss made one of the two, already an unhappy camper, unhappier.

WMB 5.146, my office, is big enough for a 3.6'x8' table and six chairs in front of a row of bookcases on the south wall, a row of book cases on the opposite wall, my desk in between facing the table. My prized window—not unnoted by colleagues considering themselves less fortunate—faces east southeast and frames the north and west façades of Parlin Hall, home to UT's English Department. Working at my table in front of that window, I have often daydreamed about life over there in the English Department as opposed to the world of Middle Eastern Languages in WMB. I teach an occasional English course, among them "Classics of World Poetry," "Khayyam and His Place in Literature," and "Autobiography as a Literary Species." Some of my Persian language classes take place in Parlin Hall basement seminar rooms.

Most of my Persian literature courses take place in WMB 5.146, where photographs of Gholamhosayn Sa'edi, Nader Naderpur, Jalal Al-e Ahmad, Forugh Farrokhzad, Sadeq Chubak, and Sohrab Sepehri, and

Nasser Ovissi's painting of Sadeq Hedayat look on. Many lucky-star-thanking moments come in sessions there on "Ferdowsi's *Shahnamé* [Book of Kings] and the Persian Epic Tradition," "Hafez and the Persian Lyric Tradition," "Rumi and the Persian Sufi Tradition," and "*The Satanic Verses* and the Sociology of Literature."

From my office to the departmental photocopier and computer network printer in an inner office at WMB 5.120 and to the men's room still farther north in Mexican-American Center territory, my language and literature reverie often gets interrupted. Except for exhibits I put up occasionally or my bulletin board collage of things Tajik(i) and two display cases of faculty publications, the quiet corridor is often empty, a place of perfunctory hellos and wariness from its days as a Middle Eastern Languages combat zone. On any given day, I'll see three colleagues more than once who filed complaints and charges against me during the war years, when I didn't even consider myself a combatant. Their nods and grunts in response to my disingenuously cheery hellos tell me that they remember those complaints and charges. On some days, the hustle and bustle of Mexican-American Center activities, or the inviting aromas of their occasional breakfasts and lunches, liven things up. To and from the photocopy room or men's room, I hum tunes and put a special bounce in my step, a sort of daytime whistling in the dark light or a subconscious determination not to let my language and literature reverie dissipate.

The word "reverie" may make what I think about seem less substantial or significant than other things other people think about and act upon or do for a living. Paradoxically, it was a sense of practicality in youth that persuaded me to pursue the reverie and a life of reading, writing, and talking about language and literature.

In college, recognizing that I had better than average quickness on my verbal feet–although it took me years to learn to write simply and eschew passive voice verbs, Latinate diction, and convoluted sentences–and a penchant for debate, I knew as well as my father, who wanted it for me, that a career in law, in litigation, would best suit that personality. But what would have suited my personality wouldn't have suited my heart. I knew from my experience of some college courses and winter holiday and summer employment that I never wanted to learn any facts or concepts or entertain any ideas that would not serve me well in the long term. I wanted to spend my days with facts and ideas which would always resonate and serve me especially well at the end of life. Nothing, I thought, would fit this two-fold objective better than the life of what Edward Shils calls a "reproductive intellectual," a person who mulls over and makes use of good ideas not necessarily his or her own. No life, it seemed to me, would fit this bill better than that of a university professor in literature. Because I knew I'd be studying languages and reading novels and poems for fun my whole life anyway, I threw personality caution to the wind and followed my heart.

At college, in a first go at graduate school, and in the Peace Corps, I didn't gravitate toward a particular literature. I found the same absorption in thinking about and teaching Steinbeck's *The Grapes of Wrath* to English majors at Mashhad University that I had found in teaching Virgil's *Aeneid* to sixth-year Latin students at Mount Michael Abbey in Elkhorn (NB). Sherwood Anderson's *Winesburg, Ohio* transported me just as effectively as Sadeq Hedayat's *Buf-e Kur* [(The) Blind Owl]. Studying Persian offered the same mysterious pleasure as studying French. I could have stayed in the company of Wordsworth and Frost or of Virgil and Horace and had just as grand a time of it.

But my impressionable personality in Mashhad's exclusively Persian environment drew me to Persian. However, before I could envision what might otherwise have happened, I fell in love with, courted, and married freshman History student Sorayya Oraee Abbasian and decided to follow university fellowship money to Persian literature rather than English. Becoming a Persianist and living in a personal and academic world of Persian made things turn out so that not one thing I learned in Mashhad or later, in class and in my professional life, seems irrelevant. I just haven't learned enough. Through a score of writers, and scores of lifelong fictional friends and acquaintances, and the lifelong habit of living some times between book covers, I keep feeling the way I want to feel.

Living and thinking in two languages, of course, has its special pleasures and lessons. One is hard put to fail to take proverbial others sufficiently into sympathetic account when one has an Other or two in his or her own head. On occasions when I've lectured on the same subject in Persian and in English, I've been unable to use the same lecture content in both cases. I don't have the same things to say in

Persian on a given subject as I do in English. I don't experience the world and respond to it the same way in both languages. Sorayya and I share different things in Persian from what we share in English. My longstanding curiosity about French has to do with my wanting to find out if speaking it well, which I never will, would add another Other to my personality.

The flip side of this coin of heads for heart and tails for personality, and I chose heads, has found me and tails in a department which hasn't cottoned to my way of talking and writing. When I responded to the announcement of a new Persian language and literature position at UT Austin in mid-1974, the three professors with whom I studied most at The University of Chicago, Heshmat Moayyad in Persian literature, Jaroslav Stetkevych in Arabic literature, and Wilferd Madelung in Islamic History, naturally wrote letters of recommendation, which I saw for the first time in 2002 when reviewing materials in my personnel file as part of litigation involving UT Middle Eastern Studies faculty. None of the three letters stopped with perfunctory praise of their just graduated student.

Wilferd Madelung wrote: "We have talked about his 'Irish temper.' He has at times here and, I understand, elsewhere criticized some of his teachers. . .in rather tactless fashion, though not completely without justification. He has also engaged in scholarly controversy in publications and his criticism of the work of others has sometimes been unnecessarily sharp-tongued, whatever the merits of the case. How far these incidents have set the pattern for the future or give way to a stronger awareness of the need of establishing fair relations with his colleagues remains to be seen." Heshmat Moayyad wrote: "There is one specific point about Mr. Hillmann's personality, not his scholarly competence, which makes his potential colleagues uncertain as to whether it is possible to collaborate peacefully and smoothly with him. . .Mr. Hillmann is straightforward and demanding. It is not easy to work with him if you are used to backbiting instead of frank exchange of opinions. He has a lot of plans, is very resourceful, and extremely active and hardworking. His presence, therefore, is always challenging and may be considered "troublesome" by those who lack these qualifications. In his criticism, no matter how sharp, he always remains. . .objective. . . He does not tolerate compromising the right and just only for the sake of maintaining a sort of peace which is based on either weakness of character or lack of competence or both. One needs to work with him instead of listening to rumors to find that Mr. Hillmann is a very friendly and indeed cordial, reliable, and amiable person." Jaroslav Stetkevych wrote: "To those who deal with him [Hillmann] professionally, he is sincere, warm and modest. He was extremely easy to teach, for instance, accepting guidance better than most other students. Yet he has his firm professional points of view and convictions, and he has also the courage to defend them. This courage to be vocal whenever truly necessary, I find something I appreciate the most."

Over the years, in those occasional situations in which I have behaved exactly as Wilfred, Heshmat, and Jaroslav had intimated I might, several administrators and colleagues privy to my personnel file have expressed surprise, despite the fact that they were getting what they had bargained for in 1974. At the same time, that UT's old Department of Oriental and African Languages and Literatures had bargained for some one like me misled me into thinking for two or three years that the department was prepared for a general American accent and unsugarcoated East Coast discourse.

UT's Department of Oriental and African Languages and Literatures had come into being in 1970, when a group of Middle Eastern, South Asian, and East Asian language faculty in the Department of Linguistics formed it, its name presumptuously echoing that of the School of Oriental and African Languages at University of London. The new department taught only one sub-Saharan African language, Swahili, and that only during the years when a Texas-trained anthropologist, who did not get promoted to tenure in 1979, was on the OALL faculty. The group also decided at the beginning to use "DO ALL" as its acronym, a hint that intellectual discourse and discipline-oriented theory would not figure in things which OALL did.

In 1970, the Department of Linguistics at Texas was seeing linguistic theory as its chief mission and activity, which left out of its mainstream a group of faculty more interested in foreign language teaching and research. The departure of the latter group from Linguistics presumably pleased both that group and the Department of Linguistics. At the same time, The University of Texas was beginning to think of itself as a national university and was hoping to become a public university of the first rank. To those ends, it began developing or expanding discrete non-western programs, regardless of how essential such programs would prove in the education of its student population of mostly Texans. A Center for Middle Eastern Studies and a Center for Asian Studies had already come into being as foci for interdisciplinary and multidisciplinary activities and as umbrellas for faculty with area-studies interests in Anthropology, Art History, Economics, Geography, Government, History, and the like.

OALL expanded in 1974–1975, when it hired three new assistant professors: Robert Stofberg, with a Ph.D. in Biblical Studies and Archaeology from The University of Pennsylvania, to teach pre-modern Jewish culture and Palestinian archaeology; Richard Williams, with a Ph.D. in South Asian Languages from The University of Chicago, to teach Sanskrit; and me to teach Persian language and literature and Arabic language. Williams left OALL seven years later for an administrative position at the University of Miami. Reginald Applegate, with a Ph.D. in South Asian Languages from University of Pennsylvania, replaced him in 1982. Interested in administration as much as if not more than teaching, Applegate later served as Director of the Center for Asian Studies, and, after an unsuccessful bid to become Dean of Graduate Studies in 1996, became Dean of the College of Liberal Arts in 1999. He thereafter played a role in the administrative fate of the Middle Eastern Languages faculty originally in OALL, some of his decisions grounded in impressions he had of colleagues back in OALL.

Throughout OALL's history, Belgian-American Edgar Polomé was its most prominent member. He was its first Chair, and stayed in the administrative fray during subsequent Chair stints by Persianist Ali Jazayery and Hindi specialist Herman van Olphen. OALL colleagues spoke with respect of Polomé as an expert in all things Indo-European. I enjoyed his company and self-confidence and even the rough edges of his English, but never learned what his relevant academic discipline was. It wasn't theoretical linguistics, applied linguistics, literary criticism, or culture studies. Maybe philology and orientalism with a focus on the Indian subcontinent were his bailiwick.

Polomé, Jazayery, and van Olphen shared a wary acquiescence toward university administration, which led OALL to suggest and request mostly things which they guessed ahead of time the college administration would approve. The vast majority of OALL faculty hailed originally from places other than America. Not only did they not have good clues as to how things might work in a faculty-run American college in general, they also had no notion about how to fight for a faculty-run department or college in the state of Texas.

In April 1977, Ehsan Yarshater invited me to interview for a Persian position at Columbia and had me teach a second-year class session. Student comments and questions, even over the noise of a lawn mower outside Kent Hall, had my kind of curiosity behind them. Ehsan offered me a job, which I turned down. Sorayya still shakes her head when she recalls that decision. News of the offer reached Paul English, Director of UT's Center for Middle Eastern Studies, who initiated a process resulting in my early promotion without my ever having had to think about promotion and tenure.

By mid-1977, the bloom off the OALL rose, I had turned to tennis, jogging, and outside consulting work. I played tennis every day it didn't rain and squeegeed off courts on rainy days as soon as the rain stopped. Outside consulting work made up for my modest university salary. With characteristic timidity vis-à-vis College Administration, Jazayery had negotiated the lowest legal salary for me in 1974. One consulting project was a Persian language program which I designed and coordinated, under the aegis of Persepolis Institute, for Bell Operations Corporation in Euless (TX) and in which nine or ten UT graduate students participated by flying to Dallas one day a week to teach six hours of elementary Persian conversation to Bell engineers and family members planning to relocate to a Bell site in Esfahan.

Then came the Iranian Revolution, a reminder of how insignificant and off-target our discourse at OALL was. Once the Iran-Iraq War began in 1980, recognizing that I wouldn't thereafter have the opportunity to live again in Iran, I decided that I couldn't stay *au courant* with contemporary Persian literature and thus decided to focus on leading pre-Islamic-Republic writers. Grants to write a book on Forugh Farrokhzad gave Sorayya, daughter Elizabeth, and me six exciting months in London in 1982 and recharged batteries for life at OALL, as well as provide notes for a series of articles and books.

In 1984, University of Texas Press published my *Persian Carpets*, a sort of culmination of teaching and research on the subject originally encouraged by kindred spirit Paul English as a Middle East Center culture course subject. In 1987, I published *A Lonely Woman: Forugh Farrokhzad and Her Poetry*, a study of someone for whom I became an advocate. In 1990, *Iranian Culture: A Persianist View* appeared, a cultural analysis on the basis of texts by Ferdowsi, Khayyam, Hafez, Hedayat, Farrokhzad, and Al-e Ahmad. Its main thesis, the significance of salutary dualities and even dipolarities in Iranian life, I still hold.

Moreover, two summers in Paris, the second with Elizabeth and then a drive with her and Sorayya to Spain, a fall term at Durham University, a summer drive from Austin to New York with Elizabeth and a memorable *Leader of the Pack* matinee, Elizabeth's years at St. Stephen's, and then off to college at Hollins in Roanoke put OALL into a perspective that made it just a place for part of living, separate from family life and travel, thinking about books, and lively classrooms. OALL was mostly languishing, conversations in it about poetry few, and its prospects of serving as the backdrop for great things nil. Only its Arabic students seemed energetic and voluble. The Arabic wing of the OALL building at 2601 University Avenue had the air of a busy overseas Peace Corps office to it. Meanwhile, around campus, pre-Revolution coverage of Iran in History, Economics, Geography, Art History, and Government disappeared.

In 1991 appeared *From Durham to Tehran*, a short autobiographical book mostly of journal entries from 1986 and 1989 about Persian Studies, Iran, and my involvement in both. It had two publishers. IranBooks in Bethesda (MD) underwrote the printing and owned the rights to the hardback edition, while the world literature annual called *Literature East & West*, which I edited at OALL, distributed paperback copies to its subscribers. A faculty colleague complained to an interim OALL Chair about *From Durham to Tehran*. In response to that complaint, the latter, who had not read the book, informed me that *Literature East & West* could no longer enjoy OALL sponsorship. That sponsorship had consisted of two things. OALL would receive mention in each special issue of *LE&W* and would pay the postage, amounting to $150 or so, for mailing copies to institutional subscribers.

Also in 1991, I organized an international conference on Sadeq Hedayat. Over the years, I had organized five or six such conferences involving leading figures in Persian literature and Persian Studies as a means of stimulating good conversation at a place far from Tehran, Paris, New York, Washington, D.C., or Los Angeles, where such conversations can take place routinely. For the first time, such a conference had its Iranian-American critics on campus. A year later, I organized the Annual Conference of the Center for Iranian Research and Analysis at UT, with Iranian-American faculty criticism louder this time. I thereafter ceased organizing Persian Studies events and turned my extra-curricular attention to renewed study of English literature in a graduate degree program at LBJ's alma mater, Texas State University at San Marcos. In 1993–1994, a visiting professorship at St. Peter's College in Jersey City gave me an energy boost.

✍ 28 December 1993, Journal entry, Perry Lane, Austin. Eliza graduated from UNM on December 18. Hurrah! Sorayya, [Sorayya's brother] Reza, and I drove to Albuquerque in Reza's Cherokee Jeep on the 16th, checking into the Albuquerque Marriott Courtyard Inn on the 17th. We ate dinner the night before at a Mexican/New Mexican restaurant called Joseph's in Santa Rosa and drove on, stopping at a motel "owned by Americans" on Central Avenue by midnight. Eliza and I met Kay Patman and Jim at the Albuquerque Airport on the 17th and that evening took our group, along with four of Eliza's PiPhi sorority sisters, Char, Stacy, Sara 1, and Sara 2, to dinner at Sadie's, their favorite and my almost least favorite Mexican Restaurant. After graduation and a cookies-and-punch reception, we had a near-gourmet lunch at La Vicino on Central Avenue. That evening, the 18th, we took the group and Eliza's beau Nathan Stalker to Café Oceana, a trendy seafood restaurant across the street from Route 66 Diner, where we had eaten lunch on the 17th. Food, with green chili sauce on most of it, was Albuquerque's chief non-graduation attraction for us. On Sunday morning, before setting out for Santa Fe and our Christmas week at La Hermosa Resort, we hosted Nathan, his grandfather, father, and stepmother to brunch at Courtyard Inn. Reza and I jogged there every day and made daily use of the swimming pool and spa. Graduation had us all even happier than usual. At our two-story, mountain-view condo unit in Santa Fe, as many as eight or nine people slept some evenings. The young people didn't mind sleeping on the floor. Sleeping bags, duffle bags with clothing spilling out of them, and skis and boots were everywhere. La Hermosa served a full breakfast in their main lodge.

Otherwise, Sorayya cooked a lot. Jim and I bought and decorated a Christmas tree. Eliza, Kay, and Nathan took me skiing every day. With a morning's worth of lessons and a day or two of practice on green runs on my own, I joined Eliza and Nathan at the top of the mountain and struggled down a terrifying blue run with the pair of them laughing at me. After an early Turkey dinner at the condo, we took Jim, Reza, Nathan, and Kay to the Albuquerque Airport on the 23rd. Back in Santa Fe, we walked up candle-lit and crowded Canyon Drive on Christmas Eve. We feasted at The Eldorado's lavish champagne and buffet dinner on Christmas. On the 26th, we drove Reza's car back to Austin, contented parents of a college graduate. We could now forget, or remember with smiles and knowing head-nodding, that Eliza had taken a semester's leave from college two years earlier, over our objections, to ski in Breckenridge. ✍

A wedding photograph of Elizabeth (Craig Hillmann Garrett) in Austin. March 1998.

Chapter 3

1994–1997

"If you are lucky enough to have lived in Paris.
then wherever you go for the rest of your life,
it stays with you, for Paris is a moveable feast."
A self-serving adaptation from Ernest Hemingway

When the telephone rang, I was talking through a keyboard to my MAC Color Classic about a new idea for a Persian textbook called *Reading Iran Reading Iranians*, an intermediate/advanced reader and guide with lessons built around authentic texts exhibiting or highlighting facets of the problems which Americans have "reading" Iran and "reading" Iranians. At the third ring, I picked up the phone and looked up and out our second-floor bedroom window down Jersey City's Glendale Avenue, a piece of Holy Name Cemetery visible at its West Side Avenue end. The last traces of snow from the stormy winter of 1994 were melting into the ground.

I had given the Convocation Address there in October in anticipation of my semester in residence from January to May. In the middle part of it, I said:

> Here follow illustrations of two reasons for holding views as strong as mine in favor of multicultural activities in American intellectual and academic life. The first has to do with how Americans see Others far away. The second has to do with how we see Others near at hand.
>
> As for the far away Other, we Americans may not be able to imagine a less sympathetic society, people, and culture today from the American vantage-point than Iran's. From that vantage-point, an ocean and a continent or two way, Iran seems home to religious fanatics. Iran, however, was the country which brought the Babylonian captivity of the Jews to an end twenty-five centuries ago. Some of those liberated Jews consequently thought the Iranian king was their messiah. More recently, a century ago, Iran was where the Baha'i Faith was born and from where it grew into the pacifist, internationalist, and egalitarian movement it is today. In short, Iran's history of religiosity has included new ideas and new beliefs and tolerance, even for Jews, Christians, and Zoroastrians in the Islamic Republic of Iran today, if not for Baha'is.

From the American vantage-point, Iran seems a violent society where dictatorial governmental terror reigns. Historians can tell us, however, that the Iranian Revolution in 1978 and 1979 was less violent than the American, Chinese, French, and Russian revolutions, while sociologists can demonstrate that the level of civil violence in places like America far exceeds that in Iran. It has always been safer for Americans to walk the streets in Tehran than for foreigners today to walk the streets of, for example, Miami.

In Iran, more space in newspapers and on radio shows is devoted to lyric poetry than to competitive sports. Persian literature has an unbroken tradition of 1,100 years, with medieval works as easy to read today as modern. Iranian homes are usually full of art, specifically Persian carpets with their civilized representations of spring-time and paradise gardens. Persian art has an unbroken tradition of nearly three thousand years.

Such facts may suggest an adjustment in perceptions from far away as to what Iran and Iranians are all about. They may suggest that such cultures as Iran's have produced veritable pearls within their apparently rough and uninviting and unfamiliar shells. Pearls may differ from culture to culture. They cost the humanist nothing in material terms to acquire. But they may be as difficult to own as real pearls are–they need diving into the deep for, they require taking the risk of separating our selves from familiar shores without knowing what we'll come back with.

As for that second arena of Others closer to home, it offers evidence that multiculturalism shouldn't just start at home, but also that it is a life-and-death endeavour that needs doing outside of and after college. My argument here is that if any of the following ifs relates to my true thoughts and feelings, I need desperately to do multicultural reading and listening and thinking: If I, as a descendant of immigrants, can easily rationalize policies to restrict immigration to this country. If I think that Cassius Clay changed his name to Mohammad Ali for no good reason and that Mohammad Ali refused to served in the American military for no good reason. If I think it's natural that anthologies of English and American literatures include no more than ten percent women authors. If I accept without thinking a politician's characterization of my country as the best or greatest in the world. If I don't think twice about media characterization of terrorists as "Muslim" or "Islamic." If I can't think right away of any objections to the proposal to make English the national language of this country. If I feel self-conscious or uncomfortable incorporating religiosity or religious beliefs into my academic or intellectual life or discourse. If I have no reservations about political nationalism as a natural and inherently good thing for human society now and in the future. If I as an Irish-American experience anxiety approaching an African-American man in a lonely place at night when I would not feel the same if the man were another Irish-American. If I can easily reach a decision about what women should and should not do to and with their bodies.

If any of these or other very real, down-to-earth ifs apply to me, I can well use this glorious new academic year at Saint Peter's to look at art, read poems, study history, learn about societies, and talk with student and faculty colleagues to grow beyond my today's monocultural self and enrich both values and self.

Then came that beautiful white winter, twenty minutes by Path Train from Manhattan. Elizabeth and I drove East from Austin in her plum Toyota Celica college graduation present to Frederick (MD), where she was beginning an M.A. program in Psychology at Hood College. Her apartment ready and stuff put in it, we drove north together to Jersey City, where she helped me settle in as Will and Ariel Durant Chair in Humanities at Will's alma mater. A month later I flew home to Austin to meet Sorayya and drive back with her to Jersey City in a family car. The travel and the novelty of life at St. Peter's had put UT life in a hazy background, a good thing for me.

For four or five years, our department had languished in a sort of college receivership and had a Chair who checked with the college administration before saying or doing anything. Conflict reportedly stewed within the Hebrew Studies program, its only star, Yair Mazor, apparently often in group hot water because he behaved and voted independently. Yair later left to become the Director of Hebrew Studies at the University of Wisconsin in Milwaukee. In Arabic Studies, Peter Abboud and Fedwa Malti-Douglas feuded. Turkish Studies, the fourth departmental area, wallowed in directionlessness and lacked a permanent faculty person.

As a group, we Middle Eastern language faculty colleagues weren't going anywhere. Almost our only saving grace was that high-stakes Middle East conflicts had not contributed to our low-stakes conflicts. Later they would. The future looked so unpromising and the departmental discourse was so uninspiring that I was planning, after finishing my M.A. degree at Texas State, to commute to College Station for a Ph.D. in English at Texas A & M University, and then either try to transfer to UT's English Department as an Adjunct Professor or look for an English literature job elsewhere.

My Durant Chair activities at St. Peter's made me optimistic about future personal prospects and further disheartened me about Middle Eastern Languages at UT. I had three responsibilities that spring. First was a seminar in Persian literature in translation for a handful of honors students, good students but a cut or two below my Persian language and literature and Iranian culture students at Texas. Second was a seminar on Humanities in Middle Eastern Culture for a group of twenty high school teachers, good teachers a cut or two above Austin compeers in terms of exposure to culture. Third was a faculty seminar for ten St. Peter's colleagues in which we investigated Salman Rushdie's *The Satanic Verses* from the perspectives of their expertise, e.g., psychology, history, literary criticism, sociology, and philosophy. I hadn't had such stimulating conversations since graduate school days in Tehran and Chicago. No such conversations ever took place among Middle Eastern Languages colleagues at Texas.

Yes, UT had receded into the back of my mind when the phone rang and interrupted my word-processing reverie in mid-design of a language lesson about an Iranian newspaper article on the June 1988 Iranian Airbus Disaster. It was Peter Abboud on the phone. He had news. A decision about our department. Our old and grandiosely misnamed Department of Oriental and African Languages and Literatures was no more. The College had created a new Department of Middle Eastern Languages and Cultures and was considering Peter as its inaugural chair. While saying more than once, "That's good news. That's wonderful. Congratulations," I mentally cancelled plans to do another Ph.D. at Texas A & M and began thinking how we might realize dreams about a Persian literature program which I had brought to Austin from Chicago twenty years earlier. Now we might attract first-rate Arabic and Persian graduate students to Austin, and hear some of those conversations which had helped persuade me in Chicago and in Tehran in the late 1960s and early 1970s to give Persian Studies a career-long try.

The day the split of OALL into a Department of Middle Eastern Languages and Cultures and a Department of Asian Studies took place, the two groups went their separate ways with no group contact thereafter. OALL's experienced and knowledgeable staff, Sandra Paschall and Anne Brokaw, sensibly chose to go to Asian Studies. Faculty also took impressions of colleagues and language groups and former colleagues with them to their two new departments. East Asian faculty felt that the new Department of Asian Studies, now administratively linked with the Center for Asian Studies, would, like CAS, be in the control of the South Asian faculty, which would mean that their status wouldn't improve any from what it had been in OALL.

MELC faculty not in Hebrew Studies wondered if the Hebrew Studies group, which could now vote in a block and carry the day in some votes, would do so in the new MELC department. They wondered if obstreperous and self-interested Jacob Levy would continue both reminiscing about days when he ran the Hebrew language program, attracting hundreds of students to it, and arguing for the restoration of a long-transferred Hebrew position. Conflict between Peter Abboud and Fedwa Malti-Douglas had resolved itself with her departure for Indiana University. Sherman Abdulkarim Jackson, who had sided with Malti-Douglas, had also left for Indiana. Most questions about who deserved responsibility for the conflict within our Arabic Studies program subsided when *The Chronicle of Higher Education* published an exposé on what happened to Middle Eastern Languages faculty at Indiana after Malti-Douglas got there.

But the Arabic Studies program still had its local critics, especially at The Center for Middle Eastern Studies, and in particular two Center faculty persons, English Lecturer Elizabeth Fernea and Geography Professor Bob Holz, neither of whom knew Arabic or anything about Foreign Language Education. Fernea, for example, objected to placement tests which Attieh and Abboud gave CMES and OALL students who took summer Arabic courses elsewhere and thereafter sought to advance a year in UT's Arabic language sequence. In at least two cases, Attieh recommended that students repeat the level of Arabic they had studied elsewhere over the summer. Complaints by at least two students would haunt Attieh and Abboud, as would Fernea's machinations behind their backs.

The conflict reached the point that CMES scheduled a meeting to review our Arabic language program. The meeting revealed that no one outside of the Arabic language faculty, except for me, had read Arabic course descriptions, course syllabi, or course textbooks, or knew about the concepts and proficiency-based and performance-based principles of Applied Linguistics upon which UT's Arabic language program rested. CMES disapproval of and interference in the Arabic language program continued after the creation of MELC, as did one other perception on the part of one faculty person in Asian Studies from OALL.

In a court deposition in November 2002, that faculty person, talking about the years from 1982 to 1994, had these things to say about Peter Abboud:

[His]. . .entire career has been invested in complaints, whining, prevarication, misrepresentation and self-inducing indignation. . .He has been
nothing but an obstacle to the Arabic program. . .At every turn [from 1982
to 1994], every hire that was ever proposed in any field, Chinese, Japanese,
Indian Studies, whatever, his first proposal was inevitably 'Let's hire [Arabic
lecturer Aman] Attieh' to the point that it became an utterly predictable
response to any proposal for hire. . .Every meeting I've ever been with Peter
Abboud since I've been here [at UT Austin], when the question of hiring
came up, Peter Abboud always proposed the hiring of Aman Attieh. And
that included proposals to hire people in fields completely removed from
Middle Eastern Studies.

Other OALL faculty recall that Abboud's interest in upgrading
Aman Attieh's position as a lecturer to a tenure-track assistant professorship ranked either fourth or fifth in faculty development items
discussed at OALL faculty meetings. First was Levy's demand that
the College of Liberal Arts restore to Hebrew a position reallocated
to Japanese. Second was Levy's demand that OALL vote for a new
Hebrew position whenever OALL might have a slot and funds for a
position in any departmental area. Third was the constant request by
me and others that OALL try to persuade the College of Liberal Arts
to fund a tenure-track position in Turkish, the only Middle Eastern
language area which lacked at least one tenure-track position. Fourth
was the constant request by me, Abboud, and others for the continued
funding of a tenure-track position in Arabic literature, a core element
in any Middle Eastern language degree program. Fifth was Abboud's
repeated request that OALL try to persuade the College of Liberal Arts
to upgrade the non-tenured Arabic language lectureship to a tenure-
track assistant professorship.

Of course, even if Abboud had raised the issue of upgrading Attieh's
position at every OALL faculty meeting, which he didn't, no logical
connection would obtain between that support or concern for a junior
Arabic colleague in a program which deserved at least two tenure-track
positions and alleged "prevarication, misrepresentation and self-inducing indignation" or Abboud's alleged role as "nothing but an obstacle
to the Arabic program."

Except for the impression recorded in the cited deposition, other
OALL colleagues recall Abboud's behavior in the 1982–1994 years with
such words as serious, straightforward, dedicated (to Arabic), energetic
(with respect to Arabic program development), and academic. In fact,

OALL colleagues who joined OALL in the 1970s think of the group of founding members Jazayery, Polomé, Roy Teele (Professor of Japanese and Editor of *Literature East & West*), van Olphen, and Abboud as sharing qualities of gentlemanliness and moral uprightness. As for the minority opinion quoted above, it is relevant to the story because it is the view of Reginald Applegate, who became Dean of the College of Liberal Arts in 1999 and relied on that impression in actions he took thereafter against Abboud and the latter's junior associate Attieh.

When I put the receiver down and went to the living room to tell Sorayya what Peter had called to say, she already knew the news from overhearing my half of the conversation. She was shaking her head. She said: "This'll never work. They'll never let an Arab manage your department. You can't have Arabs at the head of anything academic on the Middle East at UT unless there's a separate Hebrew Department and a separate Arabic Department." I dismissed Sorayya's view. Nevertheless, remembering that Hebrew Studies colleagues had always wished for a separate Hebrew Department, that no Arab(-American) had ever administered anything at Texas I knew about, and that Arab-bashing was an American media tradition, I tempered my enthusiastic reaction to Peter's news. At the same time, I saw a boldness in Dean Pederson's likely choice of Peter as Chair in a department whose chairs had been chosen over the years deliberately to avoid a microcosmic Arab-Israeli conflict.

We saw *Miss Saigon*, *Phantom of the Opera*, and most of the other Broadway shows that spring. We spent half-days at the Metropolitan Museum of Art five or six times. I gave a gallery talk in the Islamic Art Collection there on oriental carpets for my high school teachers' seminar. Sorayya and I also joined an Iranian-American poetry circle which met monthly at different homes from Princeton to Alpine. I gave a talk on Modernism in Persian Literature at the Iranian Studies Seminar at Columbia, after which we all retired to the Faculty Club for dinner. Sorayya's brother Reza flew up from Seguin in March, and the two of them took a three-week trip to Germany and Iran. In their absence I survived on salads and deli delicacies from Balducci's, which I would pick up next to a Path Train stop on the way back to Jersey City from Manhattan.

I also flew again to Austin once that spring for meetings with my Intermediate Persian Project staff and representatives of the American government language schools which had contracted with Persepolis for a new comprehensive syllabus of Intermediate/Advanced Persian instructional materials. In mid-1993, I had rented an office suite at 2701 Rio Grande Avenue, where four colleagues worked full- or half-time, and spent Fridays and Saturdays there during the academic year. The impetus which the IPP contract gave to our Persepolis instructional materials research evolved into a five-week intensive summer Persian course each summer in Austin, week-long advanced Persian seminars around the country, and the publication of Persian textbooks, readers, and glossaries/dictionaries.

On our last evening at St. Peter's, a Jesuit participant in *The Satanic Verses* Seminar invited Sorayya and me to dinner at the Jesuit college residence. Comfortable surroundings, cheerful Jesuit colleagues, a well-stocked bar, near-gourmet fare, and okay conversation made for a pleasant evening. During it, I thought off and on about my ten years in Jesuit education. By the time I had started Loyola Blakefield, the Jesuit high school in Baltimore, the Jesuit *ratio studiorum* and curriculum were out of date in content and methodology. In my college days at Holy Cross and Loyola, what the Jesuits had to say in metaphysics and ethics sounded contrived and irrelevant to students like me. But something about the Jesuit *esprit du corps* and tradition of vigorous debate inspired me. And a handful of individual Jesuits had impressed me with their this-worldly otherworldliness and life-long commitment to academics and spirituality. I had found commitment also in the Peace Corps, and at The University of Chicago, and at Tehran University, but not in our UT Middle Eastern Languages group.

In Austin, I busied myself with Persepolis's Intermediate Persian Project, organized a Persian Teachers' Workshop at the IPP office in which Michael Jerald from School for International Training (EIL-Brattleboro), Simin Karimi from The University of Arizona, and Donald Stilo from The University of Washington starred. Every so often that summer I visited my new office at WMB 5.146, less envious now than before of the English Department faculty in Parlin Hall visible from my corner window and looking forward to a second chance to be a part of a department which might accomplish things.

In our new Department of Middle Eastern Languages and Cultures, inaugural department Chair Abboud turned to his "friends" in making administrative assignments. He named Arabic Lecturer Aman Attieh Undergraduate Adviser and me Graduate Adviser. Although we had no undergraduate majors to speak of, the naming of a lecturer from Peter's own Arabic program did not sit well with some colleagues. At the time, they argued that a non-tenure-track lecturer should not serve as Undergraduate Adviser. As for my position as MELC's first Graduate Adviser–I had held the same position in the mid-1970s at the Center for Middle Eastern Studies–the former OALL Graduate Adviser later told me that he hadn't appreciated my "taking the job away" from him. Abboud's appointment of Attieh and me to cited positions would dog him for four years.

On 13 December 1994, at the end of MELC's first semester, I wrote this letter to Seth Wolitz, Gale Professor of Jewish Studies.

> At a meeting several weeks ago, Dean Larry Carver informed a group of us members of the new Department of Middle Eastern Languages and Cultures that you had submitted a written protest in response to MELC's proposal of a bachelor's degree program in Jewish Studies. As the person responsible for the proposal, I am writing to describe briefly what prompted it.
>
> As you may know, MELC is hiring an expert in Islamic Studies, which, along with Islamic Studies expertise among other MELC and Center for Middle Eastern Studies faculty, led me to suggest a B.A. track in Islamic Studies. Because it seemed inappropriate that an undergraduate Islamic Studies degree exist at a research university without a parallel Jewish Studies degree, I also proposed the latter. In so doing, I was not implying that Jewish Studies is or should be Hebrew-based or Zionist. I was also not implying that only MELC could be home base for such a new degree program. But I argued that MELC could be a home base for such a degree because its faculty offer many Jewish Studies courses and because no such degree program exists elsewhere on campus.
>
> It makes little difference to me intellectually where such a program is housed–what matters is that the program, which should have been instituted years ago, get on the books as soon as possible. . .A better plan, one that would put a Jewish Studies program under the umbrella of your Gale Professorship, would deserve adoption by definition. Even in that case, however, the bulk of the teaching of Jewish Studies subjects and issues as described in the current Course Catalogue would still take place in MELC.

Strong opposition by Hebrew Studies colleague Robert Stofberg–the name-plaque vandal, office coin-toss loser, and former Graduate Adviser–to any collaboration with Wolitz, including a proposed joint appointment for the latter in MELC, caused Jewish Studies to languish for several years. But I didn't take much notice of Stofberg's emotional response to the Wolitz proposal and his other expressions of displeasure because everything in the department was going swimmingly for me: a growing graduate student population; a stimulating trip to Tehran in January 1996 as the only American Professor of Persian to participate in the First International Congress of Professors of Persian, and only my third trip there after the Iranian Revolution; publication of *Persian Fiction Reader*; work on *Persian Newspaper Reader* and *Reading Iran Reading Iranians*; Elizabeth's career as a psychologist in Albuquerque; Sorayya's real estate career; progress on my M.A. thesis at Texas State; and plans for a semester in Paris.

I should have connected some dots between Wolitz as Gale Chair of Jewish Studies and Stofberg as a potential lifetime Associate Professor. The latter might naturally have resented Wolitz and the prestige of his position, the chief "Jewish" position a "Jewish" faculty person could hold on campus. Moreover, the person who held it was a non-observant Jew whose academic track record far outshone Stofberg's and who would outshine the latter in all regards if they served in the same department. Because Stofberg was adamant about the matter, the rest of us let it go.

Parallel and more important dots I should have connected had to do with the expanding Arabic language program, which was becoming as large as Hebrew, and this with two Arabic language faculty vis-à-vis five or six in Hebrew. Stofberg and Israeli-American Benjamin Loya, an Associate Professor of History who became Center Director in 1995, might naturally have felt apprehension about the vitality and visibility of the Arabic program. Not only were its enrollments increasing, but also its undergraduate students at the upper levels and almost all of its graduate students were superior to most of their Hebrew Studies compeers. In order to increase its enrollments of graduate students to justify its large faculty contingent, Hebrew Studies had accepted into graduate degree programs applicants who had scored 275, 325, 400 and such on the Verbal Section of the Graduate Record Examination. Hebrew Studies awarded degrees to students who couldn't read Modern Hebrew at a so-called Second-year level. Meanwhile, Arabic Studies insisted on Arabic as the language of instruction and communication with instructors in and outside of class.

Now that an Arabic professor, and the only faculty member in Semitic languages with a national reputation, had become MELC Chair and was, along with his Coordinator of the Arabic Language Program, aggressively touting Arabic program achievements with the insinuation that Hebrew, Persian, and Turkish language courses were lagging behind methodologically, Stofberg and Loya may have perceived this as a threat to a cause they held as dear as Abboud and Attieh held theirs. Moreover, Arabic Studies had the audacity to insist upon proficiency standards when placing MELC and CMES students in Arabic courses. Ever a bad judge of character and rarely aware when plots are afoot, I gave such speculation no nurturing and didn't think to tell Abboud and Attieh, two against six and CMES with the six, to cool it.

When two or three MELC staff persons left during the first two years of Abboud's tenure, I didn't give that much thought either. At the time, in conversations with others, former CMES Director Bob Holtz blamed the departure of two MELC staff persons on me. One of them, Joan Sampson reportedly registered a complaint at the Dean's office on behalf of the other, Laura Vanderhagen, stating that: "Laura Vanderhagen, who served as Graduate Coordinator for Michael Hillmann (Graduate Adviser), had complained to Joan that Hillmann, who was dissatisfied with Laura's work, took her into his office, closed the door and shouted at her. . .Joan then accompanied Laura to Employee Assistance and informed them that she had felt assaulted on an emotional level." Now, I wasn't "dissatisfied with Laura Vanderhagen's work" and had never "shouted at her." Not that I can prove my two assertions here. Moreover, I did invite her to my office to discuss both Graduate Advising matters involving student files in my possession and her performance of Graduate Coordinator responsibilities and likely closed the door to WMB 5.146 during such meetings. Graduate Adviser conversations were the business of no one but the Graduate Adviser and the Graduate Coordinator. Ms. Vanderhagen, a teacher by training, was waiting during her time at MELC for an agreeable teaching position to materialize. When it did, she left MELC to return to teaching and sent me a note expressing appreciation of the opportunity we had had to work together.

On May 23, 1996, I wrote this letter to MELC Chair Abboud about the possible transfer to MELC of a spousal hire, a visiting assistant professor temporarily housed at the Center for Middle Eastern Studies.

> I thought yesterday's meeting concerning the possible transfer of. . .[CMES's visiting assistant professor] from CMES to MELC went well. I was. . .encouraged to hear what. . .Walid Hamarneh and Khaled Abou El Fadl had to say about issues of competence, research, and scholarship in MELC fields. I also understand the perspective of MELC colleagues, honest in their non-intellectual orientations to academic matters, who made the case for. . .[the transfer] on the bases that [our CMES colleague] attracts lots of students to [CMES] classes and can perhaps learn to do more solid work in the future.
>
> By the way, Walid and Khaled likely need a pep talk. This was their first experience of non-intellectual personnel voting results, something I was used to at OALL and hoped wouldn't happen in our new department. If I were in their shoes, after yesterday's meeting, I'd likely be thinking about taking an offer elsewhere in a few years.
>
> Nevertheless, despite my negative. . .vote on. . .[the proposed] transfer to MELC, I have no strong feelings about. . .[our CMES colleague's] participation in a "Middle Eastern Cultures" program separate from Persian Studies and Islamic Studies.

At that faculty meeting, the Hebrew Studies group voted as a block in favor of accepting the CMES colleague in question into the department, while Arabic and Islamic Studies also voted as a block against the motion. Hebrew Studies carried the day. Moreover, colleagues communicated the results of the vote to the candidate who, after joining MELC, understandably harbored unfriendly feelings toward the colleagues who had voted against the transfer.

That meeting, the vote, and the uncomfortable aftermath got me thinking about our department's culture, or lack of one. We didn't share views about academic standards or a common ground with respect to humanistic study of things Middle Eastern. We also didn't exhibit any signs of American academic culture. The cultural vacuum which had always obtained in OALL/MELC left the arena in MELC open for a clique or departmental group with enough votes to influence the direction of things in other departmental areas, in this case, Hebrew Studies faculty determining the composition of and a direction in Islamic Studies. This also meant that Hebrew Studies could spearhead opposition to any departmental administration headed by another other area, in this case, Arabic Studies. I didn't think at the time that such a cultural vacuum would lead to what transpired in mid-1998 or what would ultimately happen to the department in 2002.

In early August 1997, I graduated from Texas State with an M.A. in English. Sorayya and I didn't celebrate the event and didn't need to or have the time to. For, on August 8, we hosted an engagement party at home for Elizabeth and Jeff(rey Douglas Garrett). Guests came from Baltimore, Albuquerque, and the West Coast. A Mariachi band serenaded the couple. Our houseful of guests, including in-laws-to-be, reveled in the reflected youthful happiness of the engaged couple. So, I was smiling out of two sides of my mouth for days, the Elizabeth–Jeff smile and an M.A. in English smile.

That Texas State experience, especially my exposure to African American writing and a long overdue careful study of Modernism, enriched my teaching thereafter. It also gave me a sense of having provided further symmetry to my career, which had begun with an M.A. program in English at Creighton University. There I had finished degree course work and had completed thesis research on "Steinbeck's *The Grapes of Wrath* as Epic," but lacked the discipline to get things done on time before I left Nebraska for Peace Corps training in the summer of 1965. For years, even after getting M.A. and Ph.D. degrees elsewhere, the thought that I had left something undone in Omaha came occasionally to mind. Now I could say goodbye to that thought.

The real joy about the Texas State experience and degree, however, was just that I had done it, that I had no trouble behaving like a twenty-five year old for several years, that I had relished homework, tests, oral reports, term papers, and deadlines for reading assignments. As people say less and less in their fifties, I hadn't lost a step. I had published "Hurston's *Dust Tracks on a Road* as Literary Autobiography" in *The Zora Neale Hurston Forum*. My analysis of Maya Angelou's *I Know Why the Caged Bird Sings* appeared in *Masterpieces of African-American Literature* and was quoted in an *Austin American-Statesman* article on a controversy about the book in a nearby school district.

In late August 1997, a new faculty member joined MELC. Earlier, the department had received a faculty slot for a Minority Advantage appointment in Islamic Studies, a slot for which the twin qualifications were competence in the field and African-American heritage. Sherman

Jackson long gone, Peter Abboud pursued the possibility again and, on the recommendation of Islamic Studies colleague Khaled Abou El Fadl, contacted Kamil Riyadh, a fellow graduate student back East. Riyadh interviewed for and got the position, completing and defending his dissertation just before he came to Austin. I met Riyadh at the Austin airport and had him at 3404 Perry Lane as a house guest for a week. Sorayya had left days earlier for Göttingen to spend two weeks with her sister Fahimé and then fly to Tehran and Mashhad with Fahimé to visit relatives and friends, before returning to Paris where we were to spend the fall semester.

When I left for Paris in early September, Riyadh became our tenant and occupied our house until early December. MELC staff person Trudie Redding had made the arrangements, which we thought would suit Riyadh because he said that his wife and their four children would be visiting that fall. Sorayya and I agreed to make the rent for the house and one of our cars nominal for him in the light of his situation as a beginning academic with lots of expenses.

✍ October 30, Journal entry, Paris. Sunlight framing the spaces around curtain corners wakes us up at 8:30. Opened curtains on the only window of our sixth-floor studio apartment reveal a blue sky over everything down to the top the La Tour Eiffel several kilometers to the northeast. From the top of the tower, red grey haze reaches downward. I dress, get a shopping list from Sorayya, take the elevator to the ground floor, bid the receptionist a cheery "Bon jour," and enter autumn air outside Résidence Avicenne. Walking past the soccer pitch where students yelling in French and Arabic are already busy at the world's sport and out the Cité Universitaire front gate, I cross Boulevard Jourdan, glance at a Thomas Paine statue, and enter Parc Montsouris by the gate next to the Cité Universitaire RER B Station. Down the hill to the right, making a mental note that we have to have dinner one night at the in-park patio restaurant in front of me, I leave the park and walk down Rungis Street to Rungis Square. By this time, any thoughts I had about things I should do that day or deadlines back home needing meeting have wafted out of my head skyward. At the neighborhood Marché Franprix I fill a basket with two liter boxes of red grape juice at 3F2 each (and it's not concentrate), a jar of moutarde forte de Dijon, a carton of farmer's cheese, a jar of miele fleurs de France, and a half-dozen eggs (for rare evenings when we eat in the apartment and Sorayya uses egg whites to make an omelette with tomatoes, green peppers, and dates), tomatoes, oranges, grapes, and bananas. Everything but the grapes and tomatoes go into my back pack. Back up Rungis Street, I buy a baguette from our favorite boulangerie. We've tested the bread at four different neighborhood boulangeries and like the bread here the best (even though the same baker may service all four boulangeries). Two of us eat a whole baguette for breakfast, along with meusli, fruit juice, and fruit. We put unsalted butter, jam or honey, and farmer's cheese on the bread. Almost back to the park, I buy an *International Herald Tribune* from a walk-in closet-sized magazine shop which carries as many magazines as Barnes & Noble in Chelsea. On Tuesdays, I buy *USA Today* for weekend football scores. Some afternoons I buy *France-Soir*. On Sundays we buy *Le Dimanche*. The tree-lined straight lanes behind and to the southwest of Maison Internationale seem in conversation with the curving lanes and paths leading to the buildings on the end of Cité Universitaire, beyond which runs Boulevard Périphérique. The leaves are turning red and yellow and brown on many trees. Gardeners burn little piles of them on dirt paths in the afternoon, just like they did in the garden at Mecklenburgh Square beyond the front windows of our Mecklenburgh House flat. Fifteen years between piles of burning autumn leaves have gone up in smoke. But just as many trees, some sculpted into cylindrical shapes, are ever green. Sorayya has set the window-front table for breakfast by the time my twenty-minute errand comes to its sixth-story end. At 11:15 we're still at the table. I've finished *The Tribune*. News of Monday's stock market drop doesn't bother me. Sorayya is half-way through Mary Willis Walker's *Zero at the Bone*, a mystery novel set in Austin, which she bought yesterday at Shakespeare and Company. A pile of books she has read sit on a bookcase shelf in the corner waiting to be traded on for other such books. I read one of them, Patricia Cornwell's *Post-Mortem*, one lazy day in September waiting for Sorayya to get back from Tehran. We joke about this reading, Sorayya's one vice. She has another pile of Persian books not for trading in, among them Shahrnoush Parsipour's story of her years in prison in Iran and Iran Darrudi's life story. My reading these days has a purpose: situating Sadeq Hedayat's *The Blind Owl* into a specific, early twentieth-century niche as narrative. I'm also preparing my mid-November talk on the subject at Sorbonne Nouvelle. I've tried to situate the book in Iranian, modernist, and postmodernist contexts, and in the arena of autobiographical narratives. None of these categories, or comparatist appreciation therein, gives me satisfying answers to basic questions about structure and theme in *The Blind Owl.* So I've turned to surrealistic writing and lyrical narratives, my shelf in our bookcase filled with André Breton, André Gide, Hermann Hesse, and Virginia Woolf. I took care of Rilke before coming to Paris. Today I'm in the middle of *The Waves.* After breakfast yesterday morning, we took RER B to Chatelet-Les Halles and transferred to M 1 Chateau de Vincennes. At the Chateau de Vincennes Station, I asked directions to 49 rue Defrance, where an Iranian publisher and book dealer called Khavaran is located. We walked down rue du Chateau to rue Fontenroy and turned right on it and walked on until it changed names to rue Defrance. But 49 seemed only a warehouse for several businesses, and no sign of a bookstore. Back on the street, I called the bookstore. Telecartes and their phones here are handy and cheap for long distance calls. Khavaran's owner, T. Amini, gave me directions and was waiting for us in the warehouse courtyard. Khavaran is a nicely appointed, three-room shop, with a conference room and printing press in the back. Minutes later, Sorayya and I were back in Tehran, reminded at the same time that we were not really there by all of the titles of books and magazines with the word *tab'id* [exile] in them. We bought the first three issues, published in exile, of Abbas Ma'rufi's journal *Gardoon,* banned last year in Tehran with Ma'rufi's arrest. The lead article in *Gardoon* 51 recounts his last days in Tehran. I also bought another copy of the second volume of F.F. Farzaneh's *Ashna'i ba Sadeq Hedayat* [(My) Acquaintance with Sadeq Hedayat], which Farzaneh published himself in Paris in 1998. I bought a copy of the shorter French version at José Corti's in early September right after I got to Paris. I had bought a copy of the censored Tehran edition in Tehran in 1996. Volume 1 tells the story of Farzaneh's acquaintance with Hedayat, a less useful account than Volume 2, which presents Farzaneh's recollection of what Hedayat had to say about various subjects, including his writing, specifically *The Blind Owl.* From Vincennes, and a pleasant walk through the middle of town—which I first visited years ago, the day Yannick Noah beat John McEnroe in the French Open final, as a guest at Farryar and Daryush Mehrju'i's–, we rode the metro back to Cité Universitaire, just in time for a late lunch at Maison Internationale, chicken cacciatore with green beans and mashed potatoes, carrot salad, and only sparkling mineral water to drink. The morning stroll in Vincennes had us ready to eat everything on our plates, which we whitened with bread. Lunch over by three, we boarded a PC bus to Porte de Charenton, just to see how the Petit Ceintation line works, and took a metro from there to Bastille. We walked down rue St. Antoine, turned into the alley which leads to Place des Vosges, which we like to pass through every once in a while, and then window-shopped on Francis Bourgeois until we reached the lane which leads to the Picasso Museum. We passed by Cognac and Carnavalet Museums we had visited earlier. The Picasso cost only 20 Francs, because of ongoing repairs. The reduced ticket price turned out not such a clear-cut bargain because the repairs, in Rooms 17 and up, meant that we didn't see much of the collection there of his work after 1935. His earliest paintings show his teenaged genius at drawing and communicating emotion. In its live colors, his *Acrobat* stunned us, as did his treatment of women as objects and his portraits of Dora Maar. An hour later, we were walking again, somewhat aimlessly except for shopping at Mouton à Cinq Pattes, an off-price shop Sorayya has heard about from Christophe Balaÿ. Then, we found ourselves in front of Bazar de Hôtel de Ville. I suggested hot chocolate at their Melodine Cafeteria on the sixth (their fifth) floor, which has an engaging view of rooftops. We sipped hot chocolate for an hour and talked about this and that and Picasso and dinner. We decided to look at an Iranian restaurant near Pompidou Centre. We walked up St. Martin, visited Ste. Merrie Church, and took the escalator to the top of Pompidou Centre, which is closed for renovations and won't reopen until 1999. Fortunately, Katie Meredith and I happened to decide to take in the gallery on September 28th, its last day open. I have colorful memories of Brach, Ernst, Klee, and especially Matisse's cut outs because of our good luck. Atop the Centre, Sorayya and I could see lighted buildings in three directions, from Hôtel de Ville, Notre Dame, Pantheon, Montparnasse, Invalides, and Eiffel Tower to Arc de Triomphe, St. Eustache, Bourse, and Sacre Coeur. The Iranian restaurant nearby didn't strike Sorayya's fancy as have others, among them Palais Persan and Cheminée Royale. So we walked back to rue St.

Denis, deciding en route to pay Le Luxembourg a third evening visit. Right across the street from Jardin du Luxembourg, it's a brasserie which has served us two memorable meals. But, almost there, Sorayya spied a little neon sign halfway up rue Cujas off Boul Mich. For the next two hours in Zhen Yeh, we visited China and Thailand for fish soup, shrimp salad, squid with vegetables, spicy chicken, lychees for dessert, and a carafe of house red wine, the ubiquitous Côtes du Rhone. We were back in our cozy, radiator-heated studio by 11:30, able then to read only for a half-hour or so when time disappeared until the Paris sun said hello this morning at 8:30. Our plans—if that's the right word—call for me to spend a couple hours at the Iranian Studies library at Sorbonne Nouvelle today, while Sorayya shops. We'll meet at Musée d'Orsay at 4. After another stroll through it, we'll do who knows what. ✍

Elizabeth and Jeff had set a March 1998 date for their Austin wedding. So, Sorayya went directly to wedding work from the airport on December 8, while I made plans for Christmas in Albuquerque. Before that trip, I spent pleasant hours organizing albums of Paris photographs, tickets, business cards, and restaurant bills, which we've often looked over since. I also dreamed about writing a guide book to Paris called *Hillmann's Practical Guide to Paris for American Men Who Don't Mind Stress But Don't Like Feeling Stupid*, but got no further than a two-page check list. A sample item: "6. On the plane from Paris to America eat, drink, and be merry, because you will then have memories better than what's ahead in your immediate future. But, on the way to Paris, which you want to start enjoying the minute you get out of the airport, you could do these things: drink lots of water, eat lightly at dinner (no foods with sugar, fats, salt or starch), drink more water, listen to soft sounds, and rest. Then, when sunlight hits the plane, eat breakfast with gusto to tell your body it's morning. Try to make it through the first day and crash that evening, in hopes that your confused body won't want to stir until the next Paris morning." Another sample item: "7. On that first day, head straight for the tenth floor of La Samaritaine (2, magazin principal) department store (at Pont-Neuf) and look at 360 degrees of history from the terrace, using the drawn and painted guide on the ledge surrounding you."

Chapter 4

Spring 1998 Semester

"What is a committee? A group ...
picked from the unfit, to do the unnecessary."
Richard Harkness

"Do pleasant things yourself, unpleasant things through others."
Baltasar Gracián

"It is not enough to succeed. Others must fail."
Gore Vidal

After only a couple of days back on campus in mid-January, I sensed a new mood in our department that did not bode well for the final months of Peter Abboud's tenure as MELC Chair. On the first day of the Spring 1998 Semester, Abboud memoed departmental faculty that Liberal Arts Dean Pederson wanted our views about MELC and its future during the 1998–2002 period. That request from the Dean, it turned out, had something more than the desire for a perfunctory review behind it. The Spring 1998 Semester taught me how little I knew about my fifteen Middle Eastern Languages colleagues and what they thought about our department.

Fourteen of these colleagues were parents. Eight had gone through divorces. Nine of them lived alone. Of the ten men, nine were bald or balding. One shaved his head to hide balding. One had a noticeable lack of affect in his speech. Three of the men wore coats and ties to the office and class. Only one displayed interest in sports or physical activity other than walking or swimming. Three of them professed a spectator interest in American football. Three were overweight or obese. One of them smoked (a pipe). One of them drank whiskey regularly, and one wine. Four of them engaged at least occasionally in academic discussions. The vast majority of them, according to a vote which a later department chair requested for who knows what reason at a faculty meeting, were the first individuals in their families to attend college. Two of them were the first persons in their families to attend and complete high school. Seven of them identified themselves as Jewish, five as Muslim, two as Christian, and two as without religious beliefs. Three were cancer survivors (two prostate, one stomach). Ten of these colleagues had not written books.

MELC faculty professed dedication to teaching and senses of ethical underpinnings and a belief in their own morality and sense of justice. MELC faculty made for an atypical academic departmental group at a state university in Texas in that thirteen of us had recognizable foreign accents, and in that more than half of us expressed support for or loyalty to a foreign culture or nation-state. None of us could have thought that a situation might arise in which the integrity and credibility of almost all of us would come into question. None of us could have thought that a situation might arise in which we would hear allegations against ourselves of prevarication, rumor-mongering, calumny, slander, character assassination, favoritism, incompetence, and other charges. Such charges surfaced during the Spring 1998 Semester, which began with Abboud's memo announcing the Dean's review of Abboud's four-year tenure as MELC's first Chair. Because of March 7, I wasn't listening to drumbeats or noticing handwriting on MELC's walls.

Wedding bells! George and Cathie came from Baltimore, Hammie came from Marina del Ray, John and Mary from Alexandria, Fahimé from Göttingen, Farzaneh and Chris from Colorado Springs, and Parvaneh from Los Angeles. As the ceremony began, the sky darkened, and thunder and lightening announced a rainstorm. George and Cathie sang "Panis Angelicus." Jim recited "A Wedding Poem," which began: "This wished for day is come at last / when present links love's future to past. / This holy day's a wedding way / to ring the bells and sing and dance." Nasrin recited the Persian original for the following lines from Farrokhzad's "Conquest of the Garden:"

> You and I have seen the garden from the window
> And plucked the apple from that branch beyond reach.
> You and I have joined the lamp, water, and mirror,
> And we were not afraid.
> I'm not talking about flimsy linking of two names
> And embracing in a ledger's old pages.
> I'm talking about my fortunate tresses
> With burnt anemone of your kisses.
> We asked wild rabbits one night in the green forest

And shells full of pearls in the turbulent sea
And young eagles on that strange mountain
What to do.
We found our way into the phoenix's quiet dream,
And found truth in the garden
In the shy look of a nameless flower.
We found immortality in an endless moment
When we two suns stared at each other.
I am not talking about timorous whispering in the dark.
I'm talking about daytime, open windows and fresh air
And a stove in which useless things burn.
I'm talking about our loving hands,
A bridge of the message of perfume and light and breeze.
Come to the meadow,
To the grand meadow, and call me,
From behind the breaths of silk-tasseled acacias,
Just like the deer calls its mate.

Mady Kaye's band played at the reception, attracting guests who usually dance onto the dance floor. When Mady Kay took breaks, an Iranian-American DJ presented Iranian music, which mysteriously lured everyone onto the dance floor, some to dance dances they'd never danced before.

Jeff's parents had hosted a stylish rehearsal dinner the night before at Green Pastures. The day after the wedding, guests came to 3404 Perry for lunch. Cousin Ann and her husband Jim, Parvaneh, et al. George played the piano. Cathie, Chris and others sang. John and Mary left early to catch their flight back to D.C., and sat in a plane on an Austin Airport runway for hours before taking off. A smile stayed on my face the whole week, except for the moment when Sorayya and I, who had walked Elizabeth down the aisle together, kissed and left her at the altar. Something caught in my throat, and I barely held back tears.

On March 10, I wrote the following note to Robert Stofberg.

> I've given a lot of thought to MELC issues which you cited in our conversation a couple of weeks back and which you and Deborah Cohen raised at our most recent departmental meeting. Also, I've talked to colleagues about their perceptions of MELC management and faculty-staff interaction. . .The upshot is that I've decided that my [positive] response to the Dean early in the semester about Peter Abboud's performance as chair vis-à-vis Persian Studies and Graduate Advising can stand as submitted. At the same time. . .it's appropriate for you and Ben Loya to pursue the possibility of a change in MELC leadership for the next four years and to mention your own name as potential Chair insofar as your reading of MELC on the basis of your experiences in Hebrew Studies and other MELC areas

I know little about differs from mine. Open debate and frank recommendations will make MELC a better place regardless of who serves as MELC Chair.

The next day, in response to a request from the MELC Course Committee, I wrote the following memo about a colleague's course proposal.

> In conceptual terms, the "Gender and Art in the Muslim World" course as described proposes to deal with "Islamic art" in "the Muslim world.". . . The single course text cited, Wijdan Ali's *Modern Islamic Art* (1997), defines the "Muslim world" as the Middle East, leaving out countries north and east of Iran, including the population centers of Islam in southeast Asia. . . The course description and course text imply that any art produced by artists born into Muslim families counts as "Islamic art," although many such artists have no ties with Islam and although no parallel category of "Christian art" exists. . . If the proposed course actually treats only art produced by artists from the Middle East, perhaps the title might reflect that fact in a phrase such as "Gender and Art in the Muslim Middle East."
>
> As a course, "Gender and Art in the Muslim Middle East" would call into play four sorts of knowledge: (1) familiarity with Islam, (2) familiarity with the Middle East, (3) familiarity with gender issues, and (4) familiarity with art appreciation. Good introductory surveys exist for each of these areas, e.g., John Esposito's *Islam: The Straight Path* for Islam and John Phillips, *Eve: History of an Idea* for gender issues. "Course Texts and Readings" probably needs to include titles in each of the four areas.
>
> However, two questions here present themselves. First, can one expect the freshmen and sophomores for whom the course is designed to bring to the course any knowledge in the areas of Islam, the Middle East, gender issues, and art appreciation? Second, can one expect such students to juggle bits and pieces of new information about the four areas and end up with a synthesis of some sort? If both questions get negative answers, the course might shelve its aesthetics component, gloss over Middle Eastern issues of national and regional differences, and limit the kinds of works and objects which students would study. The course might focus on Islam, gender issues, and painting (calligraphy figures prominently in contemporary Middle Eastern painting). The course might also have a prerequisite: participation in MELC's freshman survey course on Islam or a Middle East content course.
>
> Written for academic readers who know something about Islam, the Middle East, and art. . .the proposed course text, Wijdan Ali's *Modern Islamic Art* (1977). . .presents no historical or critical background and would surely try even the brightest teenaged student. The course calls for two core texts, one on pre-modern Middle Eastern art and one on contemporary Middle Eastern art. But *Modern Islamic Art* does not fit the bill for the second book for two reasons, one just cited.
>
> The main problems with Wijdan Ali's book have to do with scholarship and authorial skill. In the case of Iran, the author misrepresents (1)

nineteenth-century art (which figures prominently in such major museums as the Brooklyn Museum of Art), (2) the wonderful collection at Tehran's Museum of Contemporary Art (which Ms. Ali has apparently not visited in the 1990s), and (3) the range of contemporary Iranian painting (a much studied field with many publications featuring plates). For that matter, (4) the out-of-date Iran chapter blatantly plagiarizes a 1989 article by Farshid Diba. In more general terms, *Modern Islamic Art* (5) focuses curiously and almost exclusively on paintings in a specific and not particularly representative collection in the city of Amman. Had the author give equal billing to such collections as that at the Arab Institute in Paris, readers would have a different impression of contemporary Middle Eastern art. . .the book further suffers from a (6) paucity of sensible critical commentary based on art criticism.

An official MELC letter later submitted to UT's Office of Legal Affairs stated that the faculty colleague who wrote the course proposal filed a complaint of harassment against me because of the foregoing critique.

On April 14, Dean Pederson sent this memo to MELC Faculty.

I write to thank you for your thoughtful consideration and correspondence of the current state of your department and your suggestions related to the appointment of a Chair over the coming four years. I write also to let you know that, during these conversations, several issues arose which remain unresolved in my mind and I have, therefore, convened a committee to give me specific recommendations on the following issues: (1) Who should be appointed Chair? (2) What are the ways to strengthen relations between the Department and the Center for Middle Eastern Studies? (3) What should our standard policy be regarding the assessment of language proficiency? (4) What should our policy be regarding Senior Lecturers in supervisory roles over tenured and tenure-track faculty? Members of this committee include: Professors Robert Stofberg [and] Elizabeth Fernea, Associate Professors Ali Akbar Esfahanpur [and] Ben Loya, [and] Assistant Professors Kamil Riyadh [and] Deborah Cohen. You should feel free to contact any of these colleagues with your ideas and recommendations. I have asked that they submit their report to me on or before May 1, 1998.

Three days later, I took Pederson up on his recommendation and wrote the following:

In response to Dean Pederson's invitation to MELC faculty to communicate with members of the new MELC Chair Review Committee, I am writing to the two of you who represent MELC assistant professors, a group of MELC colleagues for whom the choice of a departmental chair has the greatest importance.

The Chair position in an academic department like ours is a full-time and thankless job without power, except insofar as departmental faculty give over their individual and collective power to a chair to coordinate and

implement things and except insofar as a Dean might accept a Chair's recommendations without review. However, in the case of untenured faculty, a
departmental Chair would appear to have power of various sorts in recommending course topics, teaching loads, teaching slots, peer evaluations and
other things in which regards an untenured faculty person may acquiesce
because of the chair's role in career development and promotions.

For these and other reasons, untenured faculty need to think carefully
about the chair position. If they think as a unified group, they would comprise in MELC's case the single largest faculty group, that fact making for
another kind of power. From my perspective, untenured faculty in MELC,
who consist of three women and a man of color, of two spousal contracts
and a minority appointment, of junior faculty in areas either undefined or
subject to unclear policies developed over the years by senior faculty, need
to assess things very carefully to make certain that within the next four years
they get every opportunity to develop academically so that consequently
their files will clearly warrant favorable promotion consideration. Let me
repeat what I've just said through a series of questions. How many tenured
female faculty does MELC have? (Five years ago, among 2,000 tenure-track
faculty at UT Austin, there were eighty or so women full professors). How
many tenured persons of African origin serve on MELC's faculty? (How
many faculty acquaintances of African origin around campus do you know
well?) How often do MELC's junior faculty get vibrations that have to do
with their dissertations, the nature of their appointment to tenure track
positions, and their juniorness?

You two are the most important members of the MELC Chair Review
Committee in one sense. Everyone else on the committee has an agenda
(and I mean by agenda a positive plan or position) that does not necessarily
have to do with MELC's internal growth and progress as an academic department. But for you two and your MELC Assistant Professor colleagues,
what happens in MELC during the next four years may determine your
academic futures.

What in a MELC Chair, besides obvious moral and academic qualities,
would seem to me to help untenured faculty develop their careers? Oral
articulateness, general writing skills, word-processing skills, skill at writing
reports and evaluations, punctuality in meeting deadlines, belief in egalitar-
ian collective policy development, consistent deportment in dealing with
colleagues of all ages and ranks, enthusiastic acceptance of policy arrived
at through faculty voting, high energy level and an eight-to-eight mentality, training and publications in a variety of MELC fields, homework preparedness for meetings and discussions, demonstrated interest in the career
development of junior faculty, a positive record of appreciation of women's
and minority issues, willingness to present frank views on all MELC-related
issues, and habitual unwillingness to talk about colleagues not present.

An official MELC letter later submitted to UT's Office of Legal
Affairs stated that the assistant professors in question, one a spousal
hire and the other a minority hire, filed separate complaints against me
because of the foregoing memo. In response to a deposition question

in September 2002, I recalled that my chief intent in the memo was to encourage junior colleagues not to recommend Stofberg for the MELC Chair position.

On the same issue, I sent this note to Pederson on April 28.

> In response to your invitation to MELC faculty to communicate with members of the MELC Chair Review Committee, I immediately wrote to three committee members in hopes that my views as a very active and committed member of the MELC faculty would get reflected in their report to you due next week. Then, yesterday afternoon, to a question on news about MELC's administrative future, Peter Abboud responded cryptically that you had decided to have the MELC Chair position rotate among faculty. Rotation of departmental and center Chair positions I think an excellent policy in principle, especially because I grew up with and in faculty-run organizations (something I have missed at UT Austin). I might have suggested rotation in my response to your request for faculty views in January except that the still unfinished department-building process seemed to call for continuity in management. And Peter seemed to me to have done an excellent job so far.

Pederson's next communication with MELC faculty came in the form of this memo dated May 1.

> Upon recommendation of the Review Committee, and to give Professor Abboud a well-deserved breather from the always difficult and sometimes thankless tasks of being Chair, I will recommend to the Provost that Professor Robert Stofberg be appointed as Chair of MELC, beginning September 1, 1998. Getting the Department off the ground has been a challenging assignment, and together you and Professor Abboud can take credit for many successes. Personally, I have enjoyed working with Professor Abboud a great deal and appreciate all he has done. Please join me in extending our heart-felt thanks to Peter for his tireless work over the past four years. I know that you will welcome and support Robert as he assumes his new duties. I look forward to working with you as we continues to address the wide range of issues which lie ahead.

Immediately after hearing the news of Stofberg's appointment as new MELC Chair, Kamil Riyadh wrote this e-message, reprinted exactly as written, to Peter Abboud on May 5.

> As a follow up to our discussion yesterday 5/4/98 concerning the note I showed you, I would formally like to request the following items ASAP: (1) A copy of the document you quoted from indicating the amount of my increase for the coming year–i.e., the % as well as the dollar amount (the Dean's review) (2) The Ex.Committe review and ranking. Other Business: A faculty member has sent me a letter during the last two weeks, the letter contains some rather inflammatory and racial remarks [Hillmann's April 17 memo], for you information I have written to the dean about that particular

letter in question and I have also spoken to the University attorney who may contact you in the near future. It is a serious matter.

Riyadh's note caught me by surprise for two reasons. First, I had assumed that he knew that his best chance to develop a decent promotion file in the area of research writing meant seeking editorial and research process advice from me and Arabic advice from Abboud. The tone he used with Abboud in his note and the bold charge he leveled at me revealed that he had joined the now-in-power anti-Abboud group, in which no Arabic or editorial expertise existed. Or, perhaps he thought that his African-American status would count for something with the University administration. Second, I hadn't expected any confrontational boldness on the part of someone who had greatly benefited from Sorayya's generosity and who could have faced consequences for his non-payment of rent and other debts to Sorayya and me. In fact, my chief concern with Riyadh's complaint had to do with the money he owed us and the possibility he'd use this show of righteous indignation to rationalize non-payment. Upon returning from Paris, telephone company threats to suspend our service because of an unpaid $3,000+ telephone bill had led us to the discovery that Riyadh had accessed Sorayya's long distance code password and made scores of telephone calls to Syria. I confronted him with the bills and forced him in mid-January to write and sign a series of post-dated checks, which I thought would make it impossible for him to renege on payment. Two of the checks bounced the first time I tried to deposit them at University Federal Credit Union, where we both banked.

The Arabic Studies faculty and most of the Persian and Arabic graduate students would later object to the process by which Abboud's tenure as MELC Chair came to an end. They alleged unfairness in the selection of MELC Chair Review Committee members and impropriety in that Committee's recommending one of its own to serve as 1998–2002 MELC Chair. I didn't share this view because I hadn't expected academic and intellectual issues to take precedence in such an administrative matter. The whole process involved politics, the kind of politics in which people participate everywhere—in the academic world and in the so-called gerrymandering and court-stuffing real world—the kind of political process which gets some people what they want and leaves some people dissatisfied. For me personally the stakes were low to begin with. The MELC Chair position had no significance in the scheme of things. No MELC Chair could interfere with, or even influence, my teaching, writing, and lecturing.

Nevertheless, I had participated energetically in the process. In response to every solicitation of views, I wrote letters and had conversations with colleagues, which I hoped would lead to a second term for Abboud. I tried to influence the views of several MELC Chair Review Committee members. The upshot was that the team for which I was rooting lost.

As Abboud's dissatisfaction and Stofberg's satisfaction at the turn of events became more pronounced, I continued to wonder about the attraction which the title and position of "Chair" could possibly have for academics whose training, qualifications and experience relate exclusively to teaching and research. A MELC staff person reported that on the morrow of his appointment as MELC Chair Stofberg went to the departmental office to cancel the bulk of his classes for 1998–1999. What particularly intrigued me about the appeal of the title "Chair" to some colleagues was that it blinded them to their own lack of personnel and management experience and skills.

In the summer of 1998, MELC again receded into the background, unable to compete with Baltimore, Los Angeles, and Midcoast Maine. Sorayya and I made our almost annual pilgrimage to ancestral haunts in Searsmont and Belfast. We met Jim in Baltimore, drove north with him, and stayed for a week in a cottage on Sennebec Pond near Appleton. I caught a pickerel for breakfast one morning. A half-century earlier, I had caught my first pickerel by the bridge over Searsmont's Anderson Stream, where Dad had taught Jim and me how to swim. That little river and Quantabacook Pond which feeds it remain almost daily conjured-up images. Jim put part of those feelings best in a poem in his 2001 chapbook called *Dream Time*.

> The pond,
> a character in our play
> muddy bottomed mirror
> of a summer day,
> ran on until the end of our imagining.
> Its part was dashing,
> full of high adventure,
> and a little dangerous.
> But all the same,
> it was a friendly body
> of frogs, pickerel, bass, and eel.

In its sparkling embrace,
we swam, and rowed,
and fished the days,
till we grew up and went away.

At cemeteries in Appleton and Searsmont, we paid our respects to six generations of Craigs, Bartletts, and Keatings, took walks on country roads, strolled around Belfast and Camden, and enjoyed our annual lobster dinner at The Lobster Pound in Lincolnville Beach. After we got back to Jim's on Bolton Hill, Sorayya returned to Austin, while I directed two, week-long Persian language seminars at University of Baltimore, watched an Orioles game at Camden Yards, and played tennis at Clifton Park. In the evenings Jim and I ate at our regular places at Fells Point and Inner Harbor, and on and near Bolton Hill.

I then flew home to Austin to pack for Los Angeles. First came a lecture on Forugh Farrokhzad's life and poetry at an annual meeting of the Iranian American Medical Association at Marina del Rey. Then came dinner with Hammie and Holly at Joe's, lacrosse on Venice Beach with Hammie, rollerblading from Venice to Santa Monica and back, and lots of time with our favorite newlyweds, who were settling into new digs in West Hollywood after migrating from Albuquerque.

Austin summoned me back for two summer courses, a university course called Classics of World Poetry, and Persepolis's annual Advanced Persian Course at University Towers. In the first course, I get to talk about the nature of lyric poetry for a month and watch the pleasure on student faces as they figure out how poems work as enjoyable vicarious experiences, rather than as off-putting anagrams, which is how most of my American students appear to think of poetry when the course begins. In the latter course, I get to supervise highly motivated students at proficiency levels beyond those in university Persian language programs as they perform in class six or seven hours a day for thirty-five days and exhibit substantial improvement in speaking and reading Persian by the end of the course.

On my first day back at WMB 5.146 in August, I noticed that someone—students later reported it was a Hebrew Studies colleague—had removed the Arabic map of the Middle East from the wall facing the Arabic language corner opposite my office. That map had the Arabic word for "Palestine" in the place where non-Arab(ic) maps put the word "Israel."

Chapter 5

Fall 1998 Semester

"What is hurtful to you, do not do to others.
That is the whole Torah; the rest is commentary."
Hillel

"Moral Indignation is jealousy with a halo."
H.G. Wells

"Mendacem memorem esse oportere."
Quintilian

"Thar ain't no sense in gettin' riled!"
'Jim,' Bret Harte

"One of the worst things in life is not how nasty the nasty people are.
You know that already. It is how nasty the nice people can be."
Anthony Powell

When MELC students returned to campus for the Fall 1998 Semester, they learned that Robert Stofberg had replaced Peter Abboud as Department Chair. By the following May, almost all of MELC's Persian and Arabic Studies graduate students had left MELC. The number of Hebrew Studies graduate students also decreased. Two of them later successfully petitioned the Office of Graduate Studies to constitute ad hoc doctoral committees not under the purview of MELC's Hebrew Studies program.

Earlier, upon hearing that Stofberg had become MELC Chair, a Middle Eastern Studies undergraduate student by the name of Annie Menzel had sent the following e-message, dated June 16, to Liberal Arts Dean Pederson, who had named Stofberg MELC Chair.

> I recently learned that Robert Stofberg has succeeded Peter Abboud as chair of the Middle Eastern Languages and Cultures department. Last summer, I participated in MELC's Archaeological Expedition to Israel and spent six weeks digging there under the directorship of Dr. Stofberg. I had previously taken two Jewish Studies Courses with Dr. Stofberg.

One day last summer as we–Dr. Stofberg, his wife, and a fellow archaeologist, and myself–drove through an Arab village on our way to Tel Aviv. . .[and]. . .passed some two-story houses on a hillside, he said: "Look at that. They live better than we do!. . .They would never have anything like that if it hadn't been given to them." At the time I had only a vague idea of the scale of the dispossession of the Palestinian people, but having seen Jerusalem and Akko, I knew at least his second statement to be patently false, and I spoke. As we argued, however, I felt frustrated at my inability to cite hard facts to counter his case, and eventually I proposed we let the issue drop. . .and we lapsed into uncomfortable silence. I was also disquieted by Dr. Stofberg's assumption of the complicity of the other student and myself, his inclusive "we" and his comfort in making the remarks at all. Unfortunately, he was accurate to a great extent. I became complicit by riding quietly all the way to Tel Aviv, and more deeply so by not investigating the injustices that I purported to deplore. Now, in light of Dr. Stofberg's installation as the MELC chair, I feel compelled to point out the irony of this development. Imagine, for example, an American Studies department headed by a professor who, upon seeing flush toilets and livable housing on a Native American reservation, wondered what in the world "they" had to complain about. Clearly, a quality of life index that would allow for such a conclusion would have to exclude from its spectrum of factors another, more fundamental kind of statistic: namely, the legacy of millions of American Indians exterminated by European invaders and removed from their land by decree of the US government in the name of God and manifest white destiny. Likewise, Dr. Stofberg's assessment of the way "they" live relies on a deliberate blindness to the tragedy of the more than 3.3 million (UN figure) Palestinian refugees removed from their homes, farms, and towns, one-third of whom live in camps in Jordan, Lebanon, Syria, Gaza, and the West Bank. Additionally, such an index, grounded as it is in a false assumption of equal footing, cannot account for the daily assault on the "universal human dignity" of the almost one million Palestinians who live within Israel's borders, as they are denied housing, work, and government services because they are Arabs. The Middle Eastern Languages and Cultures department is now under the direction of an individual whose conception of "Middle Eastern Culture[s]" is geared toward justifying the systematic destruction and displacement of a Middle Eastern people."

On August 3, Menzel sent me this e-message

Salaam Gorbon, I am afraid you are out of town teaching your crash course. In any case, in mid-June I mailed you and the rest of MELC faculty and staff a letter concerning the new chair of the department, Robert Stofberg, which I had sent to Dean Pederson. I received no response to my letter from any of the MELC faculty, but the Dean wrote me back and we scheduled an appointment to follow up on this issue. Since you are someone within the department and whose opinions I value, I was wondering if we could meet (if you are here) before I see the Dean. It's pretty short notice-my appointment is on Wednesday afternoon. Anytime you can see me between now and then is great. Khayli mamnoon.

The next day I wrote her back: "Several MELC colleagues have shown me copies of your letter to Liberal Arts Dean Arnold Pederson. But you did not include my e-mail address on your initial mailing, or I would have responded immediately to it. I'll be at the office today, from 10 to 11:15 and from 1:15 to 3:45. Tomorrow I'll be here from 9 to 11:15 and from 1:15 to 3:45. You can stop by whenever you choose." Menzel responded: "I could have sworn that you were on that list–sorry for the unfortunate exclusion. You were actually one of the people whom I wanted most to get my message. I'll be by later today."

For the rest of MELC's benighted existence, Menzel's allegations poisoned the departmental air and stayed on the minds of faculty and students in Arabic and Persian Studies. Hebrew language specialist and lexicographer Avraham Zilkha opined in private that the content of the allegation sounded like something which his Hebrew Studies colleague Stofberg might say in an unguarded moment. For my money, Stafberg's alleged statements weren't something the repercussions of which a quick apology or clarification couldn't have defused.

Instead of doing that, Stofberg accused me (and Abboud) of collusion in the composition and transmission of Menzel's e-letter and asserted that he had placed the matter in the hands of an attorney. The sole basis for alleging such collusion, Stofberg admitted, was the fact that my name did not appear among the e-addresses to which Menzel had sent copies of her letter. The foregoing exchange of e-messages between Annie Menzel and me and deposition testimony under oath by three individuals in "Attieh v. UT" verified that I had nothing to do with the Menzel e-letter. Testifying under oath in the same proceeding, Stofberg admitted that he had no evidence to support his allegation, which he had discussed openly with some MELC faculty during 1998–1999.

At the time, I couldn't fathom the "academic" mentality from which Stofberg's suspicions and accusations sprang. More significantly, his accusations contributed to MELC's unwillingness to address issues which Menzel's memo raised, other than Stofberg's understandable and predictable reaction to the Arab village he was driving through. First, a bright, articulate student had participated boldly in the most fundamental Middle Eastern discourse vis-à-vis an audience of Middle Eastern Languages faculty who refused to debate the issue. The fact that a MELC Chair would disparage Arabs in a passing comment pales in significance to the fact that some MELC faculty would think that a student of Middle Eastern Studies should not hold the views which Menzel holds or could neither have nor express those views without faculty guidance. Most MES students and faculty know that espousal of the view, which I hold as well, that an inclusive, non-religious nation-state should occupy the land which Israel today occupies and that Palestinians should live there with equal status to Christians, Jews, and Muslims, and to all local ethnic groups and with equal immigration status for those groups can evoke the charge of anti-Semitism. Four years after Menzel's e-memorandum, no discussion of the issues which she raised in her memo had taken place in our department, even though the politics of the Arab-Israeli dispute became a central force in MELC life from the first days of Stofberg's tenure as MELC Chair and CMES support for his actions against Arab-American and Arab-Canadian faculty members Attieh, Abboud, and Walid Hamarneh, and a score of Arabic students and several other MELC faculty charged with disloyalty to MELC ostensibly because they supported their Arab-American and Arab-Canadian colleagues.

On September 8, Stofberg, who seemed friendly enough when we talked, stopped by my office. The next day, I sent him this memo.

> In response to the criticisms of 1994–1998 MELC management you made in your visit to my office yesterday, i.e., that MELC then lacked openness and equity and that you received only 1% pay increases, including for 1998–1999 (with, as you stated, no pay increase for your promotion to full professor), I here repeat my astonishment at the 1% figure and lack of a raise for promotion. In fact, I'd be happy to write a letter to the College of Liberal Arts asking for some special consideration in your case, it striking me as incredible that you did not receive more than a 1% raise in any of the last four years and that you did not receive a 3%+ raise from Liberal Arts for your promotion this fall to full professor. If what you have told me is literally true, then MELC/LA certainly failed to exhibit equity in dealing with you. However, although I see no reason for MELC faculty to dwell on the past in charting a course for the future, I have to add that the Persian Studies and Graduate Studies programs, including every graduate degree student to whom I talked to last spring, have positive views about MELC's equity and openness during the 1994–1998 years. This means that MELC need not worry about mending fences in those two areas. MELC can just move forward.
>
> The report you have requested on your proposal for a MELC event on "material culture" next spring will get to you tomorrow afternoon as promised.

On September 20 Sorayya and I hosted a party for Peter Abboud. About thirty people came, all in good spirits except for Peter who still wondered why Dean Pederson, about to become Provost and in attendance, didn't let him serve as MELC Chair for four more years. Sorayya did her wonted great job with roast lamb, *baghali polow*, crème caramel, Shirazi salad, and the rest. Peter and Aman were the last to leave, at nearly two in the morning.

A month later, on October 19, Stofberg sent me this note about my ongoing work as Lecture Committee Chair:

> While the Lecturer [sic] Committee was formed approximately seven weeks ago, contrary to your statements, I have been told that the Committee has not met and that no discussions have taken place. The Lecturer Committee is not progressing in the manner that I envisioned. Moreover, because of your uncooperative spirit, your willful disregard of my instructions to the Committee and because of your offensive misuse of my Memo to the Committee, I am replacing you as Chairman of this Committee immediately.

On the same day, I sent this memo to MELC Lecture Committee members:

> Attached find a copy of today's letter to me from Robert Stofberg. . .The attached copy includes notes I added in responding to Robert and in passing along the existing fourteen pages of Lecture Committee correspondence to the new Lecture Committee Chair. For the record, my review of my activities on behalf of the Lecture Committee since September 11, when I first heard that we were to constitute that Committee in 1998–1999, leads to a characterization opposite to Robert's. . .However, discussion of such *ad hominem* phrases of Robert's as "uncooperative spirit" and "willful disregard" and "offensive misuse" would not contribute anything to MELC's goal of a successful material culture event next spring and a successful larger event in 1999–2000. I confess to avoiding dialogue at the office which does not relate to academic and intellectual issues. We'll have our planned happy hour meeting later in the fall, although without a committee agenda for an excuse.

The anger in Stofberg's memo and the martinet sense of imaginary administrative power behind it, as well as his reliance on unchecked hearsay–"I have been told"–, didn't register with me at the time because his mosquito-like buzzings in my direction paled in comparison with concomitant actions he was taking against the Arabic program.

In mid-summer Stofberg had written Attieh with the request that she vacate the Arabic Computer/Language Laboratory space and, in effect, cease to have an Arabic-only corner at my end of the WMB fifth floor corridor. Attieh refused the request. Then, in early September, Stofberg warned Attieh that she would have to make changes in her classroom and supervisory behavior if she hoped to remain on the MELC faculty. In the "Attieh v. UT" litigation, sworn deposition and affidavit testimony reveals that Stofberg had no academic basis for his comments to Attieh, that he had based his comments exclusively on hearsay from two students and two teaching assistants from among hundreds of Arabic students and a score of teaching assistants during Attieh's years in our department, without a parallel effort to verify the hearsay commentary or to discuss relevant issues with any faculty or students who might have offered more informed views about Attieh's instructional materials, teaching methods, and deportment as coordinator of lower-division Arabic language courses.

I commiserated with Attieh and expressed the hope that her worst fears wouldn't materialize. But I still regret something I didn't do then: tell Attieh to do what I do in such conflict situations, which is to write a summary of the interaction in question and send it in a letter of objection or complaint or whatever to the person who initiated the conflict. Had I done that in September 1998, my reading of judicial rulings and opinions in 2004 and 2005 tells me that Attieh's lawsuit might have ended differently. But this is getting way ahead of the story.

In mid-October 1998, Stofberg published a departmental newspaper. Because of its 40+ errors of fact, usage, spelling, and the like, which faculty colleagues brought to his attention, Stofberg did not circulate *MELC Newsletter Volume 1* beyond the department. As of mid-2003, the bulk of the copies of the newsletter, and three subsequent newsletter issues printed during the next three years, remained on bookcase shelves in the hallway outside of the WMB 5.120 departmental office.

On campus, however, this inaugural issue of a departmental newsletter got immediate attention because of what didn't appear in it. First, in its front-page article called "Message from the Chairman" in describing MELC's programs, Stofberg avoided the words "Arab," "Arabs," and "Arabic." Second, the names of Arabic Studies colleagues Peter Abboud, Aman Attieh, and Walid Hamarneh did not appear anywhere in the newsletter. The omission of Abboud's name seemed the most curious because he had just finished four years of service as MELC Chair,

and Stofberg had reported on all other changes in MELC management
by naming both the previous and new holders of positions. Third, no
names of the department's Arabic students appeared in the newsletter
either.

On October 26, six days after *MELC Newsletter Volume 1* appeared,
one of those students sent this letter, in part about the newsletter, to
Dean Pederson.

> I am writing to express my profound concern regarding developments
> in the Department of Middle Eastern Languages and Cultures (MELC) over
> the past six months–developments I and my colleagues find quite disheart-
> ening. These developments began with the nomination and appointment of
> Dr. Robert Stofberg to the chairmanship of MELC in the spring of 1998,
> and have continued to escalate and deepen since his official assumption of
> the chairmanship on September 1, 1998. The complete and intentional
> marginalization of the Arabic language and literature program constitutes
> the essence of my concerns and the basis of the proceeding complaints. I
> will endeavor to outline in the following letter the nature of these problems.
> I am convinced that the failure to address and resolve these issues will result
> in the gradual decline of the intellectual integrity of MELC.
> I. . .begin with an introductory note to explain my position as a stu-
> dent of Arabic literature of MELC. My experience with this department,
> and The University of Texas at Austin, began approximately eight months
> before I embarked upon a master's program in the fall of 1996. During my
> application process to various universities across the nation, I scheduled an
> interview with the MELC graduate adviser Dr. Michael Craig Hillmann in
> order to discuss my opportunities at MELC and the University of Texas. I
> traveled from Washington, D.C., to Austin in the fall of 1995. Upon my
> arrival at the university, Dr. Hillmann granted me an entire afternoon of his
> time, during which he introduced me to Dr. Peter Abboud and Dr. Aman
> Attieh, the former chair and former undergraduate adviser, respectively.
> Their sincere insights into the program and the generosity which they were
> willing to bestow upon a prospective student convinced me of their unfal-
> tering dedication to MELC and compelled me to choose The University of
> Texas at Austin.
> Under the instruction and guidance of Dr. Walid Hamarneh and Dr.
> Abboud, and with the constant and unselfish encouragement and advice of
> Dr. Attieh, I reached a level of competency in Arabic language and literature
> that enabled me to write my master's report in Arabic and graduate with a
> 4.0 grade point average as a member of the honor society of Phi Kappa Phi.
> Currently, I am working toward a Ph.D. in Arabic literature.
> My achievements in MELC do not represent an isolated case. Many
> of my colleagues in the Arabic department also have had remarkable suc-
> cess after graduation. To illustrate this point, Jeff Sacks, who completed his
> Master of Arts in Modern Arabic Literature, graduated as the top Arabic
> student from the prestigious CASA program at the American University in
> Cairo, Egypt. In addition, Paul Schemm, who studied Arabic in MELC and

graduated with a double Master of Arts degree from the Center for Middle Eastern Studies and the School of Journalism, is currently employed by a newspaper in Cairo, Egypt. The very number of native Arabic speakers who study both Arabic grammar and literature in MELC testifies for the quality of the Arabic program. There are numerous other examples, which, for the sake of brevity, I will omit. I state with the utmost confidence that this program represents one of the finest in the nation. The University of Texas should take pride in its outstanding Arabic language and literature faculty as well as its current and former students. I would like to summarize what I believe to represent the developments of problems which will be confronting the Arabic program in MELC, its faculty and its students.

It is my impression that the composition of the committee charged with assessing Dr. Abboud's performance precluded a fair evaluation for the following reasons. (1) Dr. Stofberg, who became chairman, sat upon the committee charged with assessing Dr. Abboud. In any other context, business or political, his presence on the committee, and his expressed desire for the chairmanship position, would represent a conflict of interest. (2) Dr. Riyadh, a member of the reviewing committee, arrived at the university only one semester prior to the chairmanship evaluation, rendering him unable to assess Dr. Abboud's chairmanship with any level of objectivity. (3) No member of the Arabic department was included in the evaluating committee. Nor was Dr. Michael Craig Hillmann, a former graduate adviser and long-time member of MELC included, though, clearly, he was equipped to provide an adequate and thorough assessment of Dr. Abboud's work as chairman. (4) After Dr. Abboud's removal from the chairmanship position, the committee did not, as far as I am able to determine, forward the reasons for its decisions regarding his termination. (5) Although asked to evaluate Dr. Abboud's chairmanship, the students of MELC were not given the opportunity to express any input regarding his potential replacement.

Since Dr. Stofberg assumed the chairmanship on September 1, the Arabic program and its students have been marginalized. This process, in my observation, has existed in the Center for Middle Eastern Studies for some time. . . (2) Dr. Loya, Director of the Center for Middle Eastern Studies, has established numerous (5–7) committees in the Center. Interestingly, not one professor from the Arabic language and literature program sits on any of these committees. (3) While the Center for Middle Eastern Studies issues numerous Foreign Language Area Studies (FLAS) fellowships, a disproportionately low number of students majoring in Arabic language or literature have received these fellowships. In fact, not one graduate student of Arabic language or literature has received a FLAS fellowship during the past two years. . .(5) Dr. Stofberg has made no effort to meet MELC students. On the contrary, the five-page department newsletter (see attached), which appeared last week, made no mention of any Arabic faculty member or Arabic language or literature student. In this letter, faculty members and students of the Hebrew, Persian, and Turkish programs were introduced and their respective endeavors were highlighted. Dr. Stofberg, as chairman of the department, should have noticed this discrepancy and acted to rectify it. No chairman of any department should allow such neglect in a departmental newsletter.

Finally, I would like to address my concern regarding Dr. Stofberg's apparent lack of dedication to the Arabic program. I have attached a letter from a colleague, Annie Menzel, expressing her concern regarding racist remarks made by Dr. Stofberg during an archaeological expedition to Israel. I am disturbed by these alleged comments, and wonder whether any action has been taken to investigate such allegations. If these comments are true, and do indeed represent Dr. Stofberg's attitude toward Arabs in general, the current marginalization of the Arabic language and literature program of MELC is explicitly clear, and can only escalate in the future.

The next day, October 27, I wrote the following letter to Stofberg about the student's letter.

I have just received a copy of the letter which MELC Ph.D. student Mark S. Sullivan, Jr., sent yesterday to Provost Pederson, with copies to the interim Dean of Liberal Arts, and assorted MELC faculty, including me.

Mark Sullivan, with whom I have spent upwards of two hundred hours in Persian language learning settings since the beginning of 1998 and who is a superior participant in an ongoing graduate course in Persian literature (involving mostly native speakers), is a first-rate graduate student with a promising career in Arabic Studies, and perhaps Persian Studies, ahead of him. He has also been a solid MELC citizen, productively active in student and extracurricular affairs since joining our program at the beginning of the 1996–1997 school year. On these bases, I surmise that his critical and challenging letter has behind it the reasonable hope that MELC work its way through what he sees as problems in MELC vis-à-vis Arabic Studies. It also strikes me that Mr. Sullivan, with whom I have never had occasion to discuss any of the matters he raises in his letter, hopes to complete his Ph.D. program with us.

As MELC Graduate Adviser until the summer of 1998, I can verify that seven or eight MELC graduate students have had the sorts of reservations which Mr. Sullivan expresses in his letter about the process for choosing a MELC chairperson for the next four years. My advice to individual students at the time was that they not worry about the process but rather write to Provost Pederson to express personal views about who as MELC chair might best serve the interests of their programs. Mr. Sullivan revisits the issue of the selection process because he appears to think a connection exists between that process and what he perceives as the subsequent marginalization of the Arabic Studies program.

That perception needs dealing with if only because at least a handful of MELC graduate students share it, with several of them making new decisions about their graduate careers because of it. You will recall my immediate reaction to the *MELC Newsletter* which came out on October 20, to the effect that it failed to give any information about Arabic Studies, our best known graduate program. MELC faculty in other areas may understandably not realize the reputation which Arabist Peter Abboud has in his field as its leading, deservedly best known, and most productive applied linguist. MELC faculty not in literary studies may understandably not appreciate the remarkable talents, knowledge, and achievements of Arabist Walid

Hamarneh who has created a first-rate Arabic Literature program here in the past six years. And our Arabic Studies graduate students, among them Shelton Henderson, Chad Kia, Mary McDermott, Dylan Oehler-Stricklin, Jeffrey Sachs, and Mark Sullivan, rank among the best in America.

If Mark Sullivan had approached me with his concerns, I might have suggested that he send you a letter with no copies to anyone outside MELC, so that MELC might attempt an internal resolution to his very resolvable concerns. But he perhaps wrote directly to the Provost because he perhaps had heard that contacting the Dean or the Provost directly with departmental problems had become a matter of course for some MELC faculty and students. If Mark Sullivan had approached me with his concerns, I might have suggested a less confrontational and critical slant in his letter. But he perhaps wrote as he did because he perhaps had heard that frank, confrontational representation of complaints and concerns had become an accepted intradepartmental approach as of last spring. In other words, I'm implying that MELC can ignore where he sent his letter and the style he uses in it and focus on the letter's content, which has serious academic and intellectual ramifications for all of us with permanent commitments to MELC's graduate enterprise.

Stofberg dismissed Sullivan as a "trouble-maker" and circulated the allegation that I, among others, had "fomented" the writing of the letter. Deposition testimony in 2002 in "Attieh v. UT" contradicted Stofberg's allegation. In his own deposition, Stofberg admitted under oath that he had no evidence for making his allegation, although he asserted that my letter in response to Sullivan's, despite its statement that Sullivan had not discussed his concerns with me, strengthened his suspicion that I had played a role in the writing of Sullivan's letter. Those suspicions and Stofberg's conspiratorial view interested me more at the time than his defensive projection and messenger-attacking. I wondered whether a culture-specific orientation lay behind his behavior toward Arab faculty and Arabic students.

Stofberg's public response to Sullivan's letter came indirectly in this note, dated November 2, from Graduate Adviser Zilkha to MELC graduate students: "I would like to invite you to a reception for the graduate students in the Department of Middle Eastern Languages and Cultures on Wednesday, November 11, from 11 to 12 in the conference room, West Mall Office Building 5.134. This gathering will give the students and faculty a chance to get acquainted in an informal setting. It will also be an opportunity for our graduate students to meet the new department chairman, Dr. Robert Stofberg. Refreshments will be served. I hope you will be able to attend."

After the meeting, a "Coalition of Concerned Graduate Students" sent this memo on November 11 to the interim Dean.

Although we were pleased at Professor Stofberg's initiative to meet with the graduate students, we were shocked at the way the meeting was conducted. Our impression of the meeting is that Professor Stofberg is more interested in the mechanics of having a meeting than addressing the issues that necessitated the meeting in the first place. Professor Stofberg came to the meeting fifteen minutes late and immediately engaged in a side discussion with the graduate advisor regarding issues that are best suited for a faculty meeting (e.g., qualifying exams and the number of conference vs. regular courses offered through the department). . .One of the students interrupted the exchange in order to bring forward the real issues which we, as graduate students, had come prepared to discuss.

The student started by stating that her decision to join UT was based on the reputation of the Arabic program and that there were allegations coming from MES faculty member Professor BJ Fernea that shed negative light on the prestige of the Arabic program as a whole. She then referred to another student present who had a list of questions already prepared, and Professor Stofberg agreed to listen to it.

CCGS Question to Professor Stofberg: One of our colleagues received a phone call from Professor BJ Fernea which was alarming. She detailed to him what she believes is the malaise of the Arabic program. She believes in short: (1) The Arabic program has a bad reputation around the country due to the poor pedagogy of the current instructors of Arabic; (2) The Arabic literature program in MELC is inadequate; (3) Islamic Studies has been compromised due to the loss of Khaled Abou El Fadl; and (4) Except for a few exceptional students, the Arabic program has failed to produce quality students. Do you share Professor Fernea's concerns? If so, what is being planned to elevate the standard of the program?

No sooner had the student read the first question when Stofberg stood up abruptly and announced that he had another meeting to attend at 11:30. He left without addressing the question. We were shocked at this turn of events. We felt marginalized, our presence disregarded, and our serious concerns blatantly trivialized. When he was asked how long he had budgeted for the meeting he informed us some time between 11:00–11:30 am. We have attached a copy of the invitation to the graduate students, which stated that the meeting was scheduled from 11:00 to noon.

In the interest of a mature and constructive dialogue, we deem it necessary that more than fifteen minutes be allowed for airing and dealing with the graduate student concerns. We sincerely hope that the meeting on Friday will not be treated as another formality but rather as a real opportunity to address and confirm the commitment of the chair and the department to the integrity of the program and specifically the continuation of the Arabic program.

In reaction to the CCGS memo, on November 13, I wrote the following to MELC Persian Studies Graduate Students:

MELC's Arabic Studies program has special importance for Persian Studies graduate students insofar as two years of Arabic are a minimal requirement, and three or four a recommendation, for Ph.D. students in Persian Studies. Consequently, concerns which Arabic Studies graduate students have recently raised about its current status in MELC and about alleged criticisms by CMES faculty deserve Persian Studies attention and response.

As a MELC faculty member who studied Arabic language and literature at Tehran University, New York University, and The University of Chicago, who taught Elementary Modern Standard Arabic for the American Peace Corps in Iran, who has published in the field of Arabic literature, and who has training and continuing involvement in the field of foreign language acquisition, I assure you Persian Studies graduate students that MELC's Arabic language program is as rigorous and substantial and as methodologically sound and up-to-date as any in the Western world, and is far and away MELC's most progressive language program, for example, MELC's only language which uses outside certified proficiency testing to gauge student achievement and teaching effectiveness. Whenever you happen to visit any other major research university with an Arabic program, e.g., Berkeley, Chicago, Michigan, Ohio State or Penn, ask about UT's program, and specifically about Peter Abboud, the leading Arabic linguist in North America, and Aman Attieh, the most energetic and dedicated Arabic program coordinator anywhere. Moreover, as someone who has lectured at major American research universities with programs in Middle Eastern languages, I have firsthand anecdotal evidence that MELC's graduate students in Arabic Studies rank among the best in America (competing well for grants and fellowships and producing first-rate theses). That means that you Persian Studies students who pursue Arabic at MELC to the advanced levels can rest assured that you will develop real competence in dealing with the Arabic texts you need to work with in Persian Studies. Rest assured also that if a problem in Arabic Studies arose with respect to instructional materials and methods, I would intervene immediately on your behalf to see to it that you were not shortchanged in any way in your study of Arabic.

At the same time, you should not give any credence to any criticisms of any Arabic program which come from. . .Elizabeth Fernea, who does not know Arabic, who has no training in Applied Linguistics, who has no graduate training in Arabic or other Middle Eastern languages or cultures, and who has not read the Arabic language program textbooks or visited classes. Now, there are MELC/CMES faculty colleagues who do not know what "Applied Linguistics" is and who think that Arabic, Persian, and Turkish likely deserve uniform teaching methods because they are all "Middle Eastern." Such unfamiliarity with language and language study is not problematic per se. MELC/CMES colleagues are in very different fields. But, in academic and intellectual terms, we MELC/CMES colleagues should refrain from voicing views about academic disciplines and programs about which we have no knowledge.

If you would like a meeting of Persian Studies faculty and students in the near future to discuss the memo which MELC's Coalition of Concerned Graduate Students distributed on November 11 or earlier letters written

61

by various students, I will gladly schedule such a meeting at 3404 Perry at happy hour or dinner time any day convenient to you between now and the end of the fall semester. I hasten to add that you need not worry about any marginalization of your Persian Studies program, regardless of changes in MELC administrative positions.

A second meeting of MELC graduate students with Stofberg took place on November 16. Two students reported afterwards that Stofberg announced upon arrival: "I'm a Jew and proud of it." Speaking of Jewish pride in America—and I was now beginning to think that Stofberg's particular brand of Judaism or personal Jewishness figured in much of his behavior at the office—Richard Bank penned this prefatory note to his *The Everything Judaism Book*:

> Though I am not a very observant "Jew," I am proud of being Jewish and feel an overwhelming sense of loss as our community diminishes. . .If demographic projections hold true, the community of American non-Orthodox Jews may disappear in fifty years. Moreover, in absolute numbers, there are fewer Jews in the United States now that there were. . .in the fifties [1950s]! One way to keep Judaism and Jewish culture alive is through knowledge. We cannot reject Judaism without first trying to know and understand it, and we have to give the same opportunity to future generations. . .*The Everything Judaism Book* is an opportunity to share in this knowledge. If, along the way, it will help some of you fortify your Jewish identity, all the better.

Stofberg would qualify as what Bank calls a "very observant Jew." An ordained Orthodox rabbi, he reportedly led a congregation in Austin for a time. At that time, in the late 1970s, Sorayya and I occasionally entertained departmental colleagues. After one such a dinner at our house, Stofberg put in my faculty mailbox a page entitled "How to Entertain the Stofbergs," which described his expectations with respect to food preparation, dishware, and eating utensils when having dinner at a home like ours. Sorayya looked at the list and thereafter did not include the Stofbergs as dinner guests. Also in the late 1970s and 1980s, Stofberg expressed puzzlement that OALL would organize 'TGIF' happy hours on Friday afternoons. In addition, he objected two or three times to my use of the phrase "Palestinian Archaeology" and insinuated, once or twice, that something I said or did smacked of anti-Semitism. In short, Stofberg was and is likely as proud of being Jewish as is Richard Bank. But the latter's pride seems to have no confrontational aspects to it. At the office, I have occasionally wondered if nurturing and perpetuating Jewishness figures as a core energizing motivation for some Hebrew Studies colleagues in their academic Hebrew Studies work.

Before their second meeting with Stofberg, CCGS had prepared this "List of Demands."

> We, Coalition of Concerned Graduate Students, deem it necessary that the chairman acknowledge publicly the following: (1) The report that he had allegedly made racist remarks towards Arabs in Israel is not true and furthermore does not represent his views personally or as a department chair. (2) In light of the serious allegations by MES faculty member Professor Elizabeth W. Fernea concerning the quality of the Arabic language and literature program in MELC, we ask that the chair issue a statement addressed to students and faculty, as well as in the *MELC Newsletter*, defending the stature of the Arabic language and literature program. (3) In order to alleviate the concerns of CCGS about the perceived systematic marginalization of the Arabic program by the new administration, we urge the chair to inform students and faculty of his agenda for a concrete advancement and continuation of the Arabic language and literature program. (4) Given that the FLAS is often the only source of funding available for language students, and given the CCGS perception that FLAS fellowships have been unfairly distributed, the CCGS urges the chair to clarify in a public statement the FLAS selection process and the FLAS committee selection. We view these demands as fair and necessary for the creation of trust and restoring the academic integrity of the Arabic language and literature program. We sincerely hope that the chair will act on these demands in a timely fashion.

On November 17, Stofberg sent this brief memo to MELC faculty: "Please be advised that there is a CALLED EMERGENCY Faculty Meeting scheduled for Monday, November 23, 1998, at 4:30 p.m. Everyone is expected to be in attendance." I scribbled this note onto the original of Stofberg's memo and left the page in his mail box: "Robert, as you know, with MELC permission, I'll be out of town on Monday, November 23." The next day, Stofberg sent a second memo to MELC faculty. It read: "Please be advised that the faculty meeting originally set for Monday, November 23rd, has been changed to this Friday, November 20th at 1:30. I expect all faculty to be present. If you have a conflict with this time please see me prior to the meeting."

Stofberg's decision to change the date of the "CALLED EMERGENCY Faculty Meeting" to fit my schedule told me that the agendaless meeting would have less to do with MELC student concerns and more to do with non-academic, *ad hominem* issues relating to me, among others, and that he would respond to serious charges made by some MELC students with an attack on MELC faculty who he would argue, albeit without evidence, fomented the student charges. I calculated that whatever Stofberg would have to say could not adversely affect me or Abboud. Hamarneh, who knew that Stofberg and Loya had just opposed his promotion to associate professor, was already thinking about a future elsewhere and had decided not to involve himself in MELC politics or meetings thereafter. That left Attieh as the only vulnerable target at the meeting. I wanted to tell her not to attend, but knew she'd insist on being there regardless of what might transpire. What transpired at the meeting would mark the beginning of the demise of our department and set in motion events and actions which would result in "Attieh v. UT."

On the same day as the second announcement of the "CALLED EMERGENCY Faculty Meeting" faculty received another memo from Stofberg, which read: "Please find attached a copy of the MEMO produced by the 'Coalition of Concerned Graduate Students' dated November 18 which they intended each of you to receive. I met with these students in hope of answering some of their concerns on Friday, November 13th. I have attached, for your benefit, the Minutes taken by Lucy of that Meeting."

Stofberg's description of the CCGS memo as something which "they intended each of you to receive" and his use of his memo as a cover statement and meeting minutes as another part of the package might not have raised any eyebrows had I not happened to walk down the MELC corridor at a specific moment on November 18. I described what I had then seen and what later transpired in the following memo to MELC faculty, which I didn't distribute right away.

> At midday on Wednesday, November 18, I passed by the WMB 5th floor corridor mailboxes and noticed that every faculty mailbox had a relatively thick stapled document in it. I removed the one in my box and, as I walked down the corridor, passed a MELC colleague to whom I mentioned that mail was waiting in the outside mailboxes.
>
> An hour or more later, I again passed by WMB 5.120 and noticed that no corridor faculty mailboxes had the cited document, which had turned out to be the CCGS 111898 Memo–cc to MELC Faculty. I wondered how all MELC colleagues could have happened by within that hour to pick up that mail. Later that afternoon, I entered WMB 5.120 and noticed that all faculty mailboxes inside the office had the same thick stapled document in them. I removed the one from my box. It consisted of the CCGS 111898 Memo–cc to MELC Faculty to which the MELC Chair 111898 Memo to MELC Faculty (consisting of a memo note and "Minutes" from

the "Meeting, November 13, 1998, with Arabic Graduate Students") had been attached as a cover memo. I said to myself then, and later to two MELC colleagues over dinner, that should CCGS find out about MELC's removal of their correspondence to faculty and alteration of its packaging, CCGS students will surely react with further questions about their perception of MELC behavior toward our Arabic Studies students and faculty colleagues.

Sure enough, on the morning of Thursday, November 19, a CCGS representative. . .knocked on my office door. He said he had been knocking on MELC faculty doors to ask if he could see the pages stapled to the CCGS memo. I pulled my copy of the doubly stapled document out of my MELC 1998–1999 file, asked the student to wait in my office, and proceeded to knock on Robert Stofberg's door. No answer. I went to WMB 5.120 and did not find MELC staffperson Lucy Billings there. Lacking any input on possible MELC policy in such matters, I proceeded to reason that CCGS probably had a legal right to read anything physically attached to a memo which they had put in faculty mailboxes but did not reach faculty in the original form. So I removed the attached three pages, cut out comments I had made in the margins (e.g., on the incorrect list of students attending the meeting on November 13 and misattribution of a statement to Mark Sullivan), photocopied the three pages, returned to my office, and gave the photocopied pages to the CCGS representative.

Throughout the rest of the day, I knocked on Robert Stofberg's door every twenty minutes or so to apprise him of the CCGS request and my response. As soon as Lucy Billings returned, I informed her of the sequence of events and also requested that, whenever she had a choice, she should hereafter remove nothing at any time from my corridor mailbox without my permission.

On the morning of Friday, November 20, Walid Hamarneh told me that he had found a page recognizable as mine from notes on it, which I had left in the office photocopier when I made a copy of the three pages of the MELC Chair 111898 Memo to MELC Faculty. Walid added that he gave the page to Lucy Billings saying that he thought it was mine. I went to Lucy Billings's office to ask for the page. She answered that she had given it to Robert Stofberg. I chanced to see Robert on the way to class a minute later and asked for the return of the page. An hour or so later the page was in my mailbox. I immediately thanked Lucy for its return.

In case the issue of how CCSG gained access to MELC's attachment to their relocated and redistributed memo comes up at the "CALLED EMERGENCY Faculty Meeting," I will distribute this explanatory page to avoid speculation and unnecessary discussion. I should add that my views on CCSG correspondence are a matter of record, in correspondence I've had with Peter Abboud, Robert Stofberg, Benjamin Loya, and Avraham Zilkha in response to receipt of correspondence from CCSG and MELC faculty. Because I haven't had a chance to talk with Arabic Graduate students Alexa Firat, Shelton Henderson, and Mark Sullivan, presumably core members of CCGS, I know nothing more about their views and aims than what I have read in copies of pieces of correspondence directed to me.

The following day, November 19, CCGS sent this memo to MELC faculty.

> On Wednesday, November 18, CCGS students delivered memos to the mailboxes of MELC faculty. Shortly afterwards, our memos were pulled from the boxes and copies of Professor Stofberg's memo and Lucy Billings's minutes were stapled to our memos. Incidentally, these "minutes" are neither comprehensive nor representative of the minutes of the meeting. The modified memos were then delivered to the faculty.
>
> We are gravely concerned as such actions represent a breach of trust between students and the department. When we asked for the reasons behind this action, we were told that professors receive their mail inside the office and that Professor Stofberg had authorized that his memo get attached to ours.
>
> These boxes are designated specifically for student-faculty correspondence (see attached *MELC Newsletter*). These actions have grievous ramifications. They violate the requisite trust, privacy, and respect between and among faculty and students.

One could hardly imagine a more inept attempt to manage an escalating situation of unrest than Stofberg's actions to this point in response to Menzel, Sullivan, and CCGS missives. And, as I had anticipated, the issue of the CCGS memo came up at the "CALLED EMERGENCY Faculty Meeting" on the afternoon of Friday, November 20. Surprisingly, it was a junior Islamic Studies faculty colleague who raised the issue and in an accusatory way, thus revealing that Stofberg had discussed the matter and the emergency faculty meeting ahead of time with at least some MELC faculty colleagues. Immediately after that junior faculty person's charge, I distributed the foregoing memo, which squelched discussion of the subject.

Stofberg opened the meeting by reading this written statement.

> I have called this emergency meeting since there are non-academic political issues that have come to dominate the time and energy of the faculty and our staff and have become common knowledge to large segments of the university community.
>
> There comes a time when all people must face themselves honestly and act in accord with the dictates of their hearts. This moment has arrived for us as a department. This is our moment of truth. To ensure total freedom of expression, no one will take minutes of this meeting. Let us put our pens and pads away. If anyone feels uncomfortable with this, feel free to leave.
>
> For me to be able to discharge my duty as Chair and successfully discharge these duties, and for the faculty to get back to research without being consumed by politically motivated agendas, the ongoing, debilitating, obstructionist, and uncouth behavior on the part of three individuals [Abboud, Attieh, Hillmann] must come to an end immediately.

The issues do not concern me alone. Therefore they cannot be resolved in private conversation. They are adversely affecting the entire department: every single faculty member, as well as our staff. Precious time that should be devoted to teaching and research is being consumed by political, non-academic concerns. There is tension in the air that is detrimental to productivity. Moreover, the staff, which simply seek to remain apolitical are unnecessarily dragged into the fray.

While there have been sub-surface issues which sapped energy earlier in the semester it has not come full-blown to the fore until the letter from Mark Sullivan to the Dean accusing me of marginalizing the Arabic program and being a racist.

I believe that this, and subsequent student letters and memos which represent harassment and vilification of me were formulated either by, or with the input of faculty members since they contain information not available to students and since the vocabulary used reflects the vocabulary of some faculty members, and since several individuals not connected to the department have recently been consulting with these faculty members. The intimate connection between faculty and the students is further demonstrated by the transmission of documents intended for faculty only to disgruntled students from outside of the department.

I further believe that these kinds of actions were orchestrated by faculty members who do not have the best interest of the department, its faculty and their own students. The faculty involvement in the incitement of the students, their attempt to discredit and harass me is now more clear than it had been before yesterday.

Yet, if I and others are wrong in this assessment, it is the obligation of these faculty to dispel these inflammatory, non-productive allegations. Tell your students to put an end to this self-defeating behavior. For you not to put a stop to it is a selfish sacrifice of your students' well-being to advance your own ends. You are misleading and isolating your students who fall victim to your deeds.

I wish to make it abundantly clear that the allegation of Mark Sullivan in his letter to the Dean are patently false. I have done nothing to marginalize the Arabic Program. (1) As is common knowledge Khalad's [sic] leaving for UCLA had nothing to do with the "negative atmosphere" created by the announcement of my becoming Chair. (2) Walid's possible leaving or his not getting tenure last year was under the former Chair. (3) The absence of an entry on Arabic faculty, Arabic Professors, or Graduate Students in the newsletter was solely the responsibility of the Arabic faculty. The deadline of October 1 was announced at two meetings. Those who care about their students made sure to submit information about them for inclusion in the *Newsletter*. It is your failure to do so, not mine, as part of an alleged marginalization. (4) The decision to replace Peter as Chair was the Dean's, in consultation with a committee he appointed, and not the result of an alleged conspiracy by the 6th Floor. (5) The allegations in Annie Menzel's letter are slanderous and the letter is in the hands of a lawyer. (6) Efforts to secure a Turkish track position was [sic] not an act of marginalization of Arabic. I have always supported a bid for a tenure track position in Arabic.

Again, if these students views are only perceptions of the students, it is up to those who are egging on the students to dispel those perceptions. The behavior of the faculty reminds me of *Fahrenheit 451* where the role of firemen was to start fires rather then to put them out.

It is incendiary to write in a letter to students in the Persian Program that they need not worry about marginalization of the Persian Program. A simple word that there is no threat of marginalization would have sufficed.

Do not out of bitterness torpedo the enterprise. It was inexcusable for Aman [Attieh] to repeatedly ignore requests to hand over material, property of the university, to a member of a duly constituted committee. Did . . . [the new undergraduate advisor] have to grovel to get this information, and by what right did Aman throw away the material since Arabic was no longer involved?

I am particularly appalled by the abusive treatment of Lucy by Michael Hillmann. On November 20th, I state clearly here and now that I will not tolerate such abusive, ill-mannered behavior: behavior which was witnessed by two faculty members. I hasten to add that this is not the first time this semester that he had spoken abusively to her. Let us not act like hooligans or thugs, and Lucy, Trudie or any of our Workstudies are not to be verbally abused, harassed or intimidated.

As is well-known, several secretaries have quit the department in the past because of similar abusive behavior on the part of a few members of the department. I will not permit such behavior to continue and I will act vigorously to defend any faculty or staff member from further abusive behavior. The reign of terror is over. I am soft spoken, but do not mistake that characteristic for lack of resolve or decisiveness.

The bald boldness of Stofberg's statement stunned me. My first thought about the audacity of his multiple attacks against me was that Stofberg could dare such a thing only if he thought he had something on me. I did a quick, reassuring review in my head of everything about my life in MELC. No unpaid photocopy bills. No purloined equipment. No pornography on my office computer. No absences ever from class. No classes in which talk went off topic. No whistling or leering at women students. No fisticuffs. No contacts with any hypothetical neo-Nazi Hillmanns back in Germany. No, he had nothing on me.

Then, how could Stofberg have dared to reveal that he was out to "get" me, that he thought he could get me? He had even written down his remarks ahead of time and had a staff person keyboard them, now a permanent record, not of an emotional outburst, but a rehearsed statement (which he obviously hadn't shown ahead of time to anyone who knew anything about writing).

My next thought was: What possible reason could Stofberg have for wanting to get me? I had to suppose that he knew that his charges were baseless. He had to know that my interactions with Lucy Billings wouldn't fulfill a dictionary definition of "abuse," much less a moral or legal definition. He had to know that he was grasping at straws in almost every allegation he made. One of those statements, with the rhetorical resonance of a television news bite, went: "The allegations in Annie Menzel's letter are slanderous and the letter is in the hands of a lawyer." The sentence has two parts, both false statements. First, Menzel and Stofberg were not alone when, Menzel alleges, Stofberg made his allegedly racist remarks against Arabs. Second, Stofberg later admitted under oath that he had never put the letter in the hands of a lawyer. On the matter of Hamarneh, Stofberg's own letter as Chair to the College Promotions Committee recommending non-promotion is a matter of public record.

In the middle of the heated and non-academic discussion, mostly attacks on Attieh, Abboud, and me, the loudest by Ali Akbar Esfahanpur against Attieh which moderator Stofberg did nothing to moderate, Hebrew Studies Lecturer Yaron Shemer expressed regret at what he construed as the first instance in departmental discourse of the Arab-Israeli conflict. Toward the end of the meeting, I said to Stofberg something to this effect. Okay, you've taken your best shot and got it out of your system. Can we move on and deal with real problems? Do you want me to tell the Concerned Students to desist from their pen-wielding until they can judge if MELC shows that it plans to mend its ways? Except for one gnawing thought, the meeting had its stimulating moments in the special way of low-stakes speech at universities. You can say what you want, and no one gets hurt. Everything that happens on the mountain stays on the mountain. The one thought that kept interrupting the rush of endorphins was Aman Attieh's situation.

Stofberg's allegation of a "reign of terror" and other allegations later became focal points in three grievance proceedings, court litigation, and now this chapter, which draws on a clear paper trail of the alleged "reign of terror," from the beginning of the Fall 1998 Semester to the date of the emergency faculty meeting. When Stofberg melodramatically announced: "The re..re..reign of terror is over," to my mind a sort of attempted reign of attempted terror had just begun, albeit not with respect to unassailable, tenured faculty compeers like me. Regardless, I'd naturally make certain henceforth to slather myself with psychological DEET at the office to keep the buzzing at a distance! No, the only person Stofberg could terrorize was Attieh. Many observers thought he did exactly that, through a series of ploys and actions that ended in the termination of her MELC employment, an eventuality which she had predicted.

✍ November 23, Journal entry, Austin Airport. Sorayya flew to Los Angeles on Tuesday. Wednesday I took an hour's walk. Saturday and Sunday I rollerbladed at Veloway and learned the value of elbow pads and wrist guards after taking a spill while attempting a semicircular stop too quickly. My elbows and hands smacked the cement. But no pain or scratches. Should I do a book on life in an obscure corner of The University of Texas? Life in that Middle Eastern corner has grown progressively bizarre this fall. For the first time in twenty-five years, since the anti-Pahlavi demonstrations before the Iranian Revolution, I'm in the middle of student protests, in this case a group of first-rate Arabic students who allege that the College of Liberal Arts, the Center for Middle Eastern Studies, and the Department of Middle Eastern Languages and Cultures are marginalizing their program and perhaps seeking the removal of Senior Arabic Lecturer Aman Attieh. Starting with Annie Menzel's allegation that MELC Chair Robert Stofberg made disparaging remarks about Arabs in Israel two summers ago and featuring letters and memos by Mark Sullivan and a group called CCGS, the situation has also involved faculty conflict, allegations by the MELC Chair that Peter Abboud, Aman Attieh, and I have incited the students. Things culminated in a "Called Emergency Faculty Meeting" last Friday, which Aman left in anger and tears after hearing and responding to allegations. Oops! They're announcing my lucky number, Southwest Flight 331! Gotta go. ✍

✍ November 28, Journal entry, West Hollywood. MELC crosses my mind more than I'd like these days. A majority of departmental colleagues found it an unpleasant place last year. I didn't have that feeling because the office staff and departmental administration operated agreeably as far as Persian Studies and my work were concerned. Moreover, Göttingen, Paris, Venice, Milan, Florence, and more Paris allowed me to miss West Mall conflicts in the fall of 1997. Last spring, when colleagues complained about Peter Abboud's style as Chair, I still didn't discern the extent of discontent. When Arnold Pederson decided against naming Peter as Chair for four more years, I didn't have a professional reaction one way or the other. Personally, of course, I sympathized with Peter because he wanted to continue as Chair. Also, I realized that now Peter, Aman Attieh, and Walid Hamarneh would begin finding MELC an unhappy place. Something else I didn't anticipate was that the unhappy majority would remain unhappy even when Peter was no longer Chair and even when the College of Liberal Arts then provided MELC with extra operating funds, a second Dean's Fellowship, a tenure-track Turkish position, approval of MELC as home to a Jewish Studies program, and who knows what else. Despite all of this and his appointment as Chair, whenever I see Robert Stofberg in the MELC corridor, he complains about something he alleges Peter did in the past. MELC junior faculty, who may average fifty-plus years of age, say they feel "marginalized" and unequal to senior faculty. Of course, student charges of racism and other biased behavior on the part of Stofberg have given MELC a black eye around campus, according to Robert, who seems incapable of feeling unoppressed. Moreover, his attacks on Peter and Aman at the emergency meeting seemed symptomatic of meanspiritedness to such colleagues as Avraham [Zilkha], Yaron [Shemer], Yildiray [Erdener], and Zilla [Goodman]. From my perspective, having had no more than a handful of conversations with Robert in the twenty-five years we have worked together at OALL/ MELC, I'll have nothing to say to or about him as MELC Chair so long as he respects intradepartmental autonomy in my Persian Studies and Tajiki programs. The rain continues, only letting up for the ninety minutes I walked up and down Melrose Boulevard window-shopping, shopping in this case for another owl figure to add to the collection. Sorayya made turkey soup for lunch and has meat loaf in the oven for tonight in case we don't go out to dinner after cocktails with Hammie and Holly on their boat at Marina del Ray. Sorayya, Eliza, Jeff, and I have an ongoing argument about life on that boat. The three of them say it's crazy. I say I'd love it except for the space problem for books, papers, notes, and writing. ✍

The last event of the Fall 1998 Semester was the following letter, dated 8 December 1998, that MELC faculty didn't learn about for almost four years. MELC Chair Stofberg and CMES Director Loya wrote and sent it to an interim Dean of Liberal Arts.

Thank you for meeting with us on Friday to discuss the problems in MELC and possible ways to address them. We appreciate your expressions of support and your commitment to help bring some resolution to what are clearly rather difficult issues.

In our meeting you proposed the idea of an outside review of MELC/ the Arabic program to be conducted in the spring by a committee of respected specialists in the field, with the expectation that based on the committee's findings the administration would be able to take corrective action. After the meeting the two of us discussed at length the merits of such a review. We have a number of thoughts and questions about its scope, timing, and possible benefits and costs that we wish to share with you.

1. Will an outside review have a mandate to investigate thoroughly the causes of the infighting in the department and possible wrongdoing by faculty? If so, will there be action, administrative or disciplinary, to deal with those shown to have engaged in unprofessional behavior, in subverting the workings of the department, or in abusive treatment of students, staff, teaching assistants, and colleagues? These questions about the scope and possible consequences of the review are crucial because the central problems plaguing the department are not the bogus marginalization of Arabic or the quality of the Arabic program but rather: (1) the campaign by a few faculty to undermine the chair–by accusing him of bias, questioning the legitimacy of his appointment, and poisoning the atmosphere in the department; (2) the predicament of the junior faculty who have spoken out against the unprofessional conduct of these colleagues and are under the threat of vindictive actions and votes that could jeopardize their promotions and careers and result in legal action against the University; and (3) the pattern of harassment and mistreatment of students, staff, teaching assistants, and colleagues. This climate is eroding the morale, productivity, and reputation of the department, whose faculty are crying out for a supportive and collegial academic environment. The principal challenge is to find ways to secure such an environment by dealing with the obstacles and threats to it. Forceful action by the department to confront instances of unprofessional behavior by faculty, such as occurred recently, and attentiveness by the higher administration to possible vindictive voting, which you suggested, are two important measures for protecting professionalism and fairness. Additional measures need to be explored, quite separately from an outside review. In our view an outside review could be helpful if it has a broad mandate to look into the fundamental problems in the department, something which will require a rather lengthy inquiry, and (4) if it can result in any real remedies which we cannot currently consider or implement; If no such remedies are likely to ensue, the usefulness of the exercise would be questionable, especially as the review process itself will generate considerable turmoil.

2. If the review is confined essentially to the evaluation of the Arabic program, that would leave some of the key issues unaddressed. The review might lead at most to the possible replacement of one instructor; the other problematic elements will remain in place. If the Arabic position is upgraded to a tenure-track or tenured line, and an outside candidate is hired to fill the new line, we can expect to have a legal suit and agitation that could

be nasty. The Arabic program wants a tenured or tenure-track position for Aman, not for a new faculty member. It is also possible that Aman would get the upgraded position.

3. We should keep in mind that the review process will be quite disruptive in itself. It will become a battlefield, stir up unpleasantness, and preoccupy faculty and students for an extended period without necessarily resolving the problems in the end. Faculty in the department have already shown their reckless readiness to engage in the incitement and misguiding of students (including non-MELC students), in fomenting a campaign of vicious attacks on the chair in raising bogus and gratuitous issues, and in playing the race card. If a review process is put in place there is every reason to believe that these tactics will be unleashed all over again to do their damage.

4. If the review is conducted in the spring or early fall, the timing is going to be detrimental to our preparations for the upcoming competition for Department of Education Title VI funding. . .A climate of infighting will compromise both the focus on preparing a strong proposal and the picture of the program that we can honestly present. If the current problems persist we stand to lose our top ranking and substantial funding. At stake are hundreds of thousands of dollars in fellowship and project funds as well as the quality and national reputation of UT's Middle East area studies program.

5. While the findings of the review committee and any action or inaction based on them could be attributed conveniently to a neutral outside body, the two of us will end up in the main line of fire. Help we provide the committee with documentation that exposes abusive and irregular behavior of faculty will put us at the center of any agitation and legal suit that may ensue. If we choose not to provide such information so as not to be hurt professionally and personally, the review process will be compromised. Our concern is not with a legal suit: the University will have a strong case and we will be ready to back it fully. Our concern is with serious harm at the hands of faculty who act as if they have nothing to lose. People ready to resort to inciting students, fabricating accusations, playing the race card, and mistreating others are a worrisome danger, to us and to the program as a whole.

When I first read this letter in 2002, I thought and said: "Wow!" The letter revealed three things. First, from the beginning of his tenure as Chair, Stofberg felt incapable of managing the department on his own and sought help from CMES and the College of Liberal Arts to achieve a modicum of his sort of order in the department. In deposition testimony under oath four years later, Stofberg stated that Loya had written the letter, while he had added comments to it. Second, after the 20 November 1998 meeting, Stofberg chose to work behind the scenes in trying to "get" me, and Abboud and Attieh. How many *mitzvot* must proscribe such behavior?

Third, in the light of non-action on the part of the College of Liberal Arts to charges of abuse, harassment, and racism which Stofberg makes in this and subsequent letters to the College, The Equal Employment Opportunity Office, and the UT Office of Legal Affairs, one perforce concludes that all allegations lacked substance. Logic and facts of American life in 1998 lead to that inevitable conclusion, which is to say that UT administrators could not possibly have then ignored any credible charge against a MELC faculty person of abuse or harassment or racist behavior toward a student, staff person, or colleague.

What then interested me about this letter, the likes of which I hadn't ever read before, was the implication that such university administrators as a Dean of Liberal Arts at one of America's largest universities actually spend time taking gossip and hearsay seriously without seeking corroborating evidence or letting faculty colleagues accused of wrongdoing in such gossip know what's transpiring behind their backs. In the 1998–2002 years, no UT administrator communicated with me even once about any of the charges circulated by DMES and CMES with my name stated or implied therein.

Departmental intrigues during the Fall 1998 Semester left me guessing what in the hearts and skulls of Stofberg and Loya inspired them to behave in the way they had to at least four people very different one from another and very different from the two conspirators. Sometimes, I thought that Loya and Stofberg wanted merely to retaliate against Peter Abboud, and that the only way they thought they could do that was to unsteady him by attacking things presumed near and/or dear or close to him: his Arabic program, his Arabic language colleague Aman Attieh, his Arabic literature colleague Walid Hamarneh, and/or his presumed American Persianist friend and presumed steadfast supporter. Years earlier, according to a CMES colleague, CMES Lecturer Fernea had suggested action to end Attieh's association with Arabic Studies as a way of bringing Abboud's Arabist career to an end, her bizarre and mistaken assumption being that Attieh managed the Arabic language program, something that Fernea ignorantly thought Abboud couldn't do without Attieh.

Behind alleged retaliation on the part of Stofberg and Loya, however, perhaps lay a possibly culture-specific animus, either a conscious or subconscious Jewish Israeli or Orthodox Jewish orientation or the culture-specific perceptions and reactions of "Others" who choose tactics not common in the culture in which they are operating. At the same time, I can feel some sadness for Stofberg and Loya sitting conspiratorially over coffee at Mozart Café, oblivious to the lake view outside, and talking about how to avoid perceived dangers to themselves, not realizing that they'd remain just as unhappy having avoided them as not having avoided them and not realizing that the real danger for them as academics would come from keyboarded and published words documenting their actions and living on within book covers on acid-free paper on climate-controlled library shelves.

If the Dean had put the letter on the table in December 1998 for all MELC faculty to see and comment on, MELC might have survived. But Stofberg presumably couldn't allow his letter to go public for a simple reason. No evidence existed for any of the charges he made in it. That is presumably the same reason that prompted him to object to an outside evaluation of MELC and its Arabic Studies program. If I had known about the letter in the Spring of 1999, I'd have demanded that Stofberg and Loya attach names to their allegations and charges. If they had attached my name to any of the allegations, who knows how many trees would have turned into paper for me to try to do my wordsmithing best to have them retract what they had been saying and writing behind my back and to have them removed from any administrative functions relating to Persian and Iranian culture. The only proper name in their letter is "Aman," the citation of such a female given name suggesting sexism on the part of Stofberg, who regularly used surnames in referring to male colleagues.

George Meredith, Hammie Dugan, Mike, and George Shehan at dinner at House of Kabob in Baltimore. May 2007.

Chapter 6

1999

*"A great many people think they are thinking
when they are merely rearranging their prejudices."*
William James

*"If you do not tell the truth about yourself,
you cannot tell it about other people."*
Virginia Woolf

1999 began quietly at MELC. It took a month or more before reemergence of bad feelings which had festered during the fall of 1998 and then erupted at the "Reign of Terror" faculty meeting. Stofberg continued to lobby against Abboud, Attieh, and me behind the scenes and was planning actions to blunt Abboud's role in and vision of Arabic Studies. Attieh remained convinced that Stofberg meant to take her job away. Hamarneh was making plans for a future elsewhere and sensibly chose to stay out of MELC group activities. Had Hamarneh succeeded in his tenure application, Stofberg would not have had the votes then or later to interfere with our Arabic Studies program.

On February 11, I sent a straightforward and transparent letter to our Persian Studies students. It read (bold script added):

> Last year Arabist colleague Walid Hamarneh suggested that **MELC** consider **host**ing **a seminar** or **symposium** this spring to give **MELC students** an opportunity to discuss their ideas and work. Such an event would get students better acquainted with compeers and with MELC fields other than their own. The event would also give MELC faculty an opportunity to appreciate student academic activity and progress.
>
> At a MELC faculty meeting last fall, I proposed that **students of Persian Studies** constitute **a** discrete **panel at this day-long symposium**. I anticipated that as many a five or six students might agree to participate, presenting papers and taking part in discussion. Papers could take from ten to twenty minutes to present. That would mean papers from five to ten pages in length.
>
> Students in the ongoing Iranian Culture Seminar can fulfill a course term paper requirement by participating in **the symposium**. Other MELC

students who have taken Persian courses can also volunteer to participate. In either case, students should talk to me about participating by February 24, when I'd like to **give MELC** a list of names and titles.

Six days later, on February 17, Stofberg sent me this note about my letter (bold script added):

> A student brought me a copy of the attached letter that you sent to the Persian Language Graduate students and wanted to know what is going on. I am also curious. . .I was surprised by the nature of your memo of 2/11/99 to the Persian students where in paragraph 1 **you make no reference to this symposium as a departmental initiative**. I also find **your scheduling a separate graduate student symposium for Persian language students** on the same day as our scheduled general student symposium odd and inappropriate. I have therefore written to the Persian Language Graduate students clarifying the position of the department.

Stofberg's letter to the students read:

> I wish to correct two misconceptions that may have been conveyed by Professor Michael Hillmann's Memo of 2/11/99 to you. (1) Though the idea of a Graduate Student Symposium, to enable graduate students to present an interim report on their thesis [sic] and dissertations originated with Professor Hamarneh, this suggestion was brought by me to the faculty. . .This is a departmental activity, not a private initiative. (2) Though Professor Hillmann asked about holding a separate symposium for Persian Language Graduate students where they would be able to discuss their studies in Persian and the idea of holding this on the same day as the general symposium to be conducted in English was not proposed and not approved.

I didn't respond directly to Stofberg. Instead, I photocopied six relevant pieces of correspondence in reduced size, numbered them in chronological order, underscored salient phrases (e.g., in bold in my February 11 memo to students and in Stofberg's February 17 response), pasted all six on a single page, and photocopied and distributed the page, without comment, to Persian Studies students. The paper trail spoke for itself: Stofberg's mindset had distorted things for him in misreading my letter to students.

The seminar session, which took place exactly as I had planned and announced it, consisted of four, twenty-minute papers: "Children of the Iranian Diaspora" by Leslie Moore (M.A. student, Persian Studies); "Reader Response to Arabic Texts: Report on a Thesis in Progress" by Mary McDermott (M.A. student, Arabic Studies); "On Writing a New Persian-English Dictionary" by Ramin Sarraf (M.A., Persian Studies,

1998, and Ph.D. student, Persian Studies); and "A Psychological Interpretation of *The Blind Owl*" by Mark Sullivan (M.A., Arabic Studies, 1998, and Ph.D. student, Arabic Studies). The McDermott and Sullivan papers, by prominent students in Arabic Studies critical of MELC management and attitudes toward the Arabic program, served as further vindication of that program and as another demonstration of the superior work of students in it.

A second disruption in the rhythm of my academic days in the Spring 1999 Semester with Stofberg's signature on it had to do with an official review of tenured faculty. In early 1998, UT administration had advised departments of a new post-tenure review process to which senior faculty should submit. Never a supporter of tenure per se because it allows the occasional senior faculty person to use last year's notes in classes, show no enthusiasm for service activities, and/or do little or no new research or writing, I volunteered as MELC's first faculty person to undergo such a review. The process began in the spring of 1998, while the review, such as it turned out to be, and the review report took place in early 1999. As of Fall 2003 Semester, I remained the only Middle Eastern Languages faculty member to have undergone such a review.

On April 13, I wrote this letter to the interim Dean.

> In response to a question I asked this morning about my Post Tenure Review, the MELC Administrative Associate informed me that the review had concluded and that MELC Chair Robert Stofberg had submitted a report on behalf of MELC to the College of Liberal Arts.
>
> For four reasons, this news surprised me. First, MELC Executive Committee members participating in meetings on the subject this spring had not looked at any of the files of teaching activities and academic writing and copies of publications which I had prepared in the summer of 1998 in anticipation of MELC Executive Committee perusal. Second, in response to a series of oral and written communications, no MELC Executive Committee members discussed any aspect of my teaching or academic writing with me. Third, no MELC Executive Committee members participating in meetings on the subject of my Post Tenure Review had visited any of my classes. Fourth, according to terms described in the memorandum dated 24 September 1998 from The Committee of Counsel on Academic Freedom and Responsibility on which you served, I was expecting to see any report and have a chance to provide input before MELC sent an official report to your office. The MELC Executive Committee had discussed this procedure at a meeting in the spring of 1998.
>
> Shortly after my brief conversation with Ms. Billings, I put a copy of the cited memorandum from The Committee of Counsel on Academic Freedom and Responsibility in Professor Stofberg's mail box. A couple of

hours later, I saw Professor Stofberg in the corridor and asked him if I could see a copy of the official report which he had sent. Ms. Billings then provided me with a copy of Professor Stofberg's letter to you of March 2, 1998 and two attachments.

The report surprised me for four reasons. First, although dated March 2, MELC had not inclined to allow me to see it in the subsequent forty days. Second, the report and the attachment called "Publication and Research Review" understates my productivity in academic writing. Third, the report lacks an attachment on my teaching activities and misstates my teaching record. Fourth, the report misrepresents my involvement with MELC faculty at large and their programs.

Two weeks later, the interim Dean answered my letter, writing in part:

> I am writing in response to your letter expressing concern about your Post-Tenure Review. You are correct in stating that you should have had the opportunity to respond to the review. . .Fortunately, I have not yet forwarded the reviews to the Provost. . . Given that Chairman Stofberg has. . . apologized. . . and given that you now have had the opportunity to respond, I propose that I forward your response and supporting materials along with Chairman Stofberg's March 2 letter. In this way, all the facts will be part of the record.

✍ June 5, Journal entry, The Chalfonte Hotel, Cape May. After no singles matches on clay in years, "Bill" something-or-other and I played two sets, 6–3 and 6–4, Thursday on HarTru at Cape May Tennis Center. Sunny, breezy, some serve-and-volley, many long points, and a pleasant chat throughout. A retired electrical engineer, Bill was out walking at 6:30 yesterday morning when I returned from breakfast I had bought to eat on the Madison Avenue Beach lifeguard chair: a bagel, a cup of yoghurt, a banana, and a can of V-8 juice. Dolphins effortlessly and unhurriedly bounded down the coast only fifteen yards from shore. Two seagulls quickly found bagel pieces I dropped in front of the chair. On Wednesday, Louisa's served me a delicious dinner. The restaurant has only ten tables, some set in Paris-style rows. Tomato bean soup, potato vegetable cakes, and apple strudel, a split bottle of Valpolicella for conversation. Beforehand, I sipped a sweet vermouth on the rocks with a twist of lemon at Pilot House, which was called Tarpon Bar in my youth. I skipped dinner on Thursday night and moved yesterday from the Blue Amber Motel to The Chalfonte, which opens this weekend for the season, but won't be serving dinner. Yesterday, Bill and I played again, this time to 6–1, 3–2, when our singles time ran out. On weekends, the club gives precedence to doubles. We then accepted an invitation to doubles, which reached 6–4, 4–1, when George Patrick and Art something-or-other retired because of a previous commitment. This morning I met my match in Jamie something-or-other from Bucks County and was lucky to lose 4–6 in the first set, and conceded the second with a sore left elbow and tired legs. I need lots of match hours on clay running down lobs to get fit. My rollerblading and walking don't help tennis muscles. Even my hard-court workouts at Westwood Country Club with Javad don't seem to help. Tomorrow I'll jog early on the beach to salve my conscience in anticipation of the Chalfonte breakfast of spoon bread, home-made biscuits, scrambled eggs and bacon I'll throw caution to the wind in eating afterwards. I tried to get a table at Louisa's again tonight, but no luck. Instead, I took an outside table at The Ugly Mug and watched people, a pint of Foster's in hand and a cup of snapper soup and a soft-shell crab sandwich on whole wheat toast with a side of coleslaw in front of me. From The Ugly Mug I walked to the boardwalk, took a half-hour stroll on it, and then found a rocking chair on the Sewell-side Chalfonte front porch. I listened to wedding reception music wafting from the hotel dining room and devoted quality time to this journal entry. ✍

✍ August 5, Journal entry, Perry Lane, Austin. My UT Second-year summer Persian language course ended on Wednesday. *Persian Fiction Reader Workbook* worked well in it. The 7th Annual Persepolis Advanced Summer Persian Course ends with dinner at 3404 Perry on Monday. *Reading Iran Reading Iranians* has served for the first time as a core textbook in the course. Carmen Nikazm taught her last Persepolis class today, after seven years of collaboration. She, Kamel, and Nina leave tomorrow for Lawrence and her new position in the German Department at University of Kansas. Mehdi Khorrami says this will be his last Persepolis course too. Students rave about his teaching. Esmael Ghadessy, who taught his first Persepolis class at Bell Operations Corporation in Euless (TX) in 1977, will be back, as will Azita Mokhtari and Ramin Sarraf. But we'll need at least one new teacher in 2002. ✍

Back at MELC, Stofberg made a change which he had first proposed in August 1998, but didn't then act on. In response, Aman Attieh immediately sent this open letter to MELC faculty.

> In response to Dr. Stofberg's memo of August 19, I would like to inform MELC faculty that I am protesting the decision of sharing my office space with the Arabic teaching assistants. Dr. Stofberg did not discuss with me or consult with the Arabic faculty about his intent to curtail the Arabic program offices. On August 9 he sent me a letter informing me that due to limited space in the department, the Arabic assistants need to vacate their offices and are to be housed with me or in the Arabic lab. I sent him a detailed letter outlining several reasons, intellectual, methodological, logistical, and my role as a coordinator, regarding the urgent need to keep that space intact for the use of the Arabic instructional team. This was to no avail. . .So I am not willingly or "graciously" accepting to take in two or three teaching assistants into my office space, but I am being forced to do so. This is not in the best interest of the students and the program. And I regret that this academic year has to start with this tense note for the Arabic program. I have the support of the Arabic faculty in this matter.

In saying that she had "the support of the Arabic faculty in this matter," Attieh meant that one person supported her, Peter Abboud. In going public with her protest at Stofberg's directive, as retaliatory and arguably meanspirited as that directive may have been, Attieh can't have been expecting support from MELC colleagues who had not objected to attacks against her at the November 1998 "emergency" faculty meeting. She also couldn't have forgotten Stofberg's threat, as unfair as it was, early in September 1998 that she wouldn't keep her job if she didn't change some of her ways. Stofberg and Loya, on the one hand, and Abboud and Attieh, on the other, had decided that the MELC world wasn't big enough for both groups. One would have to go. Despite their lack of administrative clout or friends in either low or high places, Abboud and Attieh weren't either backing down or choosing possibly winning strategies. Their reactions as aggrieved parties had something culture-specific about them, either Christians versus lions or Imam Husayn versus Yazid. Stofberg and Loya, however, felt they could proceed without taking Abboud and Attieh into account. It turns out they had a bold plan which caught Abboud and Attieh unawares.

At a September departmental meeting, Stofberg announced that the College of Liberal Arts had approved a MELC request for a new tenured position in Arabic language and linguistics. The announcement surprised everyone, especially Abboud and Attieh. Of course, no one but authors Stofberg and Loya had read their December 1998 letter to the Dean, in which they talked about the idea of a new Arabic position. I asked Stofberg how such a position could materialize with no involvement of Abboud in planning and discussions. Stofberg replied matter-of-factly that he had gone ahead on his own because he couldn't work with Abboud. Suddenly thinking that even more than hadn't already met the eye wasn't meeting the eye, I asked as nonchalantly as possible if the new position meant that MELC would now have three full-time faculty slots in Arabic language. Stofberg said that the position was an addition to existing slots and would result in three Arabic language faculty in 2000–2001. Before we voted on the proposed position, I asked twice more about the position as a third position in Arabic language. Stofberg twice more answered that the new position would be an additional position. Of course, no one at the meeting but Stofberg knew that he had referred to a new position as an "upgraded" position in the December 1998 letter.

There followed another faculty meeting and exchanges of messages among faculty over wording in the Arabic job announcement. Abboud wanted the phrase "Applied Linguistics" to appear in the statement of qualifications, which would reflect a strength of Attieh's.

On October 7, Stofberg sent the following memo to the MELC Executive Committee.

> If you wish to suggest a change in the ad for the Arabic position, please submit your suggestions no later than Monday, October 11, 1999, by 9:00 A.M. Sorry for the haste, but I wish to get the ad out as soon as possible to provide us with lead time that will enable us to select from the broadest pool for potential candidates. That, as in any ad of candidates, the ad must be approved by the Dean's office. The ad as it stands reads: "Arabic: The Department of Middle Eastern Languages and Cultures of The University of Texas at Austin announces a position at the Associate Professor level in Arabic Language beginning September, 2000. Candidates must have a Ph.D. in Arabic Language or Linguistic [sic], native or near-native competence in Arabic, five years experience teaching expertise in language instruction, involvement with national trends in the field and a commitment to scholarship and a record of publications appropriate for a senior tenured appointment. Interested individuals should send a letter of interest, current curriculum vitae, copies of relevant publications, and three original letters of recommendation to: Dr. Robert Stofberg, Chairman."

Not only did the final job description not give Attieh an inside track, on October 20 Stofberg sent a memo to MELC faculty which further threatened her faculty status. In it he wrote:

> In response to an independent issue that I discussed with the Dean [Reginald Applegate] concerning the Arabic Associate Professor position, I have received an unanticipated clarification from the Dean. Contrary to

what I believed and presented at our last Faculty Meeting, the addition is an "upgrading of the Senior Lecturer position" and not in addition to that position. Please consult the attached email received from the Dean

Date: 16 October 1999
To: Stofberg@mail.utexas.edu
From: ra@mail.utexas.edu
Subject: Arabic Position

I am writing to clarify the situation with the search for a new Assoc. Prof. for Arabic. . .This is an addition to the Arabic faculty, but it will in effect be an "upgrading" of the Senior Lecturer position. That is, when the search is successfully concluded, the teaching of Arabic will be done by tenured faculty.

Stofberg's memo, which verified the original December 1998 plan which faculty didn't know about, came four days after he had received the Dean's e-message. I wrote a response to Stofberg's memo on my copy of the memo and put it in his faculty mail box. It read in part: "Dear Robert: In light of your surprising new representation of the Arabic position, what do we do with faculty comments and voting at our last faculty meeting, based as they were on a misrepresentation of the position as defined by the College of Liberal Arts?" On the matter of who would be teaching Arabic as of 2000–2001, not only did faculty not carry out all of that teaching in subsequent years, but also the Department decided in 2006–2007 that the new faculty hire in 2000–2001 and Abboud should no longer teach lower-division language courses.

On October 20, I sent this e-message to Peter Abboud.

I have just received Robert Stofberg's memo to MELC faculty that he had misrepresented the announced Associate Professor of Arabic Language position at our most recent faculty meeting. You will recall that I asked him three or four times at that meeting if the new position was an/in addition to existing Arabic language teaching staff. He responded emphatically in the affirmative each time.

The new information. . .means that MELC faculty voted for the position on the basis of mistaken information. I would have voted for an upgraded position as well, with the twin provisos that the applicant judged most qualified by peers who have studied and taught Arabic would have the best chance to get the position and that the successful candidate's qualifications include a commitment to the use of Modern Standard Arabic as the language of classroom instruction.

I'm assuming that this "upgrading of the Senior Lecturer position" in Arabic presumes that a leading candidate for the position will be current Senior Lecturer Aman Attieh, who would appear to fulfill all of the requirements stated in the advertisement which Robert prepared. However,

I still cannot understand how the process of this "upgrading of the Senior Lecturer position" could have taken place without any communication with Aman or with you.

I didn't write in my memo to Peter that I now thought the fix was on and that Stofberg and Dean Applegate planned that Attieh not get the position and not continue as a MELC faculty member. But I couldn't imagine a scenario in which she wouldn't make a short list of candidates for the position and interview for it. But that happened, as well as something more irregular. One short-listed candidate did not meet any of the requirements stated in the job announcement.

On November 11, senior UT Persianist and OALL founding member Mohammad Ali Jazayery died, after several periods of hospitalization and a final brief stay at an assisted living hospital. Before that, in retirement from 1989, having kept an office at OALL and then MELC, he visited the department regularly and kept working on his Kasravi projects. In Jazayery's honor, CMES and MELC organized a memorial session at the College of Liberal Arts Conference Room. Jazayery's nephew Khosrow Jazayery attended. MELC Chair Stofberg invited five or six colleagues and students to speak, but predictably excluded me (and Peter Abboud). The sadness which Jazayery's death brought me, and the further sadness Sorayya and I felt when we visited Jazayery's pauper's grave in a farmer's field designated as a Muslim cemetery fifty miles from Austin, didn't give me time to ponder Stofberg's motives in not inviting me, who had known Ali since June 1965, to say a few words at his memorial service. I had prepared the following remarks for such an occasion.

No academic owes more to Ali Jazayery than I do. He directed the UT Austin Summer 1965 Peace Corps Persian language training program at which I learned the rudiments of Persian. He corresponded with me during the next two years while I studied Persian and taught English at Mashhad University. He offered me a fellowship at Texas in 1967. He offered me a job at Texas in 1974. Paul English and he spearheaded my promotion to a tenured position three years later. He gave me carte blanche in designing UT's Persian literature program and supported lecture series, symposia, film festivals, exhibits, poetry readings, and the like which I organized from the mid-1970s through the late 1980s. He hosted and entertained conference guests and lecturers, chaired meetings, made monetary contributions to some of these activities, and was the major benefactor in 'Friends of Persian Studies' support for students of mine. When he decided to retire in 1989, he made certain that Persian Studies at UT Austin would always have two tenure-track positions, something which only a handful of university Persian programs in America have ever had.

He remembered Elizabeth's birthdays and graduations. He was in good health and spirits at her wedding. He and Sorayya were friends. My brother-in-law Reza and he got along well, in large measure because of Reza's interest in Iranian intellectual and political history, including Ahmad Kasravi's writings. We have fond memories of cocktail parties and dinners at his house and his gentlemanly and often lively and sometimes quiet presence at dinners and parties at Chiappero Trail and Perry Lane. We tried to make arrangements for Essie Ghadessy to bring him to our most recent dinner party in October, but he was in the hospital. Sorayya took flowers to the hospital a day or two later. But Ali had moved. Then word reached us through the Iranian community grapevine that he had passed away. Everyone in the community in Austin knew and liked Ali.

When I think of Ali's work in the field of Persian language teaching in the 1960s, it strikes me that, contrary to my first sentence above, another academic entity owes him more than I do: The University of Texas. In the mid-1960s, when UT was still a regional university with little institutional activity relating to the non-Western world, Ali was almost single-handedly bringing Persian language teaching and instructional materials preparation into a post-grammar/translation method world with his audio-lingual *Elementary Lessons in Persian*. His influence on a new generation of Persianists extended beyond basic Persian with his co-authorship of *Persian Readers I, II*, and *III*, which hundreds of us in Iran used to learn to read newspapers and fiction. His work on mutual influences between English and Persian was then new. He was up-to-date in Linguistics. His work in Persian helped make UT Austin become a national university. He had several books in him by the end of the 1960s.

But, when the Department of Oriental and African Languages and Literatures came into being in 1970, he decided to devote himself to that enterprise. and put his books-to-be on back burners. He kept reading and taking notes, clipping out and photocopying articles, thinking about words, and attending conferences. He asked questions and made comments at every conference session. He gave his time to OALL, for years, and then to the Center for Middle Eastern Studies, for years. When he retired, he kept studying and taking notes. His library at home had an unassuming, in-progress, notes-everywhere, and books-open-and-marked personality like Ali's. But Ali never returned to a book-writing frame of mind. Some other Kasravi scholar needs to get hold of Ali's notes and unpublished essays and give the academic world at least one of Ali's unwritten books.

I've proposed to the Department of Middle Eastern Languages and Cultures that a photograph portrait of Ali with a descriptive plaque go on permanent display on MELC's WMB 5th floor corridor so that everyone can better remember someone without whose forty-plus years of commitment to our university, MELC and its Persian Studies program might not exist. I've also dedicated a new textbook called *Persian Vocabulary Acquisition: An Intermediate Reader and Guide to Word Forms and The Arabic Element in Persian* to two people among my friends who have cared most about Persian words, Ali Jazayery and Nader Naderpur. But my debt remains.

MELC Chair Stofberg rejected my proposal of a Jazayery photograph or plaque for display at MELC in his honor. At the same time, MELC posted an article on its web site about Jazayery with the title "In Memorium" [sic] and declined to change, at my request, the title's spelling.

At a MELC Executive Committee meeting on December 1, several faculty complained about leaks of information on candidates for the announced new position in Arabic language. When I denied making any leaks, Islamic Studies Assistant Professor and self-professed Muslim Kamil Riyadh averred something to the contrary. I asked if he was suggesting that I was lying, adding that a good Muslim would not suggest such a thing. At some point, Riyadh also made passing comments commending the University of Florida, which told me he was in the loop and that Florida's Arabic candidate was the loop's choice. Riyadh then left the meeting to teach a class. Either right before he left or right after, I raised the issue of the propriety of assistant professors sitting in judgment of persons at their own or higher rank.

Emory University's Mahmoud Al-Batal, Stofberg's first choice for the new Arabic position, had just removed his name from consideration. Stofberg intimated in several conversations with MELC faculty that Abboud and Attieh played a role in Al-Batal's withdrawal from consideration and also alleged that they had also removed job announcement notices posted on a bulletin board at the just concluded annual meeting of the Middle East Studies Association of North America in Boston. Several potential candidates did not apply for the announced position once they heard that it might put them in competition with Attieh.

✍ December 31, Journal entry, Perry Lane, Austin. On our Christmas trip to New Mexico, we stayed five nights at the Santa Fe Hilton and drove to Albuquerque for Christmas dinner at Karen and Ted's. We hosted them at Santa Fe's Il Piatta one evening. Il Piatta and Paul's are our favorite eateries near the square. The spare ribs at the Hilton's Canyon Café also deserve a star. I fall asleep these nights seeing the Green Santa Fe–Midland–Santa Fe Trail Runs at Santa Fe Ski Area where I spent three exhilirating days at Christmas, two with Sorayya waiting for me at the Lodge, and one with Eliza, who drove up from Albuquerque and spent the night. Eliza is cheery and expert ski company. Cheeseburgers for lunch, hot chocolate at two, and skiing until the last lift up the mountain. ✍

1999 began with the introduction of the Euro currency and ended with American transfer of the Panama Canal to Panamanian control. It ended also with a frenzy over the Millennium. Between January and December 1999, at UT's Department of Middle Eastern Languages and Cultures, low stakes machinations continued, which both kept me busy at the keyboard and occasionally challenged my upbeat attitude toward things. The machinations continued to upset Peter Abboud and to threaten Aman Attieh's job security.

Among those machinations, consequent to the realization that the Arabic search would not result in the identification of a superior candidate, was the bandying about of these allegations against Attieh, to make certain that she would not compare favorably with any other short-listed candidate. First, as a Lecturer, Attieh should not have served as departmental Undergraduate Adviser from 1994 to 1998. Second, at least one former Arabic Teaching Assistant filed a complaint of harassment and/or intimidation against Attieh. Third, Attieh was demanding in some interactions with some departmental staff. Fourth, Attieh browbeat students, chief among them an Arabic graduate student, whose allegations faculty opposed to Attieh accepted without question. Fifth, colleagues who didn't know Arabic or Applied Linguistics alleged that Attieh's teaching materials and methods were out-of-date. Sixth, Attieh had not published much. Seventh, Attieh had an aggressive, sometimes abrasive personality.

In the larger scheme of things at the beginning of 2000, the stakes in UT's Department of Middle Eastern Languages and Cultures remained low, except for Attieh and except for the health of academic integrity and principle. The record shows that what would happen to Attieh in the spring of 2000 had nothing to do with academic credentials, achievement, and potential, and everything to do with breaches of academic integrity and principle. My unequivocal views on this matter do not imply that Abboud and Attieh, on the one hand, and I, on the other, shared views about their Arabic instructional materials and the philosophy behind them. In addition, I did not rank Attieh first among announced candidates for the new Arabic language position. In my view, John Eisele was the best candidate.

As for the Attieh-Abboud approach to Arabic instructional materials preparation and classroom methodology, it got results. Moreover, good students thrived in their classes. Those two facts told me that they had a right to continue doing the efficacious things they'd been doing. But, for me, as a person who learned Persian in Iran through exposure to authentic oral and written texts in real-world situations, I've always felt comfortable writing and teaching Persian lessons and describing Persian with a primary focus on the spoken registers and forms of Persian which native speakers use in identifiable, definable situations. This means that I don't use the terms 'right' and 'wrong' or 'correct' and 'incorrect' in describing Persian morphology and syntax and that prescriptive rules and exceptions don't figure in grammar discussions in my textbooks and readers.

It also means that, if I wrote Arabic textbooks and taught Arabic, I wouldn't use Modern Standard Arabic as the language of communication in class or as the register described and taught in a beginning course. I'd start with a register which native speakers use in everyday communication with other native speakers. That register could include Colloquial and Modern Standard Arabic elements. If the colloquial elements had to be dialect-specific, I wouldn't hesitate to spend First-year Arabic presenting Cairene Arabic or Lebanese Arabic or Syrian Arabic, gradually introducing Modern Standard Arabic listening and reading. Colloquial Arabic and a hybrid of Colloquial and Modern Standard would continue throughout a four-year sequence of proficiency-based Arabic courses as the language of communication in and outside of class. My fourth-year Arabic courses would have a content basis: journalism, literature, history, religion, or whatever.

Abboud and Attieh, who use Modern Standard Arabic as the privileged register for oral communication between them and students in and out of class, would object saying that starting with a Colloquial dialect would limit students in their ability to listen, speak, and read efficiently. My two-fold answer is: first, it doesn't seem to limit native speakers of Arabic who start out in a single-dialect environment; second, there's nothing limiting about Cairene Arabic if one's native-speaker cohort numbers in the tens of millions. We teach Tajiki as an independent language, when only six million people speak it. We teach

Hebrew, which only five million people in the Middle East speak. More people speak Levantine Arabic than speak Italian.

Another notion comes to mind sometimes as a third reason. Not convinced that an Arab cultural continuum exists which encompasses the Arabic-speaking world from Qatar to Morocco, instruction of Beginning Arabic in such fashion as to treat specific dialects as having parallel and independent cultural identities could have salutary effects on students, disabusing them of the stereotypical notion that an Arabic national character or mentality exists. Their perception of something other than an Arab(ic) monolith might eventually influence similar new perceptions on the part of people beyond the academic world.

I never pursued a conversation on this subject with Attieh, whose steadfast convictions about the validity of her views on Modern Standard Arabic and teaching methods energize her teaching. After all, how a colleague manages a successful Arabic language program in which my students learn requisite skills for their Persian language work is his or her own business.

Jim's sketch of Mike and others skiing down a run at Whitetail Mountain Resort, Pennsylvania. March 2003.

Chapter 7

Spring 2000 Semester

"Life is a warfare against the malice of others."
Baltasar Gracián

"It is a good thing to follow the first law of holes; if you are in one, stop digging."
Denis Healey

"I fought for nothing—and I won."
Harry Hoston

Sorayya and I were too happy to celebrate on the night before the new year. We'd do our celebrating throughout the first half of 2000 away from Austin, our first semester away from UT since the spring of 1994. This time we were off to the Left Coast. On January 6, a day before our departure, I received an e-message which prompted this immediate e-response from me.

> Dear Kamil [Riyadh], I received this e-message [from Nora Wallstein] yesterday: "Dr. Hillman [sic], I would like to speak with you and would appreciate your calling my office at 911–1984 to set up a time when we could visit." I called 911–1984 late yesterday afternoon and set up an appointment for today at 3:30 pm. On leave and in and out of town, this was the only time I thought I could make it in the short term. On the telephone, I asked Ms. Wallstein with what office she was associated and why she wanted to meet with me. She replied that she was with the "Equal Employment Opportunity Office" and that you had gone to see her to report that I had called you "a bad Muslim" at a MELC Executive Committee meeting on 1 December 1999 and that you felt that you deserved more respect than that. If you happen to be in town, you might try to attend the meeting to make certain that you get quoted accurately and that you hear my exact responses to whatever questions Ms. Wallstein asks.

By the time Sorayya and I reached Los Angeles, Persian Studies Ph.D. student Dylan Oehler-Stricklin and Dean Applegate were exchanging e-messages which shortly thereafter came to and got my attention. First, Oehler-Stricklin wrote as follows to the Dean on January 21.

I am writing as a concerned graduate student in the Department of Middle Eastern Languages and Cultures about a situation I have only just become aware of. I am ABD in Persian Literature, and am working on my dissertation long distance from St. Louis. I recently called my advisor, Dr. Hillmann, and was horrified to learn in the course of casual conversation that Dr. Aman Attieh is in serious danger of losing her job. I have since learned that MELC's administration declared that they were upgrading her position to an Associate Professor's because you felt it necessary. Please allow me to register my serious and completely disinterested protests to this state of affairs.

I studied Arabic with Dr. Attieh in the academic year 1989–1990. I was impressed and, as one with ambitions of teaching language, influenced by her effectiveness and genuine dedication in the classroom. Much more rare in an instructor was her dedication outside the classroom. She stayed into the evening helping individual students on more occasions than I can count, and was always accessible to students, even at home. Her methods are vindicated by objective outside evaluators, in the written and verbal scores of her students—among the best in the country. Last year she won a Liberal Arts Teaching Award. I have studied five languages for many years in several countries, and am well qualified to speak as at least a student of language learning: I have never had a language teacher as talented and effective as Aman Attieh is, and it shakes my faith in academe to think that politics could conceivably have a role in her present situation—after she has taught at UT for sixteen years. This letter is completely unsolicited, and I am obviously quite out of touch with the department, having only just now learned of this.

On January 27, the Dean e-mailed this response to Oehler-Stricklin.

Thank you for your letter. Your understanding of the situation in Arabic at UT is of considerable interest. I cannot comment on what Prof. Hillman [sic] may have told you about the matter since I do not know what he told you. I can only conclude from what you have said that Prof. Hillman [sic] views the search for an Associate Prof. of Arabic as a danger to Dr. Attieh. This is the part that is interesting. As for. . .the search, I have no information. . .other than the fact that it is going on. . .Good luck with your dissertation writing. I look forward to seeing your name on the graduation rolls.

Oehler-Stricklin responded in turn to the Dean on January 28 in these words.

I must beg your pardon in giving the impression that Dr. Hillmann had any role whatsoever in my understanding of the situation in Arabic. In a recent phone conversation with him, I remarked that I had seen Hamarneh's position advertised some time ago on the *Adabiyat* e-site. He replied that it was not Hamarneh's, but a new position which would replace Attieh's. That was all, and I'm sure he would be dismayed at being the focus of your interest in this particular case. I should have made myself clearer: given Dr. Attieh's record and my own experience of her, I could not help wondering if politics were not somehow involved. At this point I would like to emphasize that no one in the department contributed to my letter or even knew of it. Thank you for your good wishes. I hope and trust that you do not look forward to my graduation only because of this situation!

On the same day, Oehler-Stricklin sent me this e-message.

> I'm sorry about the misunderstanding that my letter to the Dean caused. As soon as I received his reply, I e-mailed again and made it clear that you had nothing to do with my impressions of the situation, that you had only told me of the new position. I copied you and Dr. Stofberg, and I called the dean's office (no luck). I also called Dr. Stofberg and spoke to him, and I hope at this point everyone is clear on the independence of my thought process. I did tell Dr. Stofberg that I was a little surprised that the dean had reacted as if I had made an accusation, when all I said was that, given Attieh's record and my own experience with her, I would be dismayed if politics were a possibility. I will be writing a letter of recommendation for her, which I hope very much will not bring about the downfall of western civilization.

From October 1998 through April 2000, a dozen of UT's best undergraduate and graduate students wrote letters like those by Mark Sullivan and Dylan Oehler-Stricklin. Responses by Stofberg and the Dean to the Sullivan and Oehler-Stricklin letters would appear to typify official Department and College views of UT's best students in their distrust of the independence of the thinking of those students and typify official Department and College practice of non-answers to questions by raising *ad hominem* issues or pointing fingers elsewhere. If Department and College administrators think that their best students can't or don't think for themselves, then those administrators cannot think much of the programs they administer and perhaps should conclude that they aren't doing the job of training students to think for themselves. The exchange between Oehler-Stricklin and the Dean highlights unequivocally a non-academic and non-intellectual mindset of College administration in dealing with our Arabic language program. It also presaged a student movement during the Spring 2000 Semester that brought into question for some observers the ethics and competence of that administration.

On February 8, I sent the following e-message to the Dean from Los Angeles.

Dear Reggie, On leave and away from the office, I have just now checked my e-mail for the first time in several weeks and read the copy you sent me of the message you sent to MELC Ph.D. candidate Dylan Oehler-Stricklin. . .In your message to Ms. Oehler-Stricklin, you wrote: "I can only conclude from what you said that Prof. Hillman [sic] views the search for an Associate Prof. of Arabic as a danger to Dr. Attieh. This is the part that is interesting." You have not drawn a correct conclusion here. . .As you likely know, Dr. Attieh has many loyal students and ex-students whom the news of the end to her lectureship has likely worried. I have not had occasion to talk to those students about Dr. Attieh's position and future or to any faculty colleagues except for Avraham Zilkha and Peter Abboud, who have personal interests in what happens to our Arabic program.

✍ February 13, Journal entry, Central City Plaza, Los Angeles. Sorayya is trying on dresses at Bloomingdale's. Eliza and Jeff are watching *The Beach* at the Central City Plaza's fourteen-screen movieplex. I've got a seat at the New York Stage Deli Bar to watch the final holes of The Buick Invitational at La Jolla, sip an Amstel Light beer, and munch on a Chinese chicken salad. Of my 21,800+ days to date, most have disappeared without a trace. Despite my journals, *From Durham to Tehran*, hundreds of letters, and thousands of photographs, today is almost an exception, recorded and remembered, special only because I have happened to start a new journal with it. A half hour ago, browsing in Brentano's, I couldn't decide on a book to buy and read. So I bought a blank book to write in. We spent three days at Big Bear Lake before driving on to West Hollywood. I skied two days at Big Bear, finally graduating to all blue runs. A sore shoulder reminds me that I need more practice before I throw caution to the wind and trust speed. Sorayya and I had two cozy, delicious dinners in the Village. In Los Angeles, we've café-mocha-ed all over the west side, seen movie after movie, and learned to drive wherever we want to go. Before Big Bear, we spent four days in Arizona, three in Tucson as guests of the University of Arizona and one in Scottsdale. Cocktails at Bob and Podie Gibson's on North Campbell one night gave us as spectacular a view from a home as we've ever seen, 360 degrees of mountains and hills and city. My slide talk at the Center for Middle Eastern Studies on "An Aesthetics of Persian Carpets" drew a receptive audience of Iranian(-American)s and UofA people. Simin took us to dinner one evening. Her mother hosted a dinner party in our honor on another. First-rate accommodations at the University Marriott included a quiet exercise room. As

Eliza and Jeff's house guests, we've eaten at Club Med and Mel's Diner on Sunset Boulevard, Montana Café in Santa Monica, Bistro Italia on Wilshire, the food court on Farmer's Market on Fairfax, and elsewhere. I've spent two days researching *Iran (Revised) Bibliography* for CLIO at UCLA's beautiful, almost idyllic campus. The seafood salad at their Student Union food court, on an outdoor terrace with a view, was almost gourmet. On Thursday, I learned some things at a symposium on Islamic fundamentalism at Royce Hall. Khaled [Abou El Fadl] gave a good talk. We had a chance to chat briefly beforehand. He doesn't miss Texas, and for good reasons. Royce Hall architecture and that of other buildings on the tiered levels of campus malls invite talk and study and thought. ✍

On February 13, former CMES Director and kindred spirit Paul English replied to my late December inquiry about his health. I had written:

> I've felt that we were almost in touch during the past year or two through my association with Bill Rowe, a star Tajiki student in our Persian Studies sky and doubtless a brighter light in your larger firmament of Geography. We've talked once since his return from Tajikistan. He is helping me review exercises for a new book of mine called *Tajiki Textbook and Reader*. Then, we got your wedding announcement this past summer. Belated congratulations. Sorayya and I have thought we would take the two of you out to dinner sometime. Over dinner two nights ago, Peter Abboud and Aman Attieh casually mentioned visiting you at the hospital. We hadn't heard anything about your operation. Here's hoping you are mending as quickly as you're supposed to. I'm beginning to think that Worcester is not all that good for the health of Iranian Studies people: Jim Bill [Assumption], now you [Clark], me [Holy Cross] next? I'd like to stop by for a chat, if you can give me a home telephone number and address. Sorayya joins me in wishing you a speedy recovery. If I could do anything logistical or academic for you during the next few weeks, let me know.

Now, Paul wrote: "Not great news here. As you probably know through Bill, I was operated on for lung cancer, presumed successful, now on medical leave. This week they discovered stomach cancer (supposedly completely independent of the lung deal), and I may be having another operation shortly. I think I'll go back and be born somewhere other than Worcester. Glad you are well. Miss you."

When Sorayya and I later went to visit Paul, we couldn't see him. A nurse at his condo told us his system was shutting down and death was imminent. Paul Ward English, the best man in the history of Middle

Eastern Studies at Texas, died shortly thereafter and was buried in his beloved Cape Cod.

✍ February 15. Journal entry, above Arizona on American Airlines Flight 554. Worried about Aman Attieh's fate as an Arabic Studies colleague, Peter Abboud has arranged for me to fly to Austin for a meeting of MELC'S Executive Committee tomorrow afternoon. The meeting has two agenda items: (1) discussion of applications for a new Arabic position, and (2) recommendations for merit salary increases for 2000–2001. Attieh will likely not get more than half of the EC's votes for the new position, which comes with tenure. A Search Committee named by our College of Liberal Arts apparently ranked Aman fourth or fifth in a list of apparently qualified applicants. The Committee apparently recommended as their first choice an applicant who hasn't published a single page since 1991, hasn't published a book of any sort, did not submit any recommendation letters from Arabists, did not include his professional record as part of his résumé, apparently lacks training in foreign language teaching or applied linguistics, and, as implied in his application, has no interest in those fields. Moreover, his only Arabic language teaching has taken place at a university with no standing or degree programs in Arabic Studies. That university promoted him to Associate Professor with tenure, or perhaps without, despite his lack of the usual publication record. Politics has played a chief role in our Arabic search. Early Thursday morning I'll fly back to Los Angeles, where Jim joined us yesterday in time for a Valentine's Day dinner at the Marina del Ray Marriott Hotel Restaurant with Hammie, Holly, Eliza, Jeff, Sorayya, and me. During my forty hours in Austin, sixteen of them set aside for sleep, I have these things on my nongustatorial plate: (1) read MELC faculty annual reports and files to make recommendations at the EC meeting on merit salary increases; (2) prepare a statement on Arabic language position qualifications for discussion at the EC meeting; (3) prepare a written motion for the meeting proposing Aman Attieh as an Arabic-position applicant deserving an interview for the position; (4) start sending copies of *Short Fiction by Saudi Arabian Women Writers* to *Literature East & West* subscribers; (5) write Mark Tessler et al. thank-you notes for inviting me to UofA; (6) write Hossein Ziai et al. thank-you notes for use of UCLA facilities; (8) e-mail Faredun Hodizada an inquiry about his progress in editing *Tajiki*

Textbook and Reader and about the possibility of express mail return of the manuscript from Dushanbe by the end of February; (9) make travel plans for a March trip to Dunwoody Press in Hyattsville to review *Tajiki Textbook and Reader;* (10) check with Stofberg on the likely date of the next EC meeting, and coordinate the Hyattsville trip with that meeting; (11) make an appointment for my next colonoscopy; and (12) check the Persepolis mail box, and answer all mail. ✍

On February 16, I submitted the following written motion made to the MELC Executive Committee.

This memo responds to the announcement of today's MELC Executive Committee meeting to discuss candidates for MELC's announced new Associate Professorship in Arabic Language.

MELC's announcement for the Arabic language position states or implies that the successful candidate will have these qualifications: (1) at least near-native fluency in speaking Arabic (e.g., the ability to give a lecture in Arabic and answer questions about the lecture); (2) university training in foreign language teaching methods; (3) substantial, successful experience in teaching Arabic at the university level (e.g., reputation as a skilful, dynamic, caring language teacher); (4) productivity in foreign language instructional materials development (e.g., authorship of a standard Arabic textbook); (5) experience in language teacher training activities (e.g., a methods course for Teaching Assistant and Assistant Instructor faculty); (6) experience in supervising language teachers; (7) demonstration of interest and expertise in the cultural contexts of the Arabic language; (8) a university and academic community service record commensurate with expectations of a first-year associate professor with tenure (e.g., active membership in relevant national organizations); and (9) a publication record commensurate with expectations of a first-year associate professor with tenure (e.g., at least two books).

In terms of these qualifications, the relevant College of Liberal Arts policy statement (28 March 1996), and the Announcement of the position (*Chronicle of Higher Education,* November 1999), four or five of the applicants for our new Arabic language position. . .deserve an interview invitation and opportunity to give a lecture on a relevant subject of special research interest and teach a demonstration Arabic language class. In my view, among those four or five applicants is our Arabic Studies colleague Aman Attieh.

Therefore, I move that the Executive Committee vote to invite Aman Attieh to interview for the announced position. Besides demonstrable fulfillment of such qualifications as the foregoing, Aman Attieh's file strikes me as warranting such an invitation for the following further reasons. (1) Aman Attieh has performed the job in question since 1989 when she became Coordinator of our Arabic language program. (2) As attested to by written and oral communications from many of her undergraduate and graduate students over the years, Aman Attieh appears to have developed special loyalty among those students. (3) Aman Attieh's recent university teaching award and current presidency of the American Association of Teachers of Arabic would appear to imply qualifications beyond minimal expectations. (4) MELC's oral and written encouragement to Aman Attieh last fall to apply for the new position implies our responsibility to give her at least the same opportunity to make her case through the interview process as other candidates. (5) Because the new position apparently takes the place of the lectureship which Aman Attieh has held for over fifteen years, meaning that she apparently may face termination of employment, MELC should, in my view, give her every fair chance to maintain her association with our Department. An interview for the new position would represent that fair chance. (6) Because Aman Attieh is a MELC faculty member, her interview, lecture, and demonstration class present no scheduling, logistical or budgetary problems. She presumably can submit to the process at any time convenient to MELC at no cost to MELC. (7) In most recent MELC searches involving MELC lecturers/instructors applying for tenure-track positions, MELC chose not to invite off-campus candidates for interviews. It would thus strike me as discriminatory if MELC fails to interview the single female, UT Austin candidate among the apparently qualified four or five candidates for our new Arabic language position.

✍ February 17. Journal entry, over Arizona again, en route to Los Angeles. I completed about half of the items in my things-to-do-in-Austin check list during my day-and-a-half there. Peter took me out to dinner twice. I walked to The University yesterday, stopping at the new Kerbey Lane Café on Guadalupe for a breakfast of scrambled eggbeaters, fruit cup, orange juice, and pancakes. Copies of *Short Fiction by Saudi Arabian Women Writers* reached MELC yesterday–Doug Armstrong and Armstrong Printers did as good a job as always. MELC's Executive Committee met from four to seven yesterday afternoon. Half of it dealt with four names which the Search Committee recommended. Only John Eisele's file struck me as outstanding. All of the files hinted that applicants might want to use an offer from Texas to improve their situations at home. The second half of the meeting dealt with my motion, that MELC include Aman Attieh in the interview process. The Executive Committee voted 3–3–1 on it, whereupon Chair Stofberg cast a deciding vote against the motion. Discussion had no academic or intellectual content. No one besides Peter, Avraham, and me had a positive word to say about Aman. My focus now turns to the possibility that Aman can continue at MELC as a Senior Lecturer. ✍

Sorayya and I left the coziness of Eliza and Jeff's West Hollywood apartment for northern California on February 21. Right before then we learned that Nader Naderpour had died in Los Angeles on January

20. Eliza and I had driven by his apartment on Holt Avenue one afternoon in mid-January, but didn't stop because it looked as if no one was home.

Sorayya and I drove straight north through California to South Lake Tahoe, the last several miles almost as unnerving as the last miles to Big Bear Lake and rivaling the Karaj–Chalus Road. I skied three heavenly days at Heavenly. Sorayya walked and read and played the slot machines downstairs in our casino hotel and at nearby casinos. From South Lake Tahoe, we drove west to San Francisco for three days of invigorating walks in the drizzle, café hopping, and wonderful seafood and Chinese dinners. On the fourth day, Sorayya suddenly up and said she missed 3404 Perry Lane. We packed and drove straight home, arriving on February 28.

The third issue of *Middle Eastern Languages and Cultures Newsletter* was waiting for me at WMB 5.146. Its six pages had these headlines and featured these titles: "Message from the Chairman" by Robert Stofberg, "Judaism and Islam: Crosscurrents;" "February 8 Steinfeld Lecture (on "Jewish-Gentile Relations in Rabbinic Literature" by Zvi Stenfeld, former Chair of the Talmud Department at Bar Ilan University and Editor of *Sidra*); "Jewish Studies Major"; "Faculty Profiles" (on Jacob Levy, Professor of Hebrew, Jewish Studies, and Linguistics); "Workshop on the Teaching of Islamic and Jewish Studies"; Undergraduate Student News, Student Scholarships, MELC Faculty Awards; MELC Faculty Grants, MELC Faculty Lectures and Presentations (Zilla Goodman, Robert Stofberg, Deborah Cohen, and two others); Faculty Publications and Other Creative Work (Stofberg, Cohan [sic] and two other names); "Linda Gradstein: Reporting from Ground Xero," a program featuring Linda Gradstein, the Jerusalem correspondent for National Public Radio); Leon Yudkin to Speak April 6 ("Straining at the Leash: New Directions in Israeli Fiction" by a professor of Hebrew and Comparative Literature at University College, London, and editor of a Jews in Modern Culture Monograph Series, the lecture organized by the Gale Chair of Judaic Studies); Michael Morgan Lecture (on "Kafka, Buber, Benjamin: Themes in the Modern Jewish Experience"); A Retrospective of Haim Shiran's Films ("one of Israel's foremost personalities in the television and film industry"); and "Judaism and Islam: Cross-Currents" (with the participation of Robert

Stofberg, Benjamin Loya, Zilla Goodman, Shifra Epstein, Deborah Cohen, Yaron Shemer, Jacob Levy, Tamar Rudavsky, Reuven Firestone, Pamela Sezgin, and eleven others); and a page devoted to an essay by and photograph of Stofberg.

After the Executive Committee meeting which voted against allowing Attieh to interview for the new Arabic position, Arabic and Persian students reacted. For example, Persian M.A. student Leslie Moore had sent me this e-message on February 25.

> This is probably old news to you by now, but evidently Dr. Attieh's name did not make the short list for the new associate professor position that has been opened for the fall semester. Evidently the lecturer position that she now holds will be closed.
>
> The latest is that the students in the Arabic classes have signed a petition to urge that Dr. Attieh's credentials be reviewed more carefully and to testify to the caliber of her teaching. This petition was distributed to all MELC faculty and administrators last week. To date there has been no response. Additionally, an ad hoc committee has sent a letter to administrators expressing concern about preserving the quality of the Arabic studies program. Individual students have also sent testimonials on behalf of Dr. Attieh in an effort of keep her name under consideration before the committee.
>
> The latest step is a request to meet with members of the search committee to discuss student concerns about Dr. Attieh's candidacy in particular and the MELC Arabic program in general.
>
> You've probably already also received a copy of the letter addressed to Dr. Stofberg. In case you have not, I'm sending it as an attachment [SAAUT Letter #1].
>
> Any advice or suggestions you could offer about advancing Dr. Attieh's cause in this matter would be greatly appreciated. . .Khoda hafez.

Because I now knew that, even if Attieh had received Executive Committee endorsement to interview for the Associate Professor position, she couldn't have garnered enough Executive Committee votes to get recommended for the position, I had no advice or suggestions to offer Leslie Moore and her SAAUT confrères. All I thought I could do at this point was prepare a motion for a future Executive Committee meeting to the effect that MELC recommend renewal of Attieh's contract as Senior Lecturer for 2000–2001.

Not that I thought that the February 16 vote against my motion to allow Attieh to interview for the Associate Professor position had ended the matter. On 4 February 2000, Stofberg had added an anti-Abboud/ Attieh assistant professor member to the Executive Committee in anticipation of a vote on the issue at the February 16 meeting. On the same day as the meeting, I penned this note to Stofberg.

> As you know, I have always favored the widest participation on OALL and MELC committees and councils. The addition of another assistant professor to our EC broadens participation. But MELC needs to have a rationale both for adding a MELC colleague to the EC on the basis of gender [only females were candidates for the new EC position] and for not following Regents' Rules (e.g., Chapter 2, Section 8, Items 1,2,3). You will recall that when I raised a question about assistant professor members of our EC meeting last fall [December 1], an EC member took offense. I won't raise the issue again at today's meeting. But you might check Regents' Rules and have a rationale in case any colleagues question results of deliberations on merit increases and hiring/promotions.

The assistant professors cast two of the three votes against inviting Attieh to interview for the Associate Professor position. One, whose participation on the EC violated University rules, was on the UT faculty as a spousal hire, that is to say, assuring a job for that person was a condition in that person's spouse's UT contract. The other was on the UT faculty because he met the necessary condition of African-American origin, which his position had. Both assistant professors were Attieh's junior in terms of academic credentials—one had no graduate training in his/her field, and the other had completed a Ph.D. just two years earlier—and teaching experience. Both had filed complaints against Attieh and exhibited animosity toward her in public. Stofberg's orchestration of the EC vote against Attieh through the participation of these two assistant professors on MELC's Executive Committee seemed to me at the time a proverbial smoking gun of discrimination or retaliation against Attieh.

On March 2, Stofberg distributed a note to MELC Executive Committee members in anticipation of a visit by Arabic Associate Professor candidate Jonathan Owens. He distributed similar notes when other candidates visited. I've highlighted words in the note which suggest that MELC and the College of Liberal Arts still felt uneasy about the original, voted-on proposal of the new position as an addition to existing Arabic positions in MELC. The note reads: "In regards to the position that Dr. Jonathan Owens is applying for, it is an endowed position. His title now at the University of Bayreuth, Bayreuth, Germany is Professor and the title for the position that he is applying for is Associate Professor, as tenured. This position is **not**

in replacement of someone but **will be adding** to or **complementing** an existing program. This position is an **upgrade** of the current Senior Lecturer position to Associate Professor."

Around campus, some faculty were now reacting to the news about Attieh's situation, among them Government Professor Clement Henry, to whom I sent the following e-message on March 6.

> Thank you for e-copies of two e-mail messages which you have sent to faculty interested in UT's Arabic language program. Your second draft of a letter of faculty support read: "Dear Dean, We are seriously concerned about rumors that Dr. Aman Attieh's Senior Lectureship may be discontinued. Over the course of her career at The University of Texas at Austin, Dr. Attieh has distinguished herself as a member of the faculty. . .We realize that a lectureship is not a tenure-track position, but it is important for those of us concerned with training students for field work in Arab countries that she be encouraged to keep up her excellent work here. . .If the new recruit is to be a linguistic theorist and scholar, then she is all the more indispensable for teaching the basic language courses. If the new associate professor were to have been the principal language teacher, on the other hand, then she should have been among the finalists. We hope a satisfactory compromise can be reached which preserves the Arabic language program and the university's reputation for scholarly excellence and fairness."
>
> On leave and out of town this semester, I have returned to Austin twice: for a MELC Executive Committee meeting on February 16 and for lectures by three Arabic candidates which began last week. During my few days in town, I have not been able to respond to the thirty or so written e-communications I've received about our Arabic program. I have CMES/MELC Arabic students at my door throughout the day. In my twenty-five years at UT, I have heard of nothing like the present situation, a situation in which rumors have it that an experienced, qualified, award-winning language instructor with a national reputation in a program which needs that instructor's services is facing non-renewal of her contract, despite the views of those faculty colleagues and students and ex-students who know most about the program in question.
>
> Please e-mail me a copy of the final version your faculty letter, at which time I will add my name to it.

On March 8, a MELC-sponsored conference on "Judaism and Islam: Crosscurrents" took place. The Liberal Arts Dean's name appeared on the program as first speaker. Outside Humanities Research Center where the conference took place, Arabic and other students had congregated for a protest demonstration. After a flurry of telephone calls and a half-hour's delay, the conference session began without the Dean. Inside and out, students and faculty wondered if concerns about confronting student demonstrators had persuaded the Dean not to come.

A bizarre conference-related interaction took place later that day between Islamic Studies colleague Farshid Sepehri and me. It immediately prompted this e-message from me to him.

It was . . . good to see a full house for the afternoon session of the conference. At the office afterwards, I was stepping out of the men's room when [MELC staff person] Lucy [Billings] accosted me, abruptly asking why I had reported that the Dean had not presented opening remarks at the morning conference session because of the SAAUT demonstration outside. Lucy grew angry when I replied to the effect that my view was and is that Reggie would not miss a meeting because of a possible confrontation. . .Lucy then said that you had told her that I had said definitely that he had not come to the conference precisely because of the demonstration. I denied to Lucy that I had made such a statement, but added in the same breath that what I say, in any case–and I do not negatively characterize people in conversations–is the business only of the person to whom I may say something and to me and that what Lucy says to someone else is never my business and vice-versa. I added that MELC should not waste its time in he said-she said and gossip. Lucy replied–and at this point I thought I perceived the original bases of her anger–that she had suffered misquotation yesterday at the hands of "those students" and that an administrative mix-up had caused Reggie's absence this morning, which naturally would cause Lucy stress. I replied that I could have no comment about that since I didn't know "those students" or know about any alleged quoting or misquoting. And I didn't think at the time nor do I think now that Reggie's presence or absence would affect the intellectual content of the conference. I might tomorrow mention to someone that his name appeared on the program, but that he didn't come, in the same fashion that I might say that the conference program misspelled the word "religion" or that it looks like rain later in the day or that the water cooler outside of the HRC lecture hall makes a lot of noise or that I often think about Al-e Ahmad's experience of nothingness that night on the Hajj pilgrimage.

Because you and Zilla were the only colleagues to whom I talked after the morning session and before the afternoon session, I believe Lucy when she says you said something that led her to allege that I had said something specific to you. You will recall our brief. . .conversation in WMB 5.120. You will recall that it ended in our agreement that Reggie was not the sort of person to stay away from a confrontation, not that the presence of polite CMES/DMES students holding placards and passing out a single piece of paper and not even raising their voices above conversational whispering in front of HRC (whose staff brought them coffee this morning) would make for a confrontation. You will also recall that, before our conversation ended, we wondered about whether or not any faculty would have heard about the demonstration in time to make plans thereafter for this morning, at which point I remarked that SAAUT had announced it on its e-list last night. I did not mention to you that I had sent an e-mail to Robert the minute I got out of the SAAUT-MELC EC meeting last night, asking him to get in touch so that I could let him know what to expect this morning.

I can appreciate the stress which colleagues and staff feel in the search for a new associate professor of Arabic and in the questions raised about Aman Attieh's future in MELC. By the time candidates get to me for a visit, their first and chief question has to do with that subject. Being away most of the time this semester, I haven't felt the stress.

Oops, a reporter from *The Daily Texan* has just called to talk about guess what. Again. . .so that we do not add to the stress quotient, when we have occasion to exchange pleasantries or views in the hallway, could we mutually observe the policy I observe, which is to keep *entre nous* everything between two people when I'm one of them, because not only does poetry get lost in translation [, as Robert Frost put it], but things people say rarely get passed along exactly as said except in writing and when recorded?

In receipt of my e-message, Sepehri made his first and only visit to WMB 5.146. In our brief conversation, he advised me never to tell him anything if I was expecting that he not share it with MELC staff and faculty. He also said that he hadn't misquoted me. In response, I said that his statement that he hadn't misquoted me amounted to saying that what I said I had said and what I had written that I had said was a lie. Adding that no one had ever accused me of lying in my own office before, I told him that our conversation was over, that he was to leave my office immediately, and that if he ever misquoted me again, I'd come down on him like a proverbial ton of bricks. He left the office without comment.

Predictably enough—and a reason for why I had immediately put the narrative on paper in my e-message to Farshid—, Stofberg sent me this letter on March 9.

I have received a memo from [MELC staff person] Lucy [Billings] complaining about your discourteous and abusive behavior yesterday. Your inappropriate berating of her was overheard by Yilidray [sic] Erdener. This is the second time that I have had to draw your attention to your abusive behavior towards her. I am therefore putting this letter in your file and sending copies to appropriate parties. . .Moreover your spread of rumors of the Dean's alleged motives for not being present at the opening of the conference, suggesting that he allegedly did not wish to be confronted by the student demonstrators, was patently false. Your role in spreading this rumor is attested to in a letter to me from Farshid Sepehri, who also claims that you threatened him. I view with great gravity your pattern of discourtesy and outright abusiveness. You are hereby put on notice that your behavior, which follows a distinct pattern, will not be tolerated.

Meanwhile, Arabic candidate Jonathan Owens was visiting MELC. He presented a lecture on March 10. After the lecture, I sent this letter to Government Professor Clement Henry.

When I sat down near you before the lecture by Jonathan Owens today at The Texas Union, I couldn't help both notice the animated gestures of Jonathan Copeland with respect to the article in today's *Daily Texan* about Aman Attieh and student supporters and overhear his characterization of letters of recommendation in Dr. Attieh's file as "mixed" or some of them as coming from people who do not use her textbooks.

Not privy to Arabic Search Committee deliberations, I can only report hearsay, that is comments by one Search Committee member, to the effect that no negative discussion of Aman Attieh's file took place at Search Committee meetings. However, I can report on more than a hearsay basis that only positive discussion about her file and career and contributions to the field of Arabic language teaching took place at MELC's single Executive Committee meeting on February 16 called to discuss the "Arabic Position." At that meeting, I read the attached motion, discussed Dr. Attieh's performance with respect to the nine criteria or qualifications checked at the top of the motion's second page, and did not hear any negative commentary before the ensuing vote on the motion. I guess I can also add without violating the confidentiality of such a meeting that the written Search Committee report on their deliberations does not make mention of Aman Attieh's application.

SAAUT has announced on its e-site that a meeting of that organization will likely take place with the Liberal Arts College Dean at the end of March or in early April. I'm hoping that SAAUT can make the case that annually increasing enrollments in Arabic language classes, the likelihood that the new Associate Professor of Arabic will work as much in Linguistics as in language teaching, and Aman Attieh's track record call for renewal of her contract as Senior Lecturer.

A perception exists at CMES that MELC's Arabic program features old-fashioned or out-of-date materials and methods. A cursory look at outside evaluations in recent years and at recommendations and testimonials from almost all of the other major university Arabic programs in North America suggests the groundlessness of that perception. As someone who has read our Arabic language syllabi, visited classes, and knows a dozen Persian students who have improved their Persian skills greatly as a result of participation in our Arabic program, I know that our Arabic program is first-rate. At the same time, I know that some MELC and CMES colleagues are "down on" Peter Abboud and Aman Attieh. I have never heard the reasons why, even in informal, private conversations. I have also noticed even in the handful of days I have come to my MELC office this semester (being on leave with a Dean's Fellowship) new vibrations from three colleagues and a staff person, which I can attribute only to a possible perception on their part that my support of a departmental colleague on the grounds presented in the attached motion constitutes disloyalty to MELC.

In any case, I won't be back on campus until March 23. If you plan to move ahead with a[n announced, planned] faculty letter supporting Aman

Attieh's continued service with MELC, you need to communicate with me exclusively via e-mail. I'll be checking mchillmann@aol.com at least once a day while out of town.

Stofberg's letter of March 9 reached me right after the Owens lecture. I responded as follows.

Your letter dated 9 March 2000 on the subject of reports which you have received from Lucy Billings and Farshid Sepehri about two conversations which I had with each of them on March 8 reached me late this afternoon. . .I am answering you in this fashion [i.e., with a copy to the College of Liberal Arts] because you have communicated to the College of Liberal Arts what was hearsay to you without an attempt on your part to verify the hearsay.

Your letter of March 9 . . . makes MELC management an issue. In my view, since the fall of 1998, a series of avoidable or resolvable problems have led MELC to the brink of counterproductive public scrutiny. First came the first ever insinuation. . .of Arab-Israeli biases in our department (Menzel letter etc.). Second came Arabic student concerns and ineffective MELC responses which leave us today with only one degree-seeking MELC Arabic Studies graduate student taking courses, down from fifteen or so such students in 1997–1998. . .Third came that paragraph in the Chair's letter [of yours] in Walid Hamarneh's promotion file which contradicted other available evidence. Fourth came the bizarre November 1998 faculty meeting which led to yelling and tears overheard by students in an ongoing [Arabic Literature] class next door, adding to their confusion about MELC's commitment to Arabic Studies. Fifth came misinformation by the MELC Chair to faculty about the nature of the new Arabic position, which the Chair represented as a position to be added to the existing positions held by Peter Abboud and Aman Attieh. Sixth came a series of irregularities with respect to application procedures and the evaluation process for the new Arabic position, chronologically first among them the fact that as of the November 30 deadline none of the three candidates whom the Search Committee named as finalists had fulfilled application requirements as stated in the published official announcement for the position. For that matter, even at the time of the MELC Executive Committee meeting on February 16, at which the MELC Chair announced plans to invite three specific applicants as finalists, one file lacked letters of recommendation and samples of publications, a second file lacked a complete résumé of professional activities, and a third file exhibited letters of recommendation written for a different position at another university. Seventh was the very naming of finalists, two of whom have stated in conversations with MELC faculty and students that they would not want to commit much of their teaching time to language classes and that their presence would not help resolve the teacher-student ratio problem in Arabic language courses.

Eighth came MELC's decision not to allow Arabic Senior Lecturer Aman Attieh to interview for the new position. Enclosed find my EC motion on that subject. At no cost and no inconvenience to MELC, a head count of either Search Committee or Executive Committee membership clearly showing that Dr. Attieh would not emerge as the successful candidate, Aman Attieh's track record that spoke both to the qualifications listed in the announcement and to the experience of doing the job which the announcement called for, Aman Attieh's participation in the interview process, as I suggested in writing and in discussion, would satisfy concerned students and faculty that the process of hiring a new Associate Professor of Arabic was fair and did not give the appearance of discrimination or bias. I also informed MELC in writing before the February 16 Executive Committee meeting that the selection of a new EC member on the explicit basis of gender a week before the meeting and her participation at that meeting as a voting member perhaps to cast a deciding vote needed attention before the meeting in case the process had not followed relevant university guidelines.

Ninth came MELC responses to expression of concerns by some CMES/MELC Arabic students. Those responses, as was the case with responses to Arabic Studies graduate students in the fall of 1998, did not address the concerns but rather characterized the Arabic students in negative terms. In response to the request by members of the student group called SAAUT, the MELC Chair declined to arrange a meeting with its Executive Committee although cognizant of the fact that at least one EC member had agreed to meet with students. As it turned out, two EC members and perhaps fifteen students met for three hours at WMB 5.136 on March 7. At that meeting, students informed MELC faculty of their decision to hold demonstrations on March 8 and 9. I immediately sent an e-mail to the MELC Chair asking him to get in touch so that he might be ready on the morrow for questions by students and a reporter from *The Daily Texan*.

Tenth came the first session of the conference on "Judaism and Islam Cross-Currents" with only about fifteen non-participants in attendance (there apparently having been no prior effective public relations) and beginning with a twenty-minute delay before the first presentation. In the minds of students and faculty, that twenty-minute delay registered something negative about our department. . .The delay brought to mind: the first and unprofessional issue of MELC's *Newsletter* in the fall of 1998; the session of a MELC symposium in the spring of 1999 when two, twenty-minute papers turned into hour-long presentations without conclusions, and two slide presentations took place with faulty slide projection and mis-filed slides; compilation of a Persian Studies brochure (and perhaps other brochures) without benefit of a mailing list so that brochure copies languish at WMB 5.120; distribution of unreviewed and unedited course descriptions without clear statements of objectives, often without lists of required texts, and sometimes with substandard English and in one case the mis-spelling of a core concept in the course; department office closures beyond the noon hour without prior notice or explanation; and constant leaking of discussions at MELC faculty meetings (e.g., most recently, Elizabeth Fernea confidently asserted in a brief argument with students in front of HRC on Wednesday that the Search Committee vote not to include Aman Attieh as a finalist for the new Arabic position was unanimous—presumably a Search Committee member had told her this). The list could go on, for example, MELC's routine misspelling of faculty names, misattribution of ranks and titles, and mispronunciation of faculty names. . .The MELC Chair misspelled a faculty surname in his March 9 letter to that faculty member.

The point here is that MELC arguably needs to work to achieve adequate professionalism in its activities and interactions with the university and academic communities and the general public. I would hesitate at a faculty meeting or in conversation with the MELC Chair to bring up these issues because of another issue, my perception that the MELC Chair arguably takes even the slightest criticism personally or arguably sees criticism as having something other than the good of the department behind it. I further perceive that the MELC Chair sees friendly relations as the primary basis for successful implementation of his goals and for achievement of departmental objectives. . .American and Middle Eastern behavioral models and verbal systems exist so that organizations can operate smoothly and efficiently even when members disagree or are not personally close.

The immediate MELC issue suggests to me an *ad hominem* basis of departmental management. At least six MELC faculty have the impression that the MELC Chair sees support for inclusion of Aman Attieh's name as a finalist for the new Arabic position as having its basis in personal relationships with Dr. Attieh and as implying disloyalty to MELC. Those same faculty members have the further impression that opposition to Aman Attieh is strictly *ad hominem* insofar as no discussion of possible negative aspects of her teaching, teaching methodology, teaching materials, and publications has taken place at any faculty meetings or in any discussions involving those faculty members with the cited impression. The three MELC faculty members who voted at the February 16 Executive Committee meeting to add Aman Attieh's name to the list of candidates scheduled for interview happen to be those EC members most involved in language teaching and language materials preparation (i.e., service as coordinators, regular instruction of two language courses each semester, writing of grammars, readers, textbooks, and dictionaries). If asked, those three EC members would likely report that other faculty and administrators later questioned their vote, a situation which has its own implications. At this point, my view is that the College of Liberal Arts and MELC will have to live with reactions on the part of SAAUT, AAUP, Aman Attieh, Peter Abboud, and some faculty around campus and the country to her exclusion from the interview process for the new position. Once the vote on my motion took place at the February 16 meeting, I turned my attention to the hope that Aman Attieh could continue her service as a Senior Lecturer of Arabic during 2000–2001. I hope that MELC and the College of Liberal Arts recognize that the Arabic language program will suffer seriously next year without her participation, because none of the finalists for the new Arabic position can or perhaps wants to do the necessary teaching which she now does and because no combination of teaching assistants or assistant instructors could efficiently do that teaching either. I hope that Liberal Arts can find funding for a lectureship in Arabic for 2000–2001.

On March 22, in anticipation of a MELC Executive Committee meeting that afternoon, I prepared the following written motion for discussion and vote at that meeting.

This memo responds to recent media, faculty, and student attention on and off campus to MELC's ongoing search for a new Associate Professor of Arabic Language and controversy relating to the search process and the possibility that Arabic Senior Lecturer Aman Attieh might lose her job as of 2000–2001.

As two of the three finalists for the new Associate Professorship stated in conversations with faculty and students during the interview process, their presence and teaching would not suffice to maintain quality language instruction in our First-, Second-, and Third-year Arabic language courses if enrollments remain at current levels, not to speak of expected increases in Arabic language course enrollment. Moreover, as two of the three finalists stated in conversations with faculty and students during the interview process, their presence and teaching would not suffice to guarantee continuity in the immediate future in our tightly structured and comprehensive Arabic language program.

Therefore. . .I move that MELC's Executive Committee recommend to the College of Liberal Arts that Aman Attieh continue to serve as Senior Lecturer during the 2000–2001 academic year to assure maintenance of standards and continuity in our Arabic language program.

As Senior Lecturer in Arabic Language, Dr. Attieh would answer to the new Associate Professor of Arabic Language, who would serve as Coordinator of the Arabic Language Program. I further move that the recommendation include the proviso that the new Associate Professor of Arabic Language and Arabic Professor Peter Abboud evaluate future staffing needs of our Arabic language program in the course of the Fall 2000 Semester and communicate to MELC's Executive Committee by the end of the semester their recommendations as to any lectureships in Arabic language for 2001–2002, as well as possible changes in program philosophy, methods, and instructional materials.

If the College of Liberal Arts should have in mind, as some faculty outside of MELC have opined, the college-wide reduction or elimination of lectureship positions in its language programs in the near future, the time table described in the foregoing motion would allow Dr. Attieh the same amount of time to make other plans as is afforded tenure-track faculty not promoted to a tenured position in their up-or-out year.

The MELC-EC recommendation which this motion proposes should convince concerned UT faculty and students, and community members in Austin and elsewhere that MELC has the best interests of our Arabic language program in mind and that possible perceptions of bias or discrimination in Aman Attieh's case have no foundation in ultimate departmental behavior.

The Executive Committee voted 3–2 in favor of my motion. *The Daily Texan* later quoted the Dean as saying that MELC did not recommend that Aman Attieh continue as Senior Lecturer in Arabic in 2001–2002. Regardless, following subsequent student petitions, demonstrations, *Daily Texan* articles, meetings with the Dean of Liberal Arts, the Provost, and the President, The College of Liberal Arts reappointed Aman Attieh as Senior Lecturer of Arabic for the 2000–2001 school year.

On the same day, I responded by e-mail as follows to Jewish Studies Professor Wolitz, an Attieh supporter, who had written to the student group formed to lobby for reconsideration of the MELC decision not to allow Attieh to interview for the new Arabic position and, failing at that, for renewal of Attieh's contract.

> I have just read your message to SAAUT. You wrote: "You have every right to protest what has happened. . .I have had the pleasure and honor of knowing this wonderful person [Aman Attieh] and have seen her devotion to the teaching of Arabic and her openmindedness. . . If something "is rotten in the state of Danemark" then show by documents and facts what error of procedure took place or what should have been done and was not by omission. . ." I hope SAAUT takes your advice. I gather from the exchange of e-messages among SAAUT members that the organization is still debating issues and tactics.
>
> I share your views about Aman Attieh and Peter Abboud and am arguing in writing and in person every chance I get that the continuing effectiveness of our Arabic language program needs the continuing presence of Aman Attieh as Senior Lecturer.

Wolitz responded to my e-message the same afternoon. He wrote:

> I am glad to see that there is one levelheaded person in your complex department. My God! She has worked her head off for the Arabic section of your dept. I am fully aware that she is or was the mistress of Dr Abboud and there are people who should like to get at him via her! But that is not what is at stake. The idea of throwing out a person who has given so many years of good service and without any redress or recourse to a grievance committee is a poisonous way to operate a university. She is a Senior Lecturer after all and a certain respect for her as a human being and a superb performer of her duties deserves a fair treatment. The nonsense of arguing that she has no publications is absurd. A lecturer according to the rules of the Regents is not to be judged on publications but the classroom performance. (God knows if one were to look into Stofberg's publications the dearth would be resounding!)
>
> Prof. Stofberg no doubt believes he is acting with grace and judicious sensitivity but knowing how he has performed for the past 20 years, I can only smile quietly. The university obtained what they never expected so fully: a toddy. He is so enthused with a pinch of power that he acts just like the Judenrat types obliging them when they should be defending the mem-

bers. Perhaps the department reflects what it has as chair. From what I have gathered from other members, one is of his clique or one is not.

I am saddened for you! To have to contend all these years with the pettiness about you!

I wrote my few words to show some solidarity and to make clear one need not be Muslim or Arab to appreciate a first-rate professional who teaches Arabic language and culture. I am responding as an American academic who esteems individual accomplishment. . .What the administration never understood upstairs is that Stofberg is a reactionary who does not really distinguish between his beliefs off campus and on! He is a Rabbi and expects that his dignity carries weight besides his Ph.D. in all places. We are seeing the wonderments of Nietzschean Ressentiment being played out.

Wolitz's casual observation that Attieh "is or was the mistress of Dr Abboud" surprised me, because I had never thought of the relationship between Attieh and Abboud in those terms. Not that any sort of relationship between them would per se make any sort of difference in anything. In the MELC past, two MELC faculty members had reportedly gotten their jobs as "spousal hires" in part precisely as a result of having slept with faculty members in departments in other UT colleges! Two years later, at my "Attieh v. UT" deposition, Assistant Attorney General Horowitz referred to Wolitz's e-mails and implied that he was mentally unbalanced.

The Arabic search and Attieh's job situation started appearing in *The Daily Texan*. Some students and faculty were questioning the Arabic search process and alleging irregularities in it. Dean Applegate decided to meet with the MELC Executive Committee to discuss the matter. On April 13, before the meeting, I wrote this letter to the Dean.

In response to MELC Chair Robert Stofberg's request that MELC Executive Committee members meet with you today presumably to discuss the ongoing search for a new Associate Professor of Arabic Language, I am writing as a member of that committee who submitted a written motion at an EC meeting on February 16 that MELC invite Aman Attieh to interview for the new position and a second written motion at an EC meeting on March 22 that MELC recommend to you that Aman Attieh continue her service as Lecturer in Arabic Language in 2000–2001. Attached find copies of both motions. The February 16 motion failed. The March 22 motion passed. On April 4, MELC Chair Robert Stofberg informed MELC faculty by written memo that you had rejected the March 22 recommendation.

According to *The Daily Texan*, the currently most discussed issue relating to the search for a new Arabist has to do with alleged irregularities in the search process. My view is that irregularities which some faculty and students have perceived in the search process have probably not affected the outcome of Arabist Search Committee and MELC Executive Committee votes and recommendations on the matter.

When I first heard read the official announcement of the new position last fall, I had two reactions: (1) that Arabist colleague Aman Attieh fulfilled stated qualifications for the position and consequently deserved to have the chance to interview for the position; and (2) because Aman Attieh could not get the support of more than half of the tenured professors in MELC (i.e., Peter Abboud, Avraham Zilkha, and Michael Hillmann), the College would have no special reason to recommend her for the position, especially if more than three tenured MELC faculty would support another candidate.

For the record, however,–and I will submit this letter only if you ask at today's meeting for views of MELC EC members about the Arabic search progress–here follow Arabic search events, which outside observers might characterize as instances of irregularities. Inside observers might bear such things in mind for future reference so that MELC and the College do not again get similar negative publicity.

1. MELC announced at a faculty meeting in October that it had joined CMES in discussions with the College of Liberal Arts, but without consultation of Arabic Studies faculty, on the subject of a new position in Arabic language. In response to a query as to why discussions had begun and proceeded without input from the Arabic Studies program, the MELC Chair stated that he frankly could not work with the Arabic Studies faculty.

2. At a MELC faculty meeting, the MELC Chair announced the new Arabic Associate Professor position as an addition to the Arabic Studies faculty, resulting in three full-time faculty positions in 2000–2001: a senior lecturer, an associate professor, and a full professor. The MELC Chair affirmed this new staffing pattern three or four times, as a result of which MELC faculty voted its approval of adding the position to MELC.

3. The MELC Chair sent Aman Attieh a short note encouraging her to apply for the new position and wishing her good luck. Any suggestion that Aman Attieh's in-class or outside-of-class comportment might figure in a decision to terminate her services as of the end of 1999–2000 evaporated with this official note, insofar as no MELC Chair would encourage an application from a faculty member whose work he/she found wanting and whose services he/she no longer found compatible with departmental goals.

4. As of 30 November 1999, the MELC Chair announced to one or more MELC faculty members that only four applications had reached MELC. MELC staff put the number at eleven or twelve. MELC faculty perusal of files revealed fifteen or sixteen names and files.

5. As of 30 December 1999, the MELC Chair stated to one or more MELC faculty members that word had reached him that copies of the Associate Professor of Arabic job announcement kept getting removed from the bulletin board at the Annual Meeting of the Middle East Association of North America in Washington, D.C., that weekend and that Aman Attieh or Peter Abboud or supporters of Aman Attieh might be responsible for the alleged disappearance of copies of the job announcement.

6. MELC removed from the list of candidates under consideration the name of a candidate with a complete file, on the basis of a rumor, source uncited, presented at the 16 February 2000 MELC Executive Committee meeting, that the applicant was planning to withdraw his or her name from consideration.

7. MELC did not arrange for appointments for one or more full professors to meet for customary half-hour private conversations with two finalists.

8. MELC expanded its Executive Committee membership a week before it met to vote on Arabic Position matters, including a motion that Aman Attieh qualify for an interview for the position. The basis for the expansion of the MELC EC was that MELC Assistant Professors wanted a female Assistant Professor representative to serve along with an already elected male Assistant Professor representative. Without the vote of the new member, who joined the Executive Committee without undergoing the process stipulated in university regulations, Aman Attieh would have received an invitation to interview for the new Arabic position. If Aman Attieh had interviewed for the position, SAAUT would have likely restricted its advocacy activities to the maintenance of MELC's lectureship in Arabic.

9. After promising in writing to communicate one faculty member's written view of candidates for the new Arabic position to the Arabic Search Committee, the MELC Chair did not do so. At an Executive Committee meeting on March 28, the MELC Chair said that his failure to do so was the result of inadvertent oversight.

10. At the MELC Executive Committee meeting on March 28, the MELC Chair declined to discuss the rationale for the Arabic Search Committee's decision not to rank finalists for the new Arabic position and for the Search Committee's decision to recommend Mohammad Mohammad for the position. The MELC Chair stated his concerns about the leaking of confidential information at Executive Committee meetings as his reason for refusing to discuss the twin matters. However, at an agendaless MELC faculty meeting held an hour before the Executive Committee meeting, the MELC Chair reportedly discussed the Search Committee decision and aspects of Mohammad Mohammad's file and career.

11. The MELC Chair announced the decision of the Arabic Search Committee at an agendaless and suddenly called faculty meeting before the MELC Executive Committee learned of the Search Committee's recommendation or decision and before the MELC Executive Committee had the opportunity to discuss and vote on MELC's recommendation to the College of Liberal Arts for a new Associate Professor of Arabic Language. Subsequent to that MELC faculty meeting, presumably attended by one or more graduate students, word reached *The Daily Texan* that the Search Committee had chosen Mohammad Mohammad for the new Arabic position.

12. One or more MELC faculty members heard an Arabic Search Committee member discuss and negatively characterize in public (at Jonathan Owens's lecture) confidential letters of recommendation in the file of applicant Aman Attieh.

13. One or more MELC faculty members heard a member of the faculty of the Center for Middle Eastern Studies describe categorically in public (outside HRC on the occasion of the Islam–Judaism Crosscurrents Conference) the nature of Aman Attieh's participation in the Arabic Search Committee process and that Committee's vote on her application.

14. Reports about the Arabic search process in *The Daily Texan* would appear to demonstrate that other leaks to the press took place with respect to both Search Committee and MELC Executive Committee deliberations. Fortunately, no leaks reached the press connecting characterizations of parts or aspects of the search with specific named candidates.

Having had no prior experience or involvement, however peripheral, in the process of hiring a tenured faculty colleague, I cannot characterize the foregoing items in terms of administrative seriousness or frequency of occurrence in the College of Liberal Arts.

Two years later, in November 2002, at the end of a deposition session in "Attieh v. UT," Dean Applegate (A) and Attieh attorney Notzon (Q) had this exchange on the subject of the Arabic search process.

Q. Did you review her [Attieh's] file and compare it to Mohammad Mohammad's?

A. No. There would be no reason for me to do so.

Q. Well, if there were complaints about the process, you might want to look at it, wouldn't you?

A. Complaints about the process did not come from anyone involved in the process except Peter Abboud.

Q. And Dr. Hillmann?

A. And Dr. Hillmann.

Q. And other students?

A. Students weren't involved in the process.

Q. They didn't complain?

A. They complained, but they were not involved in the process. The students were lied to—repeatedly lied to by someone on that faculty.

Q. What's the biggest lie. . .that you recall being told?

A. That I was told?

Q. That you understand the students were told. What's the biggest lie?

A. That this process was irregular and unfair.

A comparison of the Dean's statements here with the numbered items in my letter to him on April 13 (above) illustrates the gap between academic and administrative perspectives on the subject of the process of selecting a new Arabic faculty person. Not only did no one tell students any lies on the various Arabic faculty issues, the voluminous written record on the conflict between students and administrators does not offer a single instance I'm aware of where the students proposed or asserted anything not arguably true. Moreover, no evidence appears to exist that faculty told truths to students, much less lies. On that matter, the following exchanges of e-messages between the Dean and me offer incontrovertible evidence of truth as the students' standard and something else which administrators were waving.

After the meeting on April 13, I sent this e-message to the Dean.

Thanks for scheduling this morning's meeting with our MELC Executive Committee. If memory serves me correctly, it gave me my first opportunity in twenty-five years to meet with a Dean of Liberal Arts in his or her office. I found the meeting. . .useful. . .More importantly, it was encouraging to hear that options exist so that our Arabic Language program next fall will have suffered only bad publicity during these months of meetings and talk about the new Arabic Associate Professorship and the future of our Arabic Lectureship.

On the latter issue, if I can do anything to help foster the possibility that Aman Attieh might continue her service as Arabic Lecturer in 2000–2001, please let me know. My rationale for support of her continued service appears in the two pages of copies I submitted to you this morning of two written motions I made at February and March MELC EC meetings.

The third page I submitted to you this morning lists. . . "irregularities" in the Arabic search process. . .But, as I said at our meeting. . .any real or supposed "irregularities" did not affect the outcome of the search.

At our March MELC EC meeting, I voted against the Search Committee's single recommendation for the new position for two reasons: (1) that candidate's file did not strike me as on a par with files of comparable language/literature/culture specialists at the associate professor level at major research universities; and (2) another candidate struck me as meeting wonted UT Austin requirements for an Associate Professor. That candidate's name and file did not get discussion in any discussion at MELC EC meetings. I hasten to add. . .I will have no difficulty living academically with our new Arabist colleague, whether or not he or she turns out to be a person I would vote for if asked to vote.

In early December, I mentioned in passing at a MELC faculty meeting a special interest in the candidacy of John Eisele for our new Arabic position from my Persian Studies perspective. At our February MELC EC meeting I repeated that favorable impression, with benefit of a careful reading of his application file and samples of his publications. In light of your statement this morning that you were now planning to read the files of the candidates for the new Arabic position. . .I am here taking the liberty of suggesting that you include Professor Eisele's file in your reading. If you haven't heard much about him in discussions to date, what you find in his file may pleasantly surprise you.

For example, here follows a checklist which has led me to the view that John Eisele is our best choice for Associate Professor of Arabic Language in comparison with other candidates: (1) superior undergraduate education; (2) superior graduate education; (3) better training in Middle Eastern language teaching and Islamic culture; (4) better and more comprehensive Arabic language teaching experience at higher-ranked universities; (5) more significant Arabic language program coordination experience, and at first-tier universities; (6) greater involvement in national Arabic language teacher organizations and trends; (7) greater career advancement at a younger age (do other short-listed candidates have tenured posts?); (8) more significant publications (e.g., an already published monograph and an article in *Language*); (9) better track record of appreciating American university student needs in the arduous study of Arabic at all levels; (10) a superior, more exciting, and more relevant, long-term research plan for a "language and culture" department; (11) significantly better immediate rapport with UT undergraduate and graduate Arabic students; (12) significantly better immediate rapport with several MELC faculty and with UT undergraduate and graduate Arabic heritage students; (13) significantly better immediate rapport with several MELC faculty with whom the new Arabist will interact in Arabic Studies on a daily basis; and (14) apparent approval by all Search Committee and MELC EC members (in contrast to other candidates, about each of whom several faculty have stated reservations).

Later that day, the Dean sent me this brief e-response: "Thanks for the note. I too found the discussions helpful. On one point, there seems to be some confusion. I am not going to read the files of the applicants for the position. The file that I will read. . .is the file of Mohammad Mohammad."

Six days later, in receipt of an e-message from the SAAUT student group, I sent this e-message to the Dean.

Right when I thought it was safe to go swimming again, the dorsal fin of the following SAAUT e-message appeared, presenting part of the transcript of your most recent meeting with SAAUT members:

Sameena: The Executive Committee, I understand, has asked that she (Dr. Attieh) be rehired next year in some capacity and the students are coming to you saying "we want her to be rehired next year in some capacity."

Dean: Actually, I asked about that yesterday. There was a motion to that effect put before the Executive Committee and was turned down. It was voted down.

Sameena: It was voted down?!

Dean: Yes, Yeah, you see, this is. . .this is part of the problem. And this is. . .may be a lack of communication. But this is. . .How did. . .Just out of curiosity, how did you know that the Executive Committee had recommended that she be rehired?

Sameena: Dr. Hillman [sic] told me.

Dean: Yeah. . .(Sameena interrupts)

Sameena: And he told me because. . .(Dean interrupts)

Dean: You know who told me yesterday that there was a motion and that it was turned down?

Sameena: Dr. Hillmann?

Dean: Yeah.

Sameena:	So, we should talk to him.
Dean:	Yeah, please do.
Sameena:	I probably misunderstood.
Dean:	Well. . .and I. . .you know, at this time I'm scrambling to step back and say, "this could all be a misunderstanding." And that's my position still.
Chaouki:	Did the motion pass the Executive Committee.
Dean:	No, did it not. . .No, it did not. . .(Chaouki interrupts)
Chaouki:	It did not pass the Executive Committee?
Dean:	It did not pass the Executive Committee.
Chaouki:	It did not get the votes to pass the Executive Committee.
Dean:	That's right. It was voted (assertively) down by the Executive Committee.
Chaouki:	And the motion was to rehire Dr. Attieh next year?
Dean:	I don't remember the exact language of the motion but yes some. . .(Dean interrupts)
Dean:	Yes. Right, yes.
Sameena:	. . .some motion of some kind did pass the Executive Committee.
Dean:	I was told it did not and all the Executive Committee were in the room. And no one said: "Oh, no Mike, you're wrong." So, I have to assume that. . . I don't have the records of the Executive Committee meeting and I hope I don't have to go look at them. But, yes. That's my understanding.

As I reported at your meeting with our Executive Committee, the EC. . .voted in favor of recommending to you that Aman Attieh continue as Lecturer next year (3–2–1). In two memos, Robert Stofberg described that passed motion and the request he would make and then made on MELC's behalf to you. In the second of these memos, he wrote on April 4: "Yesterday I met with the Dean to discuss, among other things, the Executive Committee's request that the Dean consider keeping Aman on as Senior Lecturer for the 2000–2001 academic year. He denied the request." You will recall that I gave you copies of [the] motion. . .at our meeting and that you took a couple of notes about them and votes on them.

The persistence of Ms. Karmally and Mr. Moussa in their questions to the Dean stemmed from their disbelieving shock that the latter could boldly and repeatedly mouth untruths in the face of written documentation to the contrary in the possession of students, faculty, and the Dean. The recorded exchange left the students in despair, because they realized that they were negotiating with two administrators, Stofberg and Applegate, who would facilely disregard the written record if they felt the need to do so. If Attieh hadn't been rehired for the 2000–2001 academic year, I'd have used just this one issue, the Dean's statements vis-à-vis the Executive Committee vote on March 15 and subsequent paper trail, to seek redress.

By this time, redress was what Attieh had decided to seek for MELC administrative behavior which she construed as harassment, discrimination, and retaliation. In that regard and also to inquire about the harassment charge which Kamil Riyadh had made to UT's Equal Employment Opportunity Office, I wrote the following letter to EEOO Director Nora Wallstein.

> Arabic Studies colleague Aman Attieh has informed me that she has given my name to you in the course of registering a complaint of harassment and discrimination with your office. That news has prompted this letter.
>
> First, I want to inquire about the status of the report which I seem to recall you saying would reach me this spring on the charge of harassment which Islamic Studies colleague Kamil Riyadh filed against me last December. . .Earlier in the spring, I informed MELC Chair Robert Stofberg that, in light of Professor Riyadh's allegation, I would not be participating in any merit increase discussions or votes concerning him. And I will not participate in the discussion of his promotion to associate professor when the MELC Executive Committee meets on the subject several years hence.
>
> Second, the dynamics of MELC EC meetings this spring which have focused on a new Arabic associate professorship and the future of our Arabic lectureship have led me to the conclude that Professor Riyadh's complaint in December had something to do with the controversy about our Arabic Studies program. As it has turned out, the role of new assistant professor members on our Executive Committee has proved crucial in MELC's vote not to invite Dr. Attieh to interview for the new Arabic position and in minority opposition to MELC's recommendation to the College of Liberal Arts that Dr. Attieh continue to serve as Arabic Lecturer during 2000–2001. Professor Riyadh's dislike of our Arabic Studies program and faculty can have carried over to me, a longtime and steadfast supporter of that program.
>
> Third, as for Dr. Attieh's allegations of harassment and discrimination, attached find copies of three relevant communications, which present my unequivocal views on the subject. In support of my views, I have prepared a chronology of documented MELC events from September 1998 through last week. On leave during this spring semester, I expect to be in Austin from now until May 4 in case you wish to discuss Dr. Attieh's complaint with me in the near future.

Wallstein's report on the Riyadh harassment charge, sent to Stofberg on April 20, got to me in May. As expected, it stated that no discrimination or harassment on my part had taken place toward Riyadh. As for Attieh's complaint of harassment and discrimination against Stofberg, to Attieh's surprise and chagrin, the Dean attended and participated actively in the meeting which Wallstein, reportedly a Dell Jewish Community Center administrator in her spare time, called to investigate those charges. It was only then that MELC faculty realized that Wallstein's Equal Employment Opportunity Office did not have administratively independent status. That being the case, Attieh's grievance filing apparently did not receive the same attention as had Riyadh's.

On May 9, the Dean announced that Attieh would return as Senior Lecturer in Arabic for the 2000–2001 academic year. That news prompted this letter from me to SAAUT members.

> The decision which the Liberal Arts Dean announced in his *Daily Texan* Guest Column on May 9 gives First-year Arabic students the opportunity they deserve to take Second-year Arabic with Aman Attieh, thus having desirable continuity in their study of the language. The decision also gives Aman Attieh the opportunity to think about and plan her academic future in 2001–2002 and beyond. Who knows, if she and the new Arabic Language Coordinator Mohammad Mohammad see eye-to-eye and if Arabic language course enrollments continue to rise, Arabic Studies might recommend that MELC request an Arabic lectureship for 2001–2002, for which Aman Attieh would likely prove the best candidate. In short, the Dean's compromise decision, in which SAAUT's expression of concerns and support for Aman Attieh in the past several months played a significant part, is good for MELC and MELC's Arabic language program.
>
> As for SAAUT's take on the rest of the Guest Column, you need to remember that the Dean's representation of the past history and present situation in a small program in the College of Liberal Arts like Arabic Studies is only as good as the information he receives. The Dean does not have to know and can't be expected to know many things about a program like Arabic Studies first-hand. For that reason, you needn't find troubling the Dean's misstatements about: (1) Arabic course enrollments (their highest ever in 1999–2000); (2) reasons for the withdrawal of Arabic graduate degree students from the program since December 1998 (dissatisfaction with MELC administration and disappointment at the announcement of the departure of Walid Hamarneh); (3) the decrease in Arabic language instructional staff concomitant with increases in Hebrew, Persian, and Turkish; (4) the status of proficiency- or performance-based methodology in Arabic language courses (recommended by the U.S. Office of Education) and MELC's Arabic instructional materials (e.g., a Cambridge University publication which reportedly sells better than other comparable textbooks); (5) mischaracterization of Sherman Jackson as a scholar of Arabic literature, of his departure from UT Austin, and his status in his field (that Sherman reportedly stayed at several universities for only a year or two each is not a criticism of him, but evidence that his departure from UT had much to do with dreams of greener pastures); (6) misrepresentation of Fedwa Malti-Douglas's present situation (transfer students from Indiana at UT and cur-

rent Indiana colleagues in Arabic and Persian tell a complicated story of a department's failure there with conflicts not dissimilar to those to which Fedwa was party at UT's OALL/MELC). . . . (8) the Dean's apparent misapprehension about MELC support for Aman Attieh (a poll of MELC's 1999–2000 instructional staff would likely show that a majority think her a good teacher who deserves to continue her work in MELC, while MELC's Executive Committee voted to recommend to the College of Liberal Arts a one-year renewal of Aman's lectureship); and (9) misreading of SAAUT's activities in characterizing you as "manipulated and misled" (you yourselves know first-hand that you were neither manipulated nor [mis]led).

✍ May 25, Journal entry, on a MARC commuter train en route from Baltimore to D.C. Today is Day 4 of my Persian Minicourse at Bolling Air Force Base for the Iran Desk group at the Defense Intelligence Agency. Larry Franklin, who took last year's May course in Baltimore with Mark Sullivan, has organized the course. Sorayya arrives at the Hyatt Regency in Bethesda this afternoon, where I'll go after class, for the weekend and a talk on Hafez's poetry at the Biennial Iranian Studies Conference. Last Saturday, I spent the afternoon and evening at George and Cathie's celebrating his 60th birthday. Last night I took in an Orioles game, a 4–3 victory over Seattle. I sat in the Camden Yards bleachers, ate a hot dog, and drank a Coors Light beer. Jim and I went to Jimmy's in Fells Point for breakfast on Sunday and then looked at 19th-century French paintings at Baltimore Museum of Art. Rodin's 'The Thinker' no longer mulls things over out front. Otherwise, I've been commuting, which has a life rhythm of its own. Up at 6. Shower, breakfast, *The Morning Sun*, and the walk to Penn Station by 6:50. Board the 7:10 MARC and look over work for the day on the train. Follow the crowd at Union Station to the Metro and buy a $1.20 ticket from the machine. Take the Red Line to Gallery Place and the Green Line to Anacostia. Ride the W-9 Bus to the DIA Building. Wait for an escort in the lobby at 8:50. Begin class at 9, three hours after waking up. We're expecting eighteen participants in our annual Intensive Persian course next month at University Towers in Austin. After that, Sorayya and I will drive to Augusta for two weeks of Persian seminars at Georgia Center for Language. *Tajiki Textbook and Reader* is in press. Persepolis has also begun work on parts of a Persian language test for use by the FBI in their screening of Persian language specialists-to-be. Thanks, as ever, go to my lucky stars! ✍

Chapter 8

2000–2001 Academic Year

> *"I always divide people into two groups.*
> *Those who live by what they know to be a lie,*
> *and those who live by what they believe, falsely, to be the truth."*
> Christopher Hampton

In August 2000, Mohammad Mohammad joined the department as Associate Professor of Arabic with tenure. He proceeded to work tirelessly in the Arabic language program, understaffed even with Attieh's full-time participation in 2000–2001. When Attieh left Texas for a similar position at Rice University in August 2001, Mohammad's work load increased, in part offset by Peter Abboud's addition of an extra language course to his already full teaching schedule. The department remained understaffed in Arabic, Mohammad teaching no courses except for language. As for the reason why understaffing continued, an interim Department Chair told me in 2004 that the University Administration could not rectify the situation as long as "Attieh v. UT" litigation continued, because the hiring of a new lecturer in addition to the appointment of Mohammad Mohammad might signal something untoward in the non-reappointment of Attieh in 2001–2002.

Even though Attieh had a new contract for 2000–2001, events of the previous spring and during the first days of the Fall 2000 Semester, as well as MELC actions dating back to September 1998, led her to seek redress off-campus for what she construed as harassment, discrimination, and retaliation at the hands of MELC. In that regard, the Equal Employment Opportunity Commission requested an affidavit from me. Part of that affidavit, which I submitted to EEOC on September 6, read:

> In a letter to me dated 31 August 2000 on the subject of EEOC Charge No. 360 A0 1714–Employer: The University of Texas at Austin, Federal Investigator E. Thomas Price requested of me "the following specific information concerning" these six "issues: (1) She [Aman Attieh] was denied

120

an interview for an Associate Professor's position. (2) Her contract was not renewed. (3) She was removed from her coordinator's position. (4) She was instructed to vacate her office. (5) She was not given a merit increase for the year 2000–2001. (6) Her entire work history came under attack.

1. Explain what specific information you have which shows that each of these issues happened because of Ms. Attieh's sex or complaint about discriminatory practices. 2. If you do not have any information that these things happened because of Ms. Attieh's sex or complaint about discriminatory practices, please tell me that on your affidavit."

This affidavit presents specific information relevant to the foregoing request in three sections.

In my most recent conversation with him [several days ago, in the MELC corridor outside of WMB 5.136], Professor Robert Stofberg asserted two things, among others: first, that he is a very good judge of character; and, second, that he does not trust anything which people tell him. He also observed that he considers friendliness an important component in faculty interactions in MELC. Dr. Stofberg stated that he does not like MELC colleagues who are not, in his view, friendly or likable and that any efforts to make it possible for Dr. Attieh to continue her career in MELC would signal to him unfriendliness not consonant with collegial behavior in MELC.

In conversation with me during the last week of August 2000, new Associate Professor of Arabic Language and new Arabic Language Program Coordinator Mohammad Mohammad stated that he planned no changes in MELC's existing Arabic Language Program, that what was not broken did not need fixing, and that he would continue for the foreseeable future to use course descriptions, syllabi, and textbooks in First-year Arabic classes which Aman Attieh had employed as Arabic Language Coordinator.

On Tuesday, August 29, 2000, MELC Chair Robert Stofberg informed me in a brief hallway conversation that he would be moving his office into the former Arabic Language Laboratory, that an assistant professor of Islamic Studies would be moving into his office, that Associate Professor Mohammad Mohammad would occupy Aman Attieh's former office, and that another assistant professor of Islamic Studies would be moving into the office vacated by departing Assistant Professor of Arabic Literature Walid Hamarneh. Professor Stofberg added that the moves, subsequent to Aman Attieh's involuntary evacuation of the office she had occupied from August 1994 to late August 2000, would leave the office across the corridor from Aman Attieh's former office vacant until a new Assistant Professor of Arabic Literature joins MELC in 2001–2002. In other words, MELC Chair Robert Stofberg had and has a MELC office available for Aman Attieh, who has moved to the second floor of the Flawn Academic Center. At the same time, Professor Stofberg announced in a late August 2000 memo to MELC faculty that MELC had changed the lock on its main office (WMB 5.120) which houses faculty mail boxes, photocopying machine, and supplies. MELC provided all instructional faculty with letters authorizing the issuance of keys to that office and also the new MELC Language Laboratory (FAC 27), except for Aman Attieh. On Thursday, 31 August 2000, I took Aman Attieh to the MELC Language Laboratory, using my own key to open the door and giving her that key to use for her MELC work, insofar as Language Laboratory work is part of the syllabus in the three Arabic language classes which she is teaching each semester during 2000–2001. . .On the same day on which MELC faculty received the MELC Chair's memo about the rekeying of WMB 5.120, one senior MELC faculty member and one senior MELC TA/AI expressed their assumption in conversation with me that the aim behind the decision to rekey WMB 5.120 was to keep Aman Attieh from having access to that office. A MELC staff person who overhead that faculty member's comments from behind a closed door accosted him and then me in the corridor to assert that no politics figured in the decision.

In light of Aman Attieh's teaching awards, presidency of the American Association of Teachers of Arabic, above-average teaching load in 1998–1999 and 1999–2000, and publication of *Short Fiction by Arabian Women Writers*, if she has not received a merit increase for 2000–2001, the lack of merit increase would have to derive from *ad hominem* grounds.

✍ September 24, Journal entry, On a Southwest Airlines plane in El Paso. We're about to take off on the second leg home after Eliza's birthday celebration in Las Vegas. Sorayya won $350 from the slot machines at MGM Grand Hotel Casino. Over the weekend, we walked through most of the major hotels on The Strip, which I can't imagine having a reason to visit again. Big-name restaurants with comfort food. Smokers everywhere. Long corridors and high towers for sardining people at $200 and more per night. Bad dressers. $$$ theme-park culture. Once home in Austin, I'll have a day and a half to ready myself for twelve hours of lectures for government Persian specialists on Wednesday, Thursday, and Friday at a McNeil Technologies' Glen Burnie office, an afternoon meeting on Friday at Language Research Center in Hyattsville with Jack Jones and Mel Deatheridge about Dari and Farsi voice and graphics texts, and a meeting in North Bethesda on Saturday with Charles Stansfield at Second Language Testing, Inc., on FBI Persian reading and listening tests. We are now airborne, ninety minutes from Austin. I'll doodle on the next page about my week's plans. Not that I ever look over journal lists after I make them. Just making a list, however, makes me feel that I've already done something about things in it. Like feeling good after buying a book I should read, before I've started reading it. ✍

✍ November 4, Journal entry, Perry Lane Austin. Eliza called last night to tell us the she is one month pregnant. She and Jeff plan to call the baby "something + Craig + Garrett." I've got to get cracking on *To and from A Village in Maine* now. "Something Craig Garrett" is

due in late June. Early August would suit me better because Persepolis Institute Persian and Arabic courses both end July 25th, when we usually host an awards dinner for which Sorayya prepares an Iranian meal.
✍

Now that Mohammad Mohammad had joined the MELC faculty and could neutralize Abboud's voice and views about directions which the Arabic Studies should take, Liberal Arts and MELC announced a search for an Assistant Professor of Arabic Literature to replace Walid Hamarneh. MELC was offering no Arabic literature courses during 2000–2001. Three of the candidates for the Arabic literature position hailed from my alma mater. That led to this e-message, dated 22 February 2001, from me to my friend Bruce Craig, Director of the Near Eastern Collection at The University of Chicago Library.

> At a meeting several weeks ago, MELC's Arabic Search Committee decided to invite three applicants among twenty or so to interview for UT's advertised junior position in Arabic literature. Those applicants have come and gone, with an offer perhaps already made to one of them.
>
> The review and selection process did not involve expert or discipline-based scrutiny of files, which means that applicants not invited for interviews have no reason to conclude that more qualified applicants got invited.
>
> Although probably the only Search Committee member to have studied Arabic in a university graduate program or to have read some pre-modern Arabic literature, I had a peripheral role in the selection process, primarily because of a series of problems which MELC's Arabic Studies program has faced since early in the 1998–1999 academic year, problems in which Middle East conflicts, non-application of standards, and *ad hominem* views and decisions have played parts. MELC quietly and unceremoniously let Walid Hamarneh go last year, is loudly and un-neatly letting Aman Attieh go this year, and appears to be harassing Peter Abboud into a less active role in things next year. In all three conflict situations, I have vigorously supported the losing side, in the process gradually distancing myself from MELC politics.
>
> These three paragraphs are a roundabout way of saying that my interest in the files of Clarissa Burt, Mustapha Kamal, and Yaseen Noorani had no effect on MELC Arabic Literature recommendations.
>
> Reading between and behind foregoing lines notwithstanding, Sorayya and I remain as joyous as ever about everything, which, as your "age gracefully" phrase reminds me, adds up to thirty-four years together, a lucky piece of business for which my personality deserves no credit. And, unless I hear that you've stopped laughing when you hear something foolish or have started biting your tongue when you hear something stupid or have chosen silence when someone asks you what you think, I don't plan to strive even for what you call "moderate success" in dealing with either the march of time or people I encounter along the way.

I've tried on and off in the past several years to get CMES to invite you down for a talk about issues present and future in university Arabic and Persian library development. But no luck so far. I also keep thinking about putting Chicago on an itinerary for a trip north. But we are usually farther east before we get that far north.

✍ March 28, Journal entry, Perry Lane, Austin. During Spring Break, while my World Literature Plan II Honors students were working on poems for Writing Assignment #5, I was also thinking about trying to write a poem to suggest one possible process to the class. I had decided if a moment or scene or person caught and kept my attention, I'd jot notes down about it and rework them until they got as close to a poem as I can do. At a sunny March 12 noon in Baltimore, I was eating a crab sandwich platter on the front patio at Phillip's Harborside when I noticed a down-and-out, middle-aged woman and sea gulls around her on a bench at water's edge. She wasn't paying attention to anything but her lunch, although I couldn't tell if she was busy with it because she liked it or because she hadn't eaten for a long time. I took notes, thinking that the contrast in our two meals might turn into a poem. The notes led to thirteen drafts, and then this.

> Her gull companions fled
> the moment she stood up.
> She smoothed her patched great coat
> and combed her grey-blond hair.
> She looked above at blue,
> and squinted, maybe smiled.
> She daintily retrieved
> a tea-stained plastic cup,
> an empty cardboard box,
> and napkins she'd balled up,
> then walked from Harborside.
> She paused, to drop those things
> into a wire-mesh bin
> from which she'd lifted them
> an hour ago for lunch. ✍

In mid-April, MELC Chair Stofberg informed Peter Abboud that the latter would have to add a section of First-year Arabic to his teaching schedule for 2001–2002. Abboud replied by saying that he had a full teaching load for the following fall and couldn't add another course. The Dean thereupon sent Abboud a letter threatening him with a reduction in salary or termination of employment if he didn't teach the extra course. Peter visited WMB 5.146 on the afternoon of April

24 to seek my advice on the matter. I listened, not believing that a Department Chair or College Dean had the right, or would dare, to make such a demand, and told Peter I'd think about it and get back to him on the morrow. My response took the form of the following e-message I sent Peter the next afternoon.

> Last night I described for Sorayya the sequence of paper events leading to [Associate Dean] Larry Carver's visit with you yesterday. We then talked about the situation at length. For what it's worth, we agreed that, if the same thing were to happen to me, I would: (1) propose the compromise which you have proposed, i.e., division of labor in language classes according to First-year (professor x) and Second-year (professor y) for the obvious reasons (differences in methodology, pace, and standards); and (2), if MELC/LA/Provost did not approve the compromise, I would inform MELC/LA that I would continue with my three-year plan for 2001–2002 (commitment to students and to a personal research plan and interests) and adjust my plan to include First- or Second-year Arabic in 2002–2003. In other words, I would ignore any threats of a reprimand or decrease in salary (on the assumption that news of such action would redound to the discredit of MELC/LA and that the fact of such action might have untoward legal ramifications for MELC/LA).
>
> In all of this, I cannot comprehend the non-academic. . .[and] non-intellectual MELC/LA orientation. In MELC's actions affecting the Arabic Studies program without consultation with Arabic Studies faculty, one might characterize the administrative orientation as anti-academic. . .and anti-intellectual. That characterization would apply even if unilateral MELC actions met with your ex post facto approval insofar as a premise of our academic lives is that only compeers expert in a given field should have prerogatives in program planning and decision-making in that field. I can't imagine a MELC Chair not expert in Persian making any unilateral decision affecting the content of Persian Studies. [In May 2007, my imagination learned a new lesson.]
>
> Good luck with your decision about 2001–2002 teaching.

In his later deposition for the "Attieh v. UT" litigation, Dean Applegate (A) describes his role in the matter and his take on Abboud's decision, in response to questions by Attorney Robert Notzon (Q).

> A. I had to intervene. And this is the only time I've ever heard of this being done at a university–any university. I had to write a letter to him saying that if he did not comply with the department chair's request–perfectly legitimate request to teach First-year Arabic, which he claims to be the great leader and expert in, that we would have to discipline him, and that discipline would and could include termination. If I did not hear from him by 5:00 o'clock on x date, he would be fired or I would initiate efforts to have him disciplined, the exact language. . .At 4:55 on that date, he snuck into my office and dropped his letter of acceptance into my mailbox.

Q. Snuck in?
A. Yes.
Q. You saw him sneak in?
A. No. One of my staff did.
Q. And what was he doing, tiptoeing?
A. I think on one toe he was tipping and on the other he was toeing. I have no idea. What kind of question is that?
Q. Well, you said snuck in?
A. Yes, snuck in. He looked around. He would not respond to a query from this secretary. He snuck in and put it into the mailbox. Yes, he snuck into my office. That is my characterization. He snuck into my office.

Shortly after Abboud acquiesced and agreed to teach First-year Arabic in 2001–2002, he filed a grievance against Robert Stofberg over the issue. The Dean had curious deposition responses to questions on this matter.

Q. Did he [Abboud] file a grievance on that?
A. He was thinking about filing a grievance.
Q. He did file a grievance, didn't he?
A. I don't know.
Q. Are you involved in that grievance?
A. I'm not sure what the status of that is.
Q. Didn't they ask you to be a decision maker in—with regard to Robert Stofberg in relation to that?
A. I don't know that he ever filed a grievance on that. And the reason I say that is, two members of the grievance panel came to me, and they wanted to talk about this complaint that Peter Abboud has.
Q. Who were they?
A. Julius Getman and David Raban [sic].
Q. They're law professors?
A. Yes. They began with a statement of amazement of Julius Getman of the load that Peter Abboud bore, and I said, "Please tell me about that." And he explained to me all these courses he was teaching. . .And I said, "Have you seen anything more about that?" He said, "No." I said, "Please investigate and see whether or not they meet at the same time and the students are cross-listed. I think if you do that you'll find that he's teaching one or maybe two courses at the most." Mr. Getman was very surprised that he had been lied to by Mr. Abboud in that case. . .The reason I'm not sure that a grievance was every really filed is Jack–Julius Getman and David Raban [sic] came to me in the hope that there would be some accommodation for this. So I said that there would be no accommodation on the question of whether or not the chairman can assign courses for people to teach because that's what chairmen do.

According to Abboud, Grievance Committee members Julius Getman and David Nancarrow, in a later letter, characterized Applegate's actions in this matter as treating faculty like "menial workers."

As for Abboud's teaching load, *The University of Texas Course Schedule*, published in advance of each semester and the summer sessions as a guide to students in their selection of courses, states that he taught at least two courses (two being the official requirement in DMES) each semester from the fall of 1998 onward. For example, during the Fall 2005 Semester, in addition to a section of First-year Arabic, Abboud taught: ARA 320K (Arabic Readings and Grammar 1), which met on MWF from 10 to 11am, and ARA 330K (Advanced Readings in Arabic 1), which met on MWF from 12 to 1 pm.

The Dean also erred in declaring that the MELC Department Chair assigns courses for people to teach, an impossibility in a department with multiple language and discipline areas about which the chair may know nothing. When I joined OALL in 1974, the Chair asked me what courses I thought most appropriate for the development of a Persian literature program. Neither that Chair nor any subsequent Chair (until May 2007) ever made even a veiled suggestion about courses I should teach.

In a foreign language area, especially in the less commonly taught languages, faculty in the area have to decide among themselves how to administer the sequence of language courses, which they teach in addition to their discipline-oriented courses in Linguistics or Literature or History or Culture. In Abboud's case, he has always taught one or two courses in the Arabic language course sequence, as I have in Persian, but as Jacob Levy in Hebrew has not. Moreover, the Dean's mischaracterization of Abboud's teaching vis-à-vis Levy has a further Arab-Israeli dimension. Since the early 1970s, students have reported to administrators that Levy, who refuses to teach lower-division Hebrew language courses, often comes to class unprepared and often digresses on non-class subjects in class. But, only Abboud, never unprepared for class and never off-message, has faced criticism from MELC, CMES, and Liberal Arts for what he teaches and doesn't teach. Some observers have long thought that apprehension about possible charges of anti-Semitism has kept MELC, CMES, and Liberal Arts over the years from doing something about Levy's alleged shortchanging of students.

In April, Aman Attieh hired an attorney. In response to a voice mail message from that attorney's office, I wrote the following letter on April 26.

I have prepared the enclosed folder of correspondence involving the Department of Middle Eastern Languages and Cultures and myself since the beginning of the 1998–1999 academic year.

I have tabbed correspondence which strikes me as particularly relevant to Dr. Attieh's problems with MELC administration since the beginning of the 1998–1999 academic year. As stated in several tabbed documents in the folder, in my view MELC routinely harassed Dr. Attieh during much of the past three academic years and discriminated against her in the spring of 2000 in not allowing her to interview for a new, advertised Arabic language position. I have shared my views in this regard with colleagues on the MELC Executive Committee and with the College of Liberal Arts in the form of photocopies of written motions and other correspondence distributed at meetings.

More generally, the enclosed correspondence paints a picture of an often non-intellectual and non-academic atmosphere in MELC. A dispassionate reader of the correspondence might well conclude that MELC is the sort of place where departmental administration might take *ad hominem* discriminatory, harassing, and retaliatory action against one or more of its members.

That is one reason why I have included materials in the file not directly relevant to Dr. Attieh's case. A second reason has to do with fairness to MELC administration. I do not see eye-to-eye with MELC administration on many things. By MELC administration I mean Chair Robert Stofberg. In my view, Professor Stofberg has engaged in a series of anti-intellectual, *ad hominem* attacks against me during the past three years, which attacks might have gained credence beyond his pen and voice, if my twenty-five year record of teaching, writing, publishing, and lecturing did not speak emphatically to the contrary. In other words, you and other readers need to know that I disapprove of Professor Stofberg's personal conduct toward MELC faculty, his inadequate management skills, the lack of professionalism in his MELC publications, events, and communications, and the current lack of standards in MELC program requirements and policies. That disapproval you and other readers need to bear in mind in assessing the credibility of my judgment about MELC's behavior toward Dr. Attieh. Having said that, however, my problems with Professor Stofberg vis-à-vis Dr. Attieh's may actually help establish a point relating to the twin issues of harassment and discrimination. Professor Stofberg cannot successfully harass or effectively discriminate against someone who has published much more, lectured much more, received much earlier promotions, and has a much firmer reputation in his or her academic field than he. But he can harass and discriminate against an Arab Muslim woman in a non-tenured teaching position.

The enclosed documentation correctly suggests that I have minimal contacts with UT Administration beyond MELC, which means that I have no information about Administration interaction with Dr. Attieh.

The fourth issue of *Middle Eastern Languages and Cultures Newsletter* appeared in late April. Stofberg had censored out of it two articles which departmental colleagues had submitted for publication. *Newsletter #4* featured a front-page picture of Mohammad Mohammad seated in shirt and tie, a checked Palestinian kaffiyeh draped around his neck. The accompanying article, entitled "Department Welcomes New Professor of Arabic," read in part:

> On one evening, while reading to his older son the children's book "Go Dog, Go," Dr. Mohammad A. Mohammad realized that he had hit on a potential teaching tool for first-year students. And so, the University of Texas' first-year Arabic classes opened in August with an Arabic study of blue dogs, yellow dogs, red dogs, green dogs.
>
> Dr. Mohammad, who has been teaching since he earned his B.A. in English from the University of Damascus in 1970, likes to find the unusual to capture his students' attention. For example, he developed an Arabic crossword puzzle for his students while eating with his wife at a Central Florida Pizza Hut five years ago.
>
> Palestinian by birth, Dr. Mohammad was born and reared in Irbid, Jordan, with his six brothers and sisters. His extended family members today live in Irbid and Iksal, Israel. Dr. Mohammad and his wife Laura have been married for six years. His greatest joys are to hear his three-year-old son George speak and to hear his 16–month-old son Hamada laugh.

On May 2, I wrote the following note about the new issue to the *MELC Newsletter* editor, Islamic Studies junior colleague Farshid Sepehri.

> In case you will be editing MELC's next newsletter, I'd like to offer some suggestions, which I hope would remain *entre nous*.
>
> In reading the Spring 2001 issue of *MELC Newsletter*, I noticed several errors with respect to Persian Studies items. I then reread the whole issue and noted upwards of fifty questions about spelling, punctuation, capitalization, diction, and syntax. Enclosed find a list, which includes misspelling of a faculty colleague's name, misstatement of a colleague's title, wrong publication dates, and wrong names of publishers, among other things.
>
> As someone who has compiled and edited a dozen or so newsletters over the years (samples enclosed), I have found it impossible to copy-edit my own writing or writing by others which I have keyboarded. Consequently, I make certain to do four things before submitting a newsletter manuscript file to a printer: (1) use a spell-check device (even if it wastes time making bizarre suggestions about foreign words); (2) read the newsletter out loud word by word, preferably in the presence of someone else with a manuscript copy of it in hand; (3) have a colleague who teaches writing or other acquaintance who edits writing look it over; and (4) review the manuscript in terms of calendar issues, making certain that citations of past, present, and

future events relate to date of publication, rather than date of submission of newspaper items.

It would take only twenty or so minutes to do tasks 2 and 3 (above), which I'd be happy to do for *MELC Newsletter #5*, if you don't come up with another way of handling copy-editing issues.

Sepehri responded in a note that Stofberg made all decisions about newsletter content and editing and that I should communicate my views to him. *MELC Newsletter #5* never appeared.

On May 3, I sent an e-message to Stofberg on another matter, in response to an e-message from him. My message read:

Thanks for the message. . .On continuing negativism about MELC's 1994–1998 administration, you may not be aware of the fact that almost every MELC faculty and Executive Committee meeting since September 1998 has involved negative criticism of Peter Abboud's tenure as MELC Chair. If I were Peter, I'd be inclined not to attend meetings because of the criticism, which strikes me as potentially stifling his academic energy or sense of academic freedom. For example, at yesterday's Executive Committee meeting, you responded to criticism about a specific MELC procedure or policy by saying that you had "inherited" it. My quick response to that had to do with logic. Peter also had "inherited" things from OALL which he fortunately disinherited as quickly as possible thereafter.

On May 6, on yet another matter, I sent Stofberg the following e-message in response to yet another e-message from him.

You wrote: "I am puzzled by your recommendations of salary increases for Zilla Goodman and Avraham Zilkha without having seen their Annual Reports in spite of you having provided me with a detailed list of the criteria that you use in making such assessments."

In my recommendations, as a MELC EC member, for merit salary increases for colleagues of ranks lower than mine, I again this year followed precisely the guidelines which I have been using in past years. Those guidelines do not allow for a recommendation of a substantial merit increase in the case of fewer than three courses taught per semester, no substantial publications, and no significant lecturing. In the case of Avraham Zilkha, I examined his course descriptions for 1999–2000, his publication activity, and his record of lecturing. In the case of Zilla Goodman, I talked with her about her activities. I frankly pay less attention to annual reports because some of us faculty often pad them: an idea for a book becomes in-progress writing becomes ready-for-publication writing becomes a publication. As part of the process of trying to come up with merit increase recommendations, which I would prefer not to have to do, I have made an effort to read everything which our junior colleagues. . .have published in recent years and have made notes on my copies of those publications and on my copies of their course descriptions.

If you would like, we could talk any time at your convenience about my impressions of course descriptions, course methods, publications, and lectures of MELC junior colleagues. In that way, you would get a clear idea of how carefully I prepare for my merit increase recommendations.

Stofberg's e-memo revealed that he had asked a staff person to tell him which colleagues looked at annual reports and who didn't. My response speaks to my characteristic mosquito-repellant preparedness and equally characteristic invitation to *le moustique en question* to do more work than he or she would like to do. When I get an antagonistic memo one paragraph long, I respond in two paragraphs with a suggestion or question which calls for the original sender to do something. At the same time, responding immediately to such memos and letters makes it easy to forget them and not get sidetracked by them beyond the time it takes to respond.

✍ May 24, Journal entry, Bolton Hill, Baltimore. Suri's Tex-Mex dinner on the 16th celebrated the end of my seventh and final Iran Seminar in Glen Burnie. Then came a wedding in Westford (MA) on Saturday: Farzaneh and Chris's son Dan's. From Massachusetts, we drove north to Camden and Searsmont, where I fished on Monday and Tuesday. On Wednesday, on our way back to Baltimore, we saw Jacqueline Kennedy's White House Years clothing exhibit at The Metropolitan and lunched at Luke's Bar and Grill on 3rd Avenue afterwards. This morning we paid a visit to Ivy Hill Road to offer our sympathy to Cathie, whose youngest sister Peggy died last Thursday. After a quiet evening at Jim's, we'll fly back to Austin tomorrow. Everything about this mini-vacation tasted good, especially dinner at Lincolnville Beach's Lobster Pound Restaurant on Monday. But Searsmont had less appeal this year, even with my romantic memories. The village no longer has a center or style. Suri says we should stay at Lincolnville Beach when we go to Maine next year. I'd like to rent a cottage on Levenseller Pond. ✍

Entryless May 15 in the journal fell victim to a telephone conference call from a UT Austin Grievance Committee investigating Aman Attieh's complaint against MELC Chair Robert Stofberg. I answered questions for ninety minutes. One question, to which I objected, asked me to verify that Abboud and Attieh were lovers, as if proof of such a bizarre allegation would discredit Attieh and neutralize her complaints against MELC. I added that the female UT attorney asking the question should feel some shame for so doing.

In early June I learned that the Grievance Committee concluded that MLEC had management efficiency problems and that whatever discrimination and/or harassment may have taken place in its dealings with Attieh, those problems did not figure in her failure to get the position in which Mohammad Mohammad had just finished his first year. Attieh's attorney informed me that Attieh would appeal the Grievance Committee's judgment on campus and pursue the case with the US EEOC and the civil court system.

✍ June 22, Journal entry, Perry Lane, Austin. Sorayya flew to Los Angeles this morning after Eliza learned yesterday that she'd be undergoing a Caesarian section delivery today. Sorayya got to the hospital in the nick of time. John Craig "Baby Jack" Garrett and his mother are doing fine. I talked to a groggy Eliza an hour or two after delivery. I'll fly out to see her and Jack in ten days or so. ✍

On June 29, Sorayya and I hosted a party in honor of Attieh, whose teaching career at UT Austin ended on May 31 and who was getting ready to begin her new career as Senior Lecturer of Arabic at Rice University one hundred and sixty miles away. Old OALL colleagues Jeannette Faurot and Sandra Paschall attended. After dinner, Peter Abboud offered remarks on Attieh's contributions to the Arabic program at Texas and presented her with a plaque, which he, Levy, and I, as the senior faculty in Arabic, Hebrew, and Persian, respectively, had signed.

I later learned that, in mid-summer, Stofberg accused Abboud of lying on his 2000–2001 Annual Faculty Report. The former accused the latter of listing a section of Second-year Arabic under his name, which he hadn't taught. Abboud and Attieh had scheduled two sections of Second-year Arabic, but only enough students for one section registered, which section Attieh taught. Abboud forgot about the other section, which appeared under his name in the MELC-produced text in the 2000–2001 Course Schedule. In his own defense, Abboud wondered why Stofberg hadn't accused him of "lying" in two cases where Abboud forgot to list on his Annual Report a course which he had taught. When I heard about this latest charge by Stofberg, the image of a television moment from my childhood flashed across my mind. It was of Attorney Joseph Welch when he famously said to Senator Joseph

McCarthy, "Sir, have you no sense of decency?" But, again, MELC stakes were low.

Also, in mid-summer, partly in response to MELC's unabashed and documented censorship in *MELC Newsletter #4*, I wrote and printed a newsletter called *Shabnamé*, subtitled "Unofficial News at UT's Department of Middle Eastern Languages and Cultures." A blurb at the bottom of the address block on page 4 read: "*Shabnamé* 1. . .offers no-frills, upbeat sounds from MELC's quiet, summer WMB corridors. Printed and distributed with private funds, *Shabnamé* neither represents MELC nor has any connection with newsletters which MELC has occasionally published since 1998. If MELC corridors get quiet enough next summer, another *Shabnamé* may appear."

In *Shabnamé* 1 appeared tributes to departed or departing faculty colleagues Aman Attieh, Zilla Goodman, and Walid Hamarneh, along with my remembrance of Ali Jazayery. It reported on new books by MELC colleagues. It also had a report on Persepolis Institute's ongoing Levantine Colloquial Arabic Course at University Towers, in which four UT graduates and faculty were teaching.

The only feedback which spiffy, well-written, and informative *Shabnamé* 1 received from MELC colleagues was an anonymous note shoved beneath my office door. It read: "singular subjects should have singular verbs." Printed in red ink in an Iranian-looking English hand, it appeared next to this newsletter statement: "A contingent of nearly 20 graduate students are pursuing MELC M.A. and Ph.D. degrees in such disparate areas as medieval Arabic poetry, post-World War II Persian poetry, and women's roles in the Hebrew Bible." In a university language department which thinks that the word "contingent" as grammatical subject has to have a singular verb or which thinks that stopping to think about that has relevance in communication, life there be worth living only if one have classrooms to go to, an office around a corner with a view, a family where office life gets no verbal space, a home with a 180–degree view of bushes, cliffs, trees, flowers, and birds, books to read and write, skiing, Maine, gastronomy, Baltimore friends, an Iranian-American social life, and John Craig Garrett. At my September 2002 deposition in "Attieh v. UT," Assistant Attorney General Horowitz questioned my motivation in publishing *Shabnamé* 1.

Chapter 9

2001–2002 Academic Year

"Before you embark on a journey of revenge, dig two graves."
Confucius

*"Apart from the occasional saint, it is difficult for people
who have the smallest amount of power to be nice."*
Anthony Clare

"He was a self-made man. He owed his lack of success to nobody."
Joseph Heller

At the start of the new school year, I had the feeling that the Department couldn't maintain the pace of its attacks against Abboud and me and the 1994–1998 past. But Stofberg made an aggressive start at the first faculty meeting of the year. In reaction, I wrote him this letter on September 6.

> In further response to the concern which you expressed at yesterday's faculty meeting that Persian Assistant Instructor Ramin Sarraf had "disappeared," that you did not know where he was, and that he had not sought permission from MELC to be away from the office, I am stating here for the record that Mr. Sarraf has not neglected any of his Assistant Instructor responsibilities with respect to the six or so hours a week which he devotes to PRS 312K.
>
> In a letter to Mr. Sarraf in mid-summer, I described for him my expectations with respect to his assistance in PRS 312K this fall as involving (1) copy-editing of course materials which I would regularly put in his MELC mailbox, (2) substituting for me as course instructor when I have to be out of town for a conference or lecture, and (3) availability for remedial tutoring of PRS 312K students who do not perform adequately on diagnostic tests given during the first three sessions of the course.
>
> I have put two packets of PRS 312K instructional materials in Mr. Sarraf's mailbox which I expect him to correct and return to me by next Tuesday. I have made arrangements with him to teach PRS 312K in my stead next Thursday when I will have to fly to New York to participate in a film conference at Lincoln Center (I cited Mr. Sarraf's substitute teaching on that date in my travel request letter to you some time back). I have informed students who can make use of remedial tutoring that those sessions will begin as soon as I can find a room and time for them.

PRS 312K does not make use of the MELC Language Laboratory. Instead, audio course materials are Online for student listening and downloading. Thus, in that regard as well, Mr. Sarraf has not neglected any PRS 312K duties. From your comments yesterday, I gather that the MELC Language Laboratory is not yet operational and that expertise other than Mr. Sarraf's is necessary to make it so. The bulk of Mr. Sarraf's responsibilities as a Persian Teaching Assistant relate to PRS 506 in which, I understand, he teaches conversation hours and prepares materials (most of them versions of conversations appearing in my forthcoming *Persian for America(ns)* syllabus) for those hours. Although Persianist colleague Ali Akbar Esfahanpur made no comment on the matter at yesterday's meeting, it would surprise me if he and Mr. Sarraf had not reached a prior agreement about the latter's August trip to Tehran.

Then came September 11. I was running on our bedroom treadmill that morning when live television coverage from Lower Manhattan began. That afternoon, I sent the following e-message to Columbia University organizers of an Iran Film Conference scheduled for the following weekend at Lincoln Center, where I was to present a paper on "Persian Literature and the Iranian Cinema."

> Attached find preliminary drafts of my Conference paper and notes designed as a handout accompanying the talk. The drafts are not for duplication or distribution. A single copy can go to the panel chair/discussant. . .The final draft of the paper will be designed for presentation in 20–21 minutes. Because of the continuing tragic events in Manhattan today, I'm wondering if conference organizers have begun thinking about rescheduling. As it stands, I am not certain that I will be flying to New York on Thursday. I will let you know sometime tomorrow.

The next day, the Film Conference Coordinator sent this e-message to conference participants.

> After consultation with people in New York as well as hearing the responses of several of you, we feel we have little option at this point other than to postpone the holding of the Iranian cinema conference scheduled for this weekend. We will reassess things in the next few days and will let you know what we may do to convene this conference. I am certain that this comes as a great disappointment to you as to those of us who have worked for about a year to organize this conference. Of course, this is but a minor matter in the context of the horrible tragedy of yesterday. Hopefully we will be able to work towards bringing us all together to discuss Iranian cinema at some time in the near future.

On September 14, UT Communications Professor Robert Jensen wrote an op-ed piece for *The Houston Chronicle*, which began with these words: "September 11 was a day of sadness, anger and fear. Like everyone else in the United States and around the world, I shared the deep sadness at the thousands of deaths." Jensen then took a provocative tack in asserting that "this act was no more despicable than the massive acts of terrorism–the deliberate killing of civilians for political purposes–that the U.S. government has committed in my lifetime." Although that realization, Jensen continued, angered him and "that anger stayed with me off and on all day on September 11, it quickly gave way to fear, but not the fear of 'Where will the terrorists strike next?' which I heard voiced all around me. Instead, I almost immediately had to face the question: 'When will the United States, without regard for the civilian casualties, retaliate?'"

Everyone now knows the answer to Jensen's question. As for Jensen's thesis, I confess to thinking on September 11 that America didn't have to build such flaunting, aggressive structures with such a name as World Trade Center. But I didn't think of American intrusions in the lives of people in other countries from the Mosaddeq *coup d'etat* in Iran in August 1953 onward as government-sponsored terrorism. Nor did I agree with Jensen's definition of terrorism, which left out the first six letters of the word. Nevertheless, his debatable views deserved debating.

Five days later, a chilling response to Jensen came from the UT Tower. Also writing in *The Houston Chronicle*, UT President Larry Faulkner, instead of debating the issue, stated: "No aspect of his [Jensen's] remarks is. . .condoned or officially recognized by The University of Texas at Austin. He. . .may not speak in its name." Faulkner then said: "Jenson is not only misguided, but has become a fountain of undiluted foolishness on issues of public policy. . .I. . .was disgusted by Jensen's article."

As subsequent printed faculty questions and discussions show, Faulkner here lost credibility among many intellectual academics at UT for the rest of his tenure because of the anti-intellectuality of his words. Offering no counter evidence to Jensen's views–something I and every other thinking academic could do–Faulkner attacked Jensen the person from the very Tower famous for a 1966 attack on people. Jenson, of course, had not attacked any persons. He had critiqued policy and policy-making.

In early October, I flew to an almost empty Newark Airport to participate in a Conference on Sadeq Hedayat at an Iranian Cultural Center in nearby Rutherford. In my talk, I focused on conflicts and dualities in Iranian culture, which Hedayat's *The Blind Owl* seems to suggest.

✍ April 30, Journal entry, Perry Lane, Austin. Hillmann Realty closed on another property today. Sorayya and I celebrated at Wink for dinner: shrimp and salad for starters, then duck breast and drum fish, and *vinho verde* on the trip. . .a perfect time. Wink deserves a star. Sorayya deserves multiple stars for Hillmann Realty's contributions over the years to our life style. Jack is coming to town on May 10th. ✍

Spring classes over, I wrote the following to Stofberg on May 15 to tie up the semester's loose ends.

> (1) Enclosed find two copies of the report you requested of Yaron Shemer's Community Service Activities for his promotion file. (2) If I can do anything else besides put out a newsletter-like flyer for our four summer courses before classes begin, please let me know. I haven't heard anything from you or summer-course colleagues in response to my e-message about current enrollments. My 'Classics of World Poetry' is full. But I can't access enrollment figures for the other three courses. (3) Enclosed find two signed copies of my 2001–2002 Annual Faculty Report. (4) Thank you for your approval of my request to be off campus from 13 to 23 September 2002 in order to present a paper at an international conference in Dushanbe, Tajikistan. Could MELC now begin the travel authorization process and considering my request for travel support? (5) For the following manuscripts I need typing/keyboarding assistance in making corrections and additions in existing Nisus computer files: '*The Blind Owl' as Narrative* (150+ pages) and *Sounds That Remain*: *Essays on Persian Poetry* (195+ pages). Would it be possible to have some work-study assistant hours assigned to me during 2002–2003 for this project?

Stofberg did not respond to this memo, for good reason. On May 21, a week after Spring 2002 final examinations, the Dean called a special meeting of the faculty of the Department of Middle Eastern Languages and Cultures in the College Conference Room in the Gebauer Building. Because faculty meetings rarely take place after final examinations when most faculty begin their summer activities, including travel (despite the fact that faculty contracts call for us to continue to come to the office until May 31), upon receipt of the Dean's e-message, MELC faculty knew that something special would happen at this special meeting. Peter Abboud called me to ask what I thought about the meeting announcement. Working at my home office on Fridays, I hadn't bothered to check my university e-mail for several days. I had an ophthalmologist's appointment on the day of the meeting, but told Abboud that I'd change the appointment time if it conflicted with the meeting time. I also told Abboud that the meeting meant that the College had decided to dissolve MELC. Abboud asked me how I knew this. I said that the delay in College announcement of a new MELC Chair (current Chair Stofberg's tenure scheduled to end at the end of August and the MELC faculty vote for a successor having taken place over a month earlier with results known by the College), coupled with the many problems in MELC administration, allowed for no other meeting agenda.

Eleven or twelve of MELC's fifteen full-time faculty attended the meeting. When the first several of us arrived at the Dean's outer office to ask about the location of the meeting, Liberal Arts staff did not know about it and could not find a note on it in their computer calendar. The outer office displayed two recent paintings by Bill Wiman. Staff did not know, in response to my question, how the paintings got there. They didn't know who painted them, or who Bill Wiman was.

The meeting started promptly at nine. Without substantial preliminary remarks, Dean Applegate announced the immediate dissolution of MELC, the establishment of a new entity called Department of Middle Eastern Studies in which Center for Middle Eastern Studies faculty from various departments around campus would also participate alongside MELC faculty. Middle East Center Director Benjamin Loya would serve as the new department's interim chair.

The news stunned Stofberg. Surprise turned to embarrassment and anger when the Dean stated that the announced change resulted from incompetence and shoddiness in the management of our department. Stofberg did not defend his management vis-à-vis specific allegations, but stated that he had deserved to hear news about the decision before the meeting. Several MELC faculty, myself included, who had spent nearly four years out of MELC loops because of Stofberg's management style (e.g., excluding several senior faculty from consultation), could have felt some ungentlemanly satisfaction at his discomfort in having been excluded from this more important loop, and his dismissal. But the categorical condemnation of his report-writing and report preparation assignments–the Dean asserted that other departments in the College had expressed anger at MELC promotion and tenure files– and the dismissive abruptness of the announcement of MELC's demise caused me to feel momentary sympathy for Stofberg. No one in the room had likely before this meeting heard academic words as harsh and a firing or dismissal so abrupt and public. I immediately thought about how Applegate and Loya were thus ridding themselves of someone who had done their dirty work, in transitory compensation for which they had allowed that person some bully pulpit space.

The minute I got back to WMB 5.146, I wrote this letter to Stofberg.

> Consequent to just hearing the news about the reconstitution of MELC as Department of Middle Eastern Studies within the Center for Middle Eastern Studies–an idea which I have supported since 20 November 1998–I am writing to tie up loose ends before the announced change takes place on June 1.
>
> First, I'd like to see a copy of the negative letter which you put in my personnel file some time back. Hoping to avoid a carryover of *ad hominem* issues from MELC to DMES, I'd like the opportunity to see if I should request removal of the letter from my file.
>
> Second, with your permission, I'll check with Alma Carrillo to make certain that reports (e.g., my 2001–2002 annual faculty report) and requests (e.g., keyboarding assistance for two book projects and August and September leave requests) which I have submitted to you have found their way into active files that will get to DMES.
>
> Third, in light of the Dean's allegations of MELC sloppiness, incompetence, and the like, as a backdrop to his announcement of its merging as DMES into CMES under the leadership of the CMES Director, I here state for the record that every MELC report on faculty teaching, research, and service with my name on it meets wonted standards in content and writing and that your decision not to include me in the loop of MELC report-writing, program coordination, committee chair responsibilities, and newsletter editing. . .exonerates me from responsibility in that aspect of the dissolution of MELC.
>
> Fourth, Reginald's criticisms of MELC at the faculty meeting at Liberal Arts, which you took personally–and you had a right to do so–were unnecessary as a prologue to the announcement of his decision to establish DMES. Moreover, he and/or Ben Loya should have informed you ahead of time of the decision (which even I, out of every imaginable MELC, CMES, and CLA loop, knew the moment I received yesterday's e-announcement of the meeting).
>
> Fifth, as you know, I have disagreed with many of your decisions as MELC Chair and with your treatment of Aman Attieh, Peter Abboud, Walid Hamarneh, Zilla Goodman, Chaouki Moussa, Mark Sullivan, John

Bradford, and other faculty and student colleagues. But, once June 1 arrives, I don't plan to visit the MELC past voluntarily. For example, I'll avoid the current practice in MELC of complaining about previous administrations in touting or rationalizing present activities and future plans.

Stofberg did not respond to my letter. But, our now one-sided correspondence didn't end there because the cited letter that Stofberg had written against me on 13 April 2000 surfaced in the fall of 2002, during the first days of DMES's first semester. At the same time, Stofberg's dismissal and the establishment of a new department didn't keep departmental faculty attention for long, because word up and down DMES corridors had it that "Attieh v. UT" was likely to turn into a court trial. Then came word that the promotion file for Islamic Studies Assistant Professor Kamil Riyadh, which Stofberg had announced on May 15 as in "good shape" was in trouble, old rumors of alleged plagiarism only part of the story.

In the matter of "Attieh v. UT," I received a subpoena for materials relating to *Literature East & West*. In response, I wrote this letter to Assistant Attorney General Horowitz.

> In receipt of Subpoena for Cause No. GN1–04059, dated 17 June 2002, and its two-page Attachment A, I am writing with reference to Attachment Item 9 and request that the books needing inspection get inspected at WMB 5.146 at UT Austin at a time convenient to your office. I avoid heavy lifting. . .and would prefer not to have to tote boxes of books to my scheduled deposition at the Office of the Attorney General on September 9. Also, for the record, as stated in written documentation submitted in May 2002 to UT Austin at the request of their Legal Department, *Literature East & West* ceased operation in May 2001, immediately after my learning that one or more UT Austin colleagues had stated at a University grievance hearing that they considered *LE&W* a vanity press publication with little academic merit. Attachment Item 1.d requests records concerning *The Epic and Asian Literatures* and *The Literariness of Persian Texts*, plans for the publication of which I cancelled with the termination of *LE&W* activity.

Chapter 10

Fall 2002 Semester

*"If you do not tell the truth about yourself,
You cannot tell it about other people."*
Virginia Woolf

*"Some circumstantial evidence is very strong,
as when you find a trout in the milk."*
Henry David Thoreau

On September 9, as this book's opening scene describes, I submitted to a deposition in "Attieh v. UT." On September 12, American President George W. Bush threatened war against Iraq in a speech at The United Nations. On September 19, I wrote the following to Assistant Attorney General Horowitz. "As discussed during my recent deposition at your office, enclosed find a current *curriculum vitae* of mine to substitute for the outdated and incomplete 1993/4 *résumé* which you used during that deposition session. Also, as we discussed at the end of the deposition, I'd appreciate the expeditious return of the binders of files which I left for your staff to photocopy."

On October 1, still trying to track down the Stofberg letter in my file, I wrote the following to Benjamin Loya, the new Chair of our new Department of Middle Eastern Studies. "Pursuant to three earlier oral and written communications, what's the DMES verdict about my request to review a letter attacking me which Robert Stofberg told me in person and in writing that he had put in my DMES personnel file? You've written back twice saying that I need to be more specific about a date. Does that mean there is more than one denunciatory letter?!? My guess is that Robert wrote the letter in mid- or late 2000. . ."

On November 12, Attieh attorney Robert Notzon deposed Stofberg at the Attorney General's Office. Under oath, Stofberg made a score of untrue statements, and statements contradicting statements he had made earlier in writing. A psychologist commenting on these untrue and contradictory statements told me that he thought they suggested a delusional personality, someone who lies when threatened, for one of two reasons, one being that he or she thinks false things are true.

From an academic perspective, the most telling exchange between Notzon and Stofberg related to the latter's publication record. In a world in which publications count and in which reputations can hinge upon publications, most academics have understandably good memories about their own publication record. In fact, the most likely situation in which an academic might seem unclear or hazy about his or her publications would arise when that academic has falsely presented him- or herself as having a distinguished publication record. In such a case, not remembering details about one's own articles and books can serve a necessary purpose. Here follows the exchange between Notzon (Q) and Stofberg (A) on the subject of the latter's publication record.

Q. Are you someone who publishes a lot?
A. Yes.
Q. And when was the last time you published?
A. I have. . .art. . .published articles in 2002, 19– -, 1999. . .I have three man–I have three books; I have something like twenty articles; I have encyclopedia articles. . .so I have a respectable publish–publication record.
Q. Over thirty years?
A. Yes.
Q. When was the last book you published?
A. It's–I don't recall when it came out.
Q. Do you remember what decade it came out?
A. Must have been in the '90s.
Q. Early '90s, late '90s.
A. I don't recall.
Q. And the book before this, when did that come out?
A. That was probably in the '80s.
Q. Early '80s, late '80s.
A. I don't recall.

The General Libraries UT NetCat site at The University of Texas cited no book-length publications under the name "Robert Stofberg" at the time he was making the foregoing statements. Besides his unpublished 1972 doctoral dissertation, a search of library materials under his name at the same time revealed a total of 59 bound pages in a pamphlet/booklet dated 1988. Stofberg's own departmental web page cited even fewer pages of published "recent writing" (1992–2003), and no book titles.

A day earlier, on November 11, Mohammad Mohammad and I had talked about rumors by Avraham Zilkha and Ali Akbar Esfahanpur that MELC had recommended Kamil Riyadh's dismissal from the university for charges "more serious than plagiarism." Mohammad described to me his positive feelings about Riyadh and his hope that he and Riyadh would have a long-term collaborative academic relationship. Mohammad also expressed irritation that MELC had left him out of the loop in the matter of Riyadh's status.

Consequent to my conversation with Mohammad, I wrote the following letter to DMES Chair Loya on November 14.

> Reports began circulating in DMES last month that you, in your capacity as DMES Chair, recommended formally in writing to the College of Liberal Arts Promotions and Tenure Committee that Assistant Professor of Islamic Studies Kamil Riyadh be dismissed from DMES. A check among DMES colleagues has verified that you did not consult the senior DMES faculty most qualified to judge Professor Riyadh's academic work and with the most at stake in our Islamic Studies program in reaching conclusions leading to your recommendation. Among those unconsulted senior faculty (whom I have not consulted in writing this letter) are: Peter Abboud (who teaches courses on the Koran and other Islamic texts), Mohammad Mohammad (who has reportedly been thinking about a Koranic Arabic track in DMES), and yours truly, a colleague with more formal training in Islamic Studies than any other tenured DMES faculty colleague whom you presumably consulted and a colleague who teaches courses on Islamic art, Islamic oriental carpets as culture, and Islam in literature, as well as publishing on those subjects.
>
> The exclusion of the most senior and most knowledgeable faculty from expressing their views and/or voting on the dismissal of a junior colleague is anti-academic, anti-intellectual, and perhaps in violation of DMES, Liberal Arts, and/or university policy. Equally important, if DMES continues its 1998–2002 policy of excluding some senior faculty from important and relevant deliberations, votes, and committee work, DMES will continue to perform inadequately as a department with concomitant negative effects on the activities and reputations of faculty with career-long commitments to DMES.
>
> I...protest your actions as DMES Chair in the Riyadh promotions case, news of which has circulated around campus and off-campus because you did not make certain that whatever official deliberations took place remain confidential.
>
> The story of the first two months of the new DMES's first semester likely has much more to it, unknown to me because I am out of every conceivable DMES loop, which fact strikes me as contributory to DMES's problems. After The University announces promotions for 2002–2003, I hope that DMES can see its way clear to schedule at least one departmental meeting at which faculty hear a description of DMES's official position

with respect to the roles which senior Arabic Studies and Persian Studies colleagues should play in situations where DMES plans to recommend something as serious as the hiring or firing of a colleague. At that meeting, I would hope that DMES would allow open discussion of the issue as well as announce the ground rules and/or composition of DMES's Executive Committee for 2003–2004 and beyond. Where I come from, if everybody in a group has a chance to express his or her views (directly or to representatives) and hear the views of others and then has a chance to vote on relevant motions, that validates decisions and makes it possible for voters whose cause did not prevail to attest to the equity of the process and to support the group decision. OALL/MELC/DMES has never quite gotten to the point where it uses such procedures in building its future, which accounts in part for its unsettled and undistinguished present.

Within hours of receiving my letter, Loya met with Mohammad. The next day, Mohammad sent me the following note, with a copy of it to Loya.

> Thank you for providing me with a copy of your letter to Ben Loya. Since our meeting, some detailed and thorough information came to my attention that shed light on all of the questions and concerns that I have had. I feel I owe you an honest and frank description of my current thinking on all the issues that you and I talked about. I believe that: (a) The committee charged with reviewing Kamil's tenure was carefully and thoughtfully selected. The selection of the members was made with the interest of the. . .candidate. . .in mind. (b) The committee's subsequent deliberations were conducted professionally, fairly and with integrity. (c) Ben acted throughout the process with integrity, honesty, professionalism, and without bias.

The phraseology of Mohammad's note brought momentarily to mind the fact of his relatives in Israel and the cloud under which he remained in DMES through no fault of his own. His characterization of his note as "an honest and frank description" made a sort of sense. I never learned any details about the grounds which prompted Mohammad's new assessment of Riyadh.

Meanwhile, "Attieh" and "UT" were continuing to gear up for a possible trial. In anticipation, Plaintiff's expert witness, Roger Allen, Professor of Arabic at University of Pennsylvania, submitted the following affidavit.

Middle Eastern Studies at *The University of Texas at Austin*. Without going into details, I can suggest that the way in which departments of the MELC type operate (and the success, or lack thereof, with which they operate within the context of collegiality) varies widely across American academe. In particular, the juxtaposition of scholars in Arabic language, linguistics, and literature (who are often native-speakers of the language) and scholars in Hebrew and Biblical or Israeli Studies (who are often Jewish and/or Israeli) will often engender tensions that are a reflection of the situation on the ground in the Middle East region itself; such tensions tend to be more diffused in departments which have a broader (Asian) geographical purview. When clashing individual personalities are added to such a scenario, the entire atmosphere of the department or program can rapidly deteriorate. I know of several other institutions where tensions in Middle East Studies departments (under various titles) have been high (and sometimes remain so); on occasions this may lead to a further administrative decision, namely to split the (Middle Eastern) regional organization still further. This has happened at NYU, for example, where, whether due to internal tensions or not, the Jewish Studies program obtained its own separate endowment and split off from the rest of Middle East Studies to form an academic unit of its own. In summary, the welfare of a Department of Middle East Studies (to use a generic label) in which the study of Arabic and Hebrew and their cultural heritages are juxtaposed is directly and heavily dependent on a level of mutual, collegial respect, something that demands of administrators, both departmental and university-wide, that they exercise particularly high levels of tact and diplomacy. There are, I would suggest, several universities (including my own) where this latter model (a combination of Hebrew and Arabic studies) does work, but I would again stress that the fostering and maintenance of a collegial atmosphere has to rely heavily on the willingness of colleagues to put aside current political tensions and individual preferences in favor of the common good of the department or program in question.

On the basis of the above. . .in retrospect, the decision to subdivide OALL at UT may have turned out to be a mixed blessing. The very least that needs to be asserted is that, since its creation, MELC seems not to have been a pleasant or collegial working environment; the Dean himself describes it as "small, fraught with inter-personal animosities," and "a troubled Department." The particular conjunction of faculty has, for whatever cluster of reasons, not been able to work well together, and, it would appear, tensions have also arisen in the relationship with the Middle East Center. Against such a backdrop, the decision not to reappoint Professor Peter Abboud as chair of MELC after the submission of a committee report and instead to appoint a member of the reporting committee to replace him as chair was patently not going to improve, indeed seemed more than likely to aggravate, the situation that seems already to have existed.

I do not wish to dwell on the particular issues involved in this unfortunate general situation (one detailed version of them is provided in Professor Hillmann's EEOC document). However, before proceeding to more particular matters, I have to say that the atmosphere of confrontation with students, of accusations of conspiracy, of reigns of terror, and so on, all these phrases point inevitably to the existence of an academic context within which any discussions of the status, qualifications and candidacy for promotion of Dr. Aman Attieh were liable to be nothing less than problematic.

145

Proficiency: Definition and Implementation. One of the major points in the report on Professor Abboud's chairmanship and Dr. Amah Attieh's policies in administering the Arabic language program is concerned with the application of principles of proficiency in the context of UT students taking summer-school Arabic courses. Since there seems to be a widespread misunderstanding of the concept of proficiency, I will here endeavor, as briefly as possible, to explain what the term means (and thus, I assume, what the Federal Government's [DOE] criteria require by way of implementation within the context of the FLAS fellowship program). I should point out that certain UT faculty personnel are not alone in habitually misusing the technical term "proficiency" as a synonym for "fluency," "competence," "language-requirement," and so on.

Simply stated, proficiency involves the measurement of a learner's performance in acquiring a foreign language on the basis of criteria external to the academic context: specifically to measure performance against a graded scale of functions that replicate the behavior of native-speakers of that language. Thus, "proficiency" (I am putting the term in quotation marks here to emphasize its role as a technical term within the context of language-learning professionals and of DOE criteria for FLAS purposes) is not and cannot be linked to any one institution or teacher, to any one syllabus, to the pace of instruction, or any other similar criteria (for which the technical term "achievement" is used). For each of the various language-skills, a proficiency-based assessment procedure simply asks one basic question: can a learner perform specific communicative and receptive tasks; and on that basis what particular "rating" can they be assigned on either the ACTFL (American Council for the Teaching of Foreign Languages) or the ILR (Government Interagency Language Roundtable) scales of proficiency?

It is thus obviously the case, I would suggest, that, if a program wants to implement a rigorous and useful process of assessing students' progress, it will be necessary to test their proficiency level at least twice annually and outside the context of any particular language course. That will be especially the case after a period of study-abroad or summer school, when learners will have been exposed to the language in different contexts. Research on language acquisition makes it abundantly clear that there are radical differences in acquisition patterns in learners who study a language course, say, five times per week for one hour during the academic year on the one hand, and on the other learners who take an intensive course for four to five hours a day over the summer. The syllabi may be the same, the number of hours may even be the same, but the materials learned (and retained) cannot be the same. In some ways, summer study improves the learning of certain aspects of the language, not least because the gap between the end of a course and the beginning of a new academic year is significantly less for summer-school learners than for those who finish in May and then spend their summer on other activities. The rate and nature of language-attrition for summer-school students of a foreign language is both less and different.

My point in going into such detail here–apart from the identification of what "proficiency" is–is to suggest that summer-school courses are not the same as academic year courses; they are different. By that, I do not imply "worse" by any means, but "different." Any responsible proficiency-based program will test returning students in the fall in general (my own program does so as a matter of routine). It is, I believe, a necessary part of the process of motivating students to recuperate their language lost during the summer to show them their proficiency-level in September as opposed to the level they obtained in May.

I thus find that the process whereby returning UT students were given proficiency-tests and then assigned to the language course appropriate to their actual skill-levels in September (rather than utilizing previous course-work as a criterion) to be an appropriately rigorous application of those proficiency-based principles currently being advocated by the US Department of Education. It was in fact the failure to establish and maintain such effective standards that produced generations of linguistically incompetent "Middle East experts" identified by. . .Richard Lambert in his well-known study *Beyond Growth*. That renowned study of the results of the NDEA Act and its Title VI programs depicted a sad state of affairs in "national language readiness" (to quote the Carter Commission of 1979), something that the introduction of the entire "proficiency movement" in the 1980s was intended to address. The question to be asked was not: "how long have you studied Arabic," but "what can you do in Arabic [now]?"

As a corollary to the above views, 1 might point out that the question as to how to handle the problems of learners whose proficiency does not match the required level of a particular language-course is very much a question of policy and staffing at individual institutions. Middlebury College's School of Arabic in the summer, for example, attended by students of Arabic from institutions across the country, specifically has two "intermediate" levels of instruction for students who are "in between" the other levels. However, bearing in mind enrollment patterns in Arabic, the availability of such "inter-levels" is a luxury that few institutions can replicate during the academic year. The bottom line question, as it were, then becomes: is it to the benefit of the learner to be placed into a language-course where the proficiency-level is higher than the one that they have currently achieved, or is it better to begin at a lower level where the learner can really cement the skills that are only partially present? The answer to that question will depend on both the motivations of the individual student and the best judgment of the language-program coordinator; but it is frequently the case that pushing students up into higher levels is not the right thing for them and is—more often than not—not right for the other students in the higher-level class either.

I would acknowledge that these remarks do not address issues of the applicability of grades and transfer credit, nor the UT relationship with the Western Consortium and its institutions, and so on; and for the simple reason that, as I have tried to explain above, a rigorously based proficiency assessment procedure is not concerned with such issues but only with the learner's actual current competence. Policies regarding those "achievement-based" issues just noted (grades, transfer credit, etc.) need to be made, of course, but they have no linkage whatsoever to the application of proficiency-based principles of curriculum organization.

The Search for a New Professor in the Field of Arabic. In discussions and correspondence going on in October 1999 it appears that UT decided that, in view of enrollment pressures ("unprecedented numbers") on the Arabic language program, there was a need for an additional position in Arabic. Professor Stofberg, the Department Chair, and Professor Abboud, the former chair and head of the Arabic program, exchanged written communication on changes in a posting for an "Associate Professor of Arabic Language," to which was specifically appended reference to Applied Linguistics, Education, and Foreign Language Education (also to the need for at least five years of teaching experience and the submission of syllabi). At some point in the process, these references to Education and Foreign Language Education were omitted from the job announcement itself and "Linguistics" was substituted. It is not clear whether this substitution was merely intended as a change of nomenclature, or whether it in fact implied a different set of expectations from candidates.

In this context I think it is necessary to observe that I know of no Ph.D. field of study whose exclusive focus is "Arabic Language." Language in general, and the Arabic Language, are tools, media, texts, by which one can undertake studies in a variety of academic fields and disciplines. The actual study of any language-system at the Ph.D. level in contemporary American academe takes place within the context of a discipline/department named Linguistics; therefrom the academic study of the language-systems of the Arabic-speaking peoples is termed Arabic Linguistics (there is a professional society devoted to conferences and publication on that topic). When other fields are involved (literature, for example), the Ph.D. is said to be either in "Arabic Literature" or else "and" is used to append the discipline in question; at my own university e.g., the field is "Arabic & Islamic Studies." Thus, the use of the word "or" in the UT job announcement ("Arabic Language or Linguistics") rather than "and" ("Arabic Language and Linguistics"–implying both the medium and the discipline) is a further source of confusion. However, in spite of the confusing nomenclature used to define the position itself, the listing of subfields that follows in the UT job announcement makes it abundantly clear that the primary area of expertise was and is, in fact, Language Pedagogy and, by extension, Arabic Language Pedagogy.

Within the context of the preparation and publication of the job announcement–with its built-in ambiguities, the "unanticipated clarification" referred to in a communication from Stofberg to Abboud on October 20th 1999, noting that the new position would replace that of the Senior Lecturer (in spite of the earlier rationale about the need for an "additional faculty member") and that henceforth language-teaching would be done by tenured faculty, was a procedural move that seems to have caught everyone by surprise. The abruptness of its insertion into the search process was clearly the cause of some consternation and questioning at the time. Whatever may have been the motives involved in such a decision and at such a stage in the process, however, this exchange between Dean and Chairman of the MELC Department underscores the fact that the position in question was clearly intended for a specialist in language-pedagogy.

As the record of the [Arabic Search] Committee's deliberations makes clear, the ambiguous nature of the language utilized in the announcement seems to have attracted the attention of at least one major figure in theoretical linguistics and grammar (Owens), who was later found by the committee (and UT students) to be totally unsuited to the position, mostly because of his complete lack of experience and interest in language-pedagogy. Along with Owens, the committee looked at the files of Ferhadi (NYU), Eisele (William and Mary), and Mohammad (Florida). Records tend to suggest that the members of the committee were evaluating this set of candidates initially on the basis of their linguistic scholarship. Abboud's list meanwhile, Attieh, Ferhadi, and Younes (Cornell), suggests strongly that he was still assuming that the focus of this position needed to be on language-pedagogy and its sub-fields, not least because his own field of specialization happens to be Linguistics and the need for another specialist in Linguistics was far from obvious.

That the proceedings of the search committee could lead to a situation in which there was a 4–1 vote in favor of one candidate and the one negative vote came from the head of the Arabic program and Professor of Arabic Linguistics presented a grave situation that should have caused everyone pause.

Academic Profiles of Aman Attieh and Mohammad Mohammad. At this point I need to point out that. . .I am only addressing myself in this section of comparative evaluation to issues relating to the field and discipline of language pedagogy. Such an approach certainly seems to be justified not only by the listing of courses that Dr. Aman Attieh taught at UT before her departure and that Professor Mohammad has been teaching there since his arrival, but also by the subfields specified in the job announcement and the fact that the position had been described as a replacement for Dr. Attieh's position as Language Lecturer.

The primary UT document in which the expectations of a tenure-track language-pedagogy specialist are delineated is the Memorandum of Professor Michael Katz to then Dean Pederson in March 1998. It notes that, at UT as at many other academic institutions nation-wide, a new emphasis on the professionalization of specialists in language pedagogy was leading to situations in which those institutions would need to develop mechanisms for retaining the services of such valuable resources; I might add that, within the context of Middle Eastern Studies, this was and is particularly the case due to the extremely small number of such specialists and thus the desirability of retaining their services. While my own university does not incorporate such specialists into the usual tenure-track process (preferring a separate track of Language Lecturer and Senior Language Lecturer), UT did and does contemplate the possibility of promotion for such specialists to the ranks of Associate and even Full Professor.

The March 1998 (Katz) Memorandum identifies three primary areas in which candidates for appointment and promotion are to be evaluated: research, teaching, and administration. In that regard the UT document certainly reflects national trends in establishing such positions as these within academic departments. The research component talks in terms of published articles about pedagogy in refereed journals, tests, multimedia materials, and so on. It also mentions attendance at conferences, the reading of papers, and establishing a national reputation. The teaching component talks of applying the "usual criteria," presumably implying student evaluation procedures, classroom visits by colleagues, and the like. The administration component is the most elaborately described of the three sub-categories, and one notes that in the final paragraph of the document this particular component of the applicant's profile is to "be given more weight than usual in deliberations over promotion and tenure." Once again, the much invoked term "proficiency" is mentioned, although it is not at all clear whether it is being used here in a technical sense. Taking all three categories together, the areas that are identified in each one and the emphases sought make it clear that the "applied linguists" referred to in the title of the Katz Memorandum refer to specialists in foreign-language pedagogy. I would emphasize once again that these criteria closely match the expectations of my own university and of several others known to me in the process of hiring and retaining highly qualified foreign language pedagogy specialists.

The application file of Professor Mohammad Mohammad clearly reflects the training and development of a fine scholar in the field of Arabic Linguistics. . .What is conspicuously missing within this profile is a concern with language pedagogy and its subfields or indeed any experience in the coordination and administration of language programs. Virtually the entire set of published articles and public presentations is placed within the context of linguistic societies and their publication organs. There appears to have been no involvement in the activities and meetings of the American Association of Teachers of Arabic, the nation's major association of Arabic language pedagogues, and no writing on any aspect of language-pedagogy or its subfields: curricular planning, classroom dynamics, testing, and so on. These impressions are further underlined by a perusal of the letters of recommendation, the contexts of which concentrate heavily on Dr. Mohammad's clearly important role as a participant in the linguistics program at the University of Florida. . .In summary then it would appear that Professor Mohammad is an incipient and highly promising scholar in the field of Arabic Linguistics. His colleagues also comment very favorably on his classroom demeanor, and the teaching award nominations clearly lend further credence to their views. However, the file shows virtually no evidence of publication of or interest in the field of language pedagogy or participation in the national community of teachers involved in those fields within the Arabic language context, items specifically mentioned in the UT job announcement.

Dr. Aman Attieh taught at UT for more than 16 years, having obtained a Ph.D. at the same institution in the field of "curriculum and instruction and foundations of education." She has taught Arabic at UT, coordinated the basic-level courses of the program, and participated frequently in conferences of Arabic teachers nation-wide; she has also been selected to serve as President of the American Association of Teachers of Arabic. For many years she was curriculum coordinator for the School of Arabic at Middlebury College, where, within the context of a project to prepare proficiency-oriented materials for the various levels of instruction there, she participated in the preparation of a remarkable series of textbooks mentioned in her CV. She was in fact one of the first teachers to recognize the significant change involved in the shift towards proficiency-based curricular planning, learning, and testing, and attended the very first workshop that I held on the topic in 1986. She was runner-up for a distinguished teaching award at

UT in 1997 and did in fact receive such an award in January of 1999. As the UT President, Larry Faulkner, points out in his letter to Dr. Attieh, the award indicates "the highest compliments and expression of respect that a teacher can receive from students." The excellence of the Arabic program at UT under Dr. Attieh's coordination is also indicated in the evaluation report of the Middle East Center. Turning to Dr. Attieh's publications and public presentations, we immediately notice that the focus of her efforts is a direct reflection of her field of expertise, namely language pedagogy. The publications include program- and course-materials (specifically mentioned as appropriate subjects for evaluation in the Memorandum of Professor Katz) and a large number of lectures and presentations, in both English and Arabic, on a variety of topics within the field of curricular planning (including, I note, a paper devoted to "challenges" relating to the Western Consortium [1998]) and language-teaching, -learning, and -testing.

   Conclusion. If I have interpreted the implications of Professor Katz's memorandum correctly, then the document is calling for the use of "different" methods of "weighting" than is usual for literature specialists or theoretical linguists (final paragraph). Such different weighting should include consideration of published materials relating to other fields associated with research on pedagogy and might also include "handbooks, dictionaries, national tests, videos, multimedia materials, software, etc." As I peruse the curriculum vitae for Dr. Attieh, I see evidence of such activity in some profusion. With that in mind, I have to conclude that, if the criteria laid out in this obviously crucially important document were to have been applied in adjudicating this competition for a post at UT, then the profile offered by Dr. Attieh would have prevailed over that of Professor Mohammad. Instead however, it appears that the "different" weighting advocated in the memorandum of Professor Katz was not utilized within the selection committee's deliberations. The "usual weighting" was applied, and indeed was applied in the context of scholarship and not Language Pedagogy.

During the eight years in which the issues which Roger Allen here reviewed and assessed were almost daily topics of writing and talking, not one memo or a single letter or a piece of deposition commentary or a committee or individual report from MELC/DMES or CMES or the College of Liberal Arts or the Provost's Office displayed any of the academic and intellectual rigor, integrity, and articulateness of Allen's affidavit.

Paralleling that affidavit and written in partial answer to it was a printed statement, on behalf of the Defendant in "Attieh v. UT," describing what the Defendant's expert witness would be prepared to say under oath at trial. According to the statement, that expert:

> . . . is expected to testify that. . .based on Dr. Attieh's curriculum vitae, she does not have an adequate publication record to warrant tenure at any major academic institution in the field of applied linguistics or Arabic. . .[On

the subject of Attieh's *Modern Arabic Women Short Story Writers* (2000)] for translations to have value, they need to be translations of a substantial work of literature accompanied by an analytical section written by the translator–even then, however, they do not carry the same weight as scholarly publications when assessing qualifications for tenure. . . With respect to the proficiency method in the teaching of Arabic. . .[the Defendant's expert] believes that. . .when students of Arabic who have participated in reputable programs. . .at other institutions [and] garner good grades in such programs, it is the responsibility of their "home" institution and of its Arabic faculty to give those students full credit for their work, including promoting them to the next level. . . Arabic faculty members from Western Consortium schools have expressed surprise to. . .[the Defendant's expert] upon learning that some students from Texas who participated in the program and did well were told by Dr. Attieh that the training they received at the Western Consortium was inadequate. . . It appears that Dr. Attieh is not well regarded by others in her profession. In. . . [the Defendant's expert's view], the position of President. . . of the American Association of Teachers of Arabic [to which post Attieh was elected in 2000] is a largely ceremonial position. . . Dr. Attieh's election to that position is by no means synonymous with an endorsement of her by the membership of the AATA.

As it turned out, the Defendant's Expert did not submit to a deposition in "Attieh v. UT." If he or she had and if I had prepared the questions, his or her deposition testimony might have gone something like this.

Q. Professor Expert Witness, I'm going to ask you a series of questions, for which I need only one-word, "yes" or "no" answers. Of course, should you try to give answers other than "yes" or "no," because *From Classroom to Courtroom* is my book, I'll invoke my writer's prerogative and record only "yes" or "no." My first question is this: In your view, is The University of Texas at Austin a major academic institution in the fields of Applied Linguistics and Arabic, Hebrew, and Persian?

A. Yes.

Q. Do you consider Peter Abboud, Ali Jazayery, and Deborah Cohen, who received any and all graduate training they may have had in Applied Linguistics or Foreign Language Education at UT Austin, competent Arabic, Persian, and Hebrew language specialists, respectively?

A. Yes.

Q. Do you know that literary translations can serve as the chief component of dissertations in Arabic, Hebrew, and Persian Studies in Middle Eastern Studies and the Program in Comparative Literature at UT?

A. No.

Q. Do you know that literary translation and the editing of literary translations have figured significantly in the career progress of such UT faculty members as Ali Akbar Esfahanpur and Fedwa Malti-Douglas?

A. No.

Q. Guessing on the basis of your two "no" answers, can I assume that you are not expert in literary translation and how literary translations figure in career progress at least one major research university in North America?

A. Yes.

Q. If I presented incontrovertible evidence demonstrating that summer courses in Middle Eastern languages sponsored by the Western Consortium of Middle East Centers made use of outdated or inexpertly prepared instructional materials taught by untrained teachers using, at best, a grammar-translation method, would you admit that a member university's Arabic language program, whose Center contributes financial support to the summer courses, would have a right both to register a complaint about such courses and question the readiness of students participating in them to proceed to the next level of language study upon their return to their home university?

A. If you put it that way, yes.

Q. Professor Expert Witness, one-word answers, please. If I were to tell you that, because of problems with instructional materials and methods, the Western Consortium Summer Arabic Program will cease to exist as a formal entity with a single summer program in a couple of years, would you now rethink your statements about Aman Attieh's critique of Arabic courses in that program? Or, when the program ceases to exist, would you rethink your assertions?

A. Yes.

Q. Now, please look over the two pages of the printed statement of what you are prepared to say in court against Aman Attieh? Can you show me any sentence in that statement which, rather than just asserting your position, offers any data or evidence to support your assertions?

A. [inaudible response].

Q. Is Aman Attieh well-known in the university Arabic language teaching community in America?

A. Yes.

Q. Does that community, including yourself, think Attieh is a competent, committed, and energetic teacher of Arabic?

A. Yes.

Q. Does Attieh have the necessary qualifications and skills to serve as a university lecturer in Arabic at an American university, such as The University of Texas at Austin or Rice University, where she has held such a position?

A. Yes.

Q. Now, please take a look at these two résumés of language teacher training and experience. Then, answer this question: Does Résumé #1 exhibit greater training and experience in Arabic language teaching than Résumé #2?

A. Yes.

Q. Please look at these two lists of Arabic courses taught at UT Austin. Then, answer this question: Do both lists cite the same courses, and no other courses?

A. Yes.

Q. Look again at these second copies of the first list, this time each including the name of the Arabic instructor whose record the file presents. Then, assuming that all items cited in both lists are demonstrably factual, does your previous answer verify that Aman Attieh (Résumé #1) has more training and experience in Arabic language teaching than does Mohammad Mohammad (Résumé #2)?

A. Yes.

Q. Look again at these second copies of the second list, this time each including the name of the Arabic instructor whose record the file presents. Then, assuming that all items cited in both lists are demonstrably factual, does your previous answer verify that Aman Attieh (Arabic Courses #1) and Mohammad Mohammad (Arabic Courses #2) taught exactly the same Arabic courses at UT between 1998 and 2003, and no other courses?

A. Yes.

Q. In other words, are you saying that Aman Attieh, who you are prepared to testify does not qualify as a candidate for an Associate Professor position in Arabic at a major American university, in fact carried out competently the very tasks which Mohammad Mohammad, who you are prepared to testify does qualify for an Associate Professor position in Arabic Language at a major American university, has carried out as a tenured associate professor ?

A. . . .[inaudible]!

At end of the Fall 2002 Semester, having gained access to Stofberg's letter of 13 April 2000, I wrote to DMES colleagues who Stofberg's letter reported as having filed complaints with him against me. In my letters to those colleagues, I presented documentary evidence and argumentation negating the complaints. For example, here follows my letter, dated December 17, to junior Persianist colleague Ali Akbar Esfahanpur.

As you may know, five or six DMES colleagues, including me, have submitted to depositions in ongoing litigation concerning former colleague Aman Attieh's allegations of harassment and/or discrimination against our 1998–2002 MELC administration. In the course of my deposition, offered as a result of a subpoena, questions posed by the attorney representing MELC/DMES made me realize that four colleagues, including you, had filed complaints against me during the 1998–2002 period and that then MELC Chair Robert Stofberg had reported those complaints in a document which he put into my departmental file. Later this fall, interim DMES Chair Benjamin Loya verified the existence of that report and identified its date of composition. Here follows the substance of what Professor Stofberg stated therein about you:

"Date: April 13, 2000
From: Robert Stofberg
For: Michael Hillmann's Departmental File

Professor Esfahanpur has written to me, April 3, 2000, indicating to me that he had a history of ongoing harassment by Professor Hillmann. Michael Hillmann was opposed to his initial appointment. Voted against him for promotion to Associate Professor and has sent a negative report about his teaching for the post tenure review and his request for promotion to full professor."

For the record, none of Professor Stofberg's statements is true. Of course, even were they true, they would not constitute harassment by any definition. (1) I did not oppose your initial appointment. As you know, I wrote to you and Leonardo Alishan long before the appointment that I could not support any candidate [even such former students as the two of you] who wanted to teach what I taught, but that I would not oppose applications by such candidates. As you also know, I told you at my house a night or two before the vote that I would not oppose your application. Official documents show that the vote. . .was unanimous (3–0) for your appointment [I abstained]. (2) Written records show that I did not vote against you for promotion to Associate Professor. (3) My report on your language teaching, dated 22 March 2000, reflects my continuing views on weaknesses [in textbook materials and methodology] in PRS 506/507. But MELC did not complete your post-tenure review. If it had, you would have had the opportunity by regulation to review preliminary reports and suggest changes in them. . .(4) Written records [e.g., a recommendation letter solicited by Stofberg] show that I supported your promotion to full professor.

I have copies of all of my correspondence to you from the late 1970s to today. The file includes ten or more wholly positive, solicited letters of recommendation of mine on your behalf [to University of Virginia, University of Michigan, University of Washington, The Ohio State University, University of Arizona, et cetera]. None of it is *ad hominem*. None of it suggests that I have ever discussed you or your work with colleagues other than the MELC Chair of the moment when asked for program-related input. All of the correspondence has to do with Persian Studies. None of it hints at any sort of harassment. For that matter, as compeers born within a handful of years of one another and finishing graduate school within a handful of years of one another, how could one of us harass the other?

When I started *From Classroom to Courtroom*, I didn't know how to characterize Ali Akbar Esfahanpur as a MELC colleague during the 1994–2002 years. Of our Persian program's dozen or so language courses, he taught only the first-year Persian course sequence. That left me free rein in Second-year, Third-year, and other language courses, including our three-course sequence in Tajiki. Because Esfahanpur also did not teach mainstream Persian poetry courses, that left me free to do what I have wanted with Ferdowsi's *Shahnamé*, Sa'di's *Golestan*, Rumi, Hafezian *Ghazals*, and Modern(ist) Persian poetry.

During the 1990s, written and oral reports reached me occasionally from Loya, Abboud, Stofberg, and Persian teaching assistants and assistant instructors, as well as from four or five Persian Studies graduate students, that Esfahanpur was unhappy with me and my Persian Studies activities. But, because he never once raised an objection in my presence to anything I was doing, I saw no reason to bring such matters up in conversation with him. Nor did we once exchange heated words or even argue during those years.

Regardless, Esfahanpur's behavior toward departmental colleagues in, or supportive of, MELC's Arabic Studies program puzzled me. In 1992, he protested CIRA's talk of involving me formally in their organization. He encouraged students not to include me on their dissertation committees. When one of them, Zhaleh Hajibashi, was under consideration for a Persian teaching position at The University of Chicago, I got a call from Chicago with this question: "Why weren't you on her [modern Persian literature] dissertation committee?" I had no answer. In 1995, Esfahanpur complained to MELC that I was writing Persian textbooks for the Central Intelligence Agency. More mosquito buzzing! At an October 1998 MELC Executive Committee session, after I left the meeting, Esfahanpur reportedly attacked me in anger for supporting Walid Hamarneh's case for promotion and proceeded to attack Hamarneh and his record. A month later, at the "Reign of Terror" meeting, Esfahanpur led the verbal assault on Attieh. In the February 2000 MELC meeting, without offering a reason, he voted against allowing Attieh to interview for the new Arabic position. In April 2000, he registered the cited complaint of harassment against me. Later, he discouraged Parichehr Moin from continuing her Ph.D. studies, despite her excellent M.A. thesis on Nima Yushij. His failure to support Azita Mokhtari and Ramin Sarraf also seemed *ad hominem.*

In all of this, Esfahanpur's behavior suggested to me culture-specific possibilities relating to arguably Iranian survival techniques. I've talked about such things in analyses of writing by Hedayat, Al-e Ahmad, and others. But my thoughts didn't lead to any surmises about Esfahanpur until I read his 2005 book called *Reading Chubak*, a compilation of plot summaries and impressionistic characterizations of fictions for readers who can't read Chubak's short stories and novels in Persian.

Esfahanpur devotes a fourth of the pages in his slim paperback to a chronology of personal issues with Chubak, whom he knew only slightly, and an *ad hominem* characterization of Chubak unrelated to critical appreciation of Chubak's fictions. Esfahanpur says this about Mr. Chubak: "in the work of Chubak. . .at times one sees overt and sometimes covert traces of anti-Jewish sentiment. . .in my frequent telephone conversations and the occasional meetings with him in the 1980s, I became certain that these sentiments were deeply rooted and ingrained in the psychology and character of Chubak."

That Sadeq Chubak was a private, limelight-avoiding, unassuming, witty, observant, friendly, sensitive, and generous man who took his role as fiction writer seriously, everyone who knew him well would agree. Moreover, Esfahanpur had not confronted the live Chubak in such terms during a ten-year period in which he says he had such thoughts about the writer. Perhaps Esfahanpur's views about Chubak and his views of Arabs in MELC and me as perceived competition related to stereotypical views of some Iranians toward Jews and Arabs and stereotypical Iranian ways in which some Iranians deal with conflict and perceived affronts and/or threats to themselves.

Esfahanpur consistently opposed his Arab colleagues from 1995 to 2000 and consistently sided with Hebrew Studies faculty. One Iranian graduate student interpreted this behavior as a typical Iranian decision to support Jewish administrators because they presumably represent a group whom many Iranians in Iran and some Iranians and Iranian-Americans in America stereotypically and conspiratorially think have some control over their world. At the same time, rejection of Arab administrators and colleagues can relate to stereotypical Iranian antipathy toward Arabs. Or, a third possibility, in Sorayya's view, Esfahanpur's behavior illustrated the proverb which goes "*iraniyan hezb-e badand*" [Iranians belong to the political party which leans in the direction the wind blows]. The clearest case in point would have to be Esfahanpur's votes on Walid Hamarneh's promotion application. In September 1997, when Abboud chaired MELC, Esfahanpur participated in a unanimous Executive Committee vote in favor of promotion. A year later, with Stofberg as MELC Chair, Esfahanpur reportedly voted against promotion.

In these regards, Esfahanpur also arguably exhibited a culture-spe-cific pattern of behavior in his avoidance of direct confrontation and argument, choosing instead to work behind the scenes to achieve his goals. In the Chubak case, he waited until after the author's death, when a confrontation could no longer take place.

Another arguably culture-specific behavior arguably part of Esfahanpur's actions and reactions in MELC has to do with the im-portance which some Iranians and older Iranian-Americans appear to attach to titles and positions, with the corollary expectation that they not have to answer to such individuals in lesser positions as Lecturer Attieh and Assistant Professor Hamarneh, who "talked back" in refus-ing to acknowledge "rank" in departmental discussions. In Attieh's case, her advocacy of proficiency-based language materials and instructional methods, not part of Esfahanpur's First-year Persian syllabus, may have made him doubly uncomfortable: an Arab woman of lower rank talk-ed about relevant pedagogical issues he didn't know much about and hadn't taken into account in his own work as a language teacher.

The importance which one attaches to one's position and profes-sional standing can also lead to increased sensitivity to criticism and understandable resentment toward others one assumes are rivals or competitors, which Hamarneh as a well-read theorist in Comparative Literature certainly was. Retaliation to perceived affronts might figure in this mix, as in Esfahanpur's attacks in *Reading Chubak*. Esfahanpur's special sensitivity to my Persian Studies work may have had its roots in his mistaken perception that he and I were in competition. Had he ever asked, I could have told him that I see both my only competition and my only judge in the mirror every morning and evening. I could have told him that the chief item of my agenda in the work place is to win both that competition and the approval of that judge.

Esfahanpur's retaliatory behavior in *Reading Chubak* toward author Chubak (who had refused in 1982 to give Esfahanpur permission to publish a translation of Chubak's novel called *The Patient Stone*) and his behavior toward Attieh and Hamarneh thus could seem the result of culture-specific attitudes learned in a childhood and youth in Iran and maintained in adulthood in America. Of course, Esfahanpur had every right to express his views and vote on colleagues in person and in print and to express his views about an Iranian writer in print. In all of this, he crossed no lines. My surmise merely posits that a particular sort of inherited Iranian culture, no better or worse than the particular sort of American culture which may account for how I tick, may have colored his views and influenced his deportment and decisions.

On December 18, I wrote again to Stofberg.

> I am writing this letter to request that you request that MELC Chair Benjamin Loya remove from my departmental file the four-page, untitled memorandum dated 13 April 2000 which you put in that file without apprising me before or after of its contents. . .As written and placed in my departmental file, the only conceivable purpose your memorandum can have is character assassination or defamation of character through slander. I have begun making available to every current and former MELC faculty and staff member cited by name in your memorandum a copy of the specific statements you make about or attribute to that person.
>
> If you placed it [your 13 April 2000 memo] there [in my departmental file] to have me see it one day, I've seen it. If you placed it there to cause me inconvenience, you've succeeded: I've spent nearly three hours writing various responses to it on a day when I should have been readying the final manuscript of a new book for submission to my publisher. . .If you wrote it to get something off your chest, you have perhaps succeeded in satisfying some urge for retaliation in your own mind and heart. I even feel some retroactive sympathy for you now that I know how much time, effort, and emotional energy it must have taken, in the middle of the difficult days you were facing as MELC Chair in March and April 2000, to solicit letters and views to slander me and to write them up and keyboard them as your memorandum of 13 April 2000.

Jim and Mike on the Parsonage ledge next to the site of the "Craig Homestead" in Searsmont. June 1995.

Chapter 11

2003

"Almost every man wastes part of his life
in attempts to display qualities which he does not possess,
and to gain applause which he cannot keep."
Samuel Johnson

✍ January 20, Journal entry, Perry Lane, Austin. Behind the wheel and on the road from Austin to Colorado almost three weeks ago, I had this thought which Sorayya transcribed for me: Eliot—you can't hold onto time and you need to conquer it through it; Mike—place holds you, and you can escape it only through it. It's travel that does the trick: jogging, hiking, kayaking, rollerblading, mountain climbing, skiing, auto excursions, airplane flights, train rides, and bicycling. It's in the going, from departure to arrival, and savoring the going. Travel through a semester, maybe, through a class session, through a book project. Not life as a metaphorical journey, but trips in life. Jimmy Berger and I beside him in his parents' Opel speeding down Buckshutem to Cape May. Hammie Dugan and I in his Buick Riviera in Western Pennsylvania, singing "walk right in, set right down. . ." on the way to Omaha. Eliza and I in our Granada to New York, Florida, and back. Pan Am Flight 1 from New York to Paris to Rome to Istanbul to Tehran. Sorayya and I on a TGV from Paris to Milan. According to Einstein, time passes slightly slower for the train passenger than for the person standing near the tracks watching the train go by.

We spent a relaxing and talk-filled evening in Fort Collins with Farzaneh and Chris. Then came a week at the Sitzmark Lodge in Vail, with Mohammad and Shahla. I skied four days at Vail and two at Beaver Creek, my current favorite place to ski. We ate out every evening. But only Terra Bistro approached gourmet fare. Pepi's Antlers Room and Bar had okay game dishes and atmosphere. We walked around the Euro-Disneyish Village of Vail in the evenings. In the late afternoons, we sat in the rooftop hot tub watching the last skiers glide down the mountain and watching snowflakes fall. Fellow Sitzmarkers talk like Chalfonters of my youth. The hotel owners hosted a cocktail party in their rooftop apartment one evening. We've reserved the same room for a week next January. But I've no time here to dwell on adventures just past when Sorayya and I are making plans for a upcoming trips and when I'm still overdue with manuscripts for *Tajiki Textbook and Reader: Second Edition* and *Basic Tajiki Word List.* Over Valentine's Day weekend, we'll baby-sit Jack in Scottsdale while Eliza and Jeff pamper themselves in Las Vegas. ✍

At DMES, days before the beginning of the Spring 2003 Semester, in response to a request for the temporary use of a new toner cartridge for the office laser printer so that revised camera-ready pages in our Second-year Persian syllabus might exhibit the same density of blackness as the rest of the camera-ready manuscript printed in December, DMES staff informed me that Department Chair Loya would not approve the request. On the same day as the request rejection came, Loya approved the purchase of a paper shredder. This new paper shredder may mean that fewer documents will make it to attorneys in the next litigation involving the department than the voluminous materials that have reached them in "Attieh vs. UT."

On February 1, I wrote the following letter to Attieh attorney Robert Notzon.

> Because my late spring and summer schedule is shaping up, I need to coordinate it with any obligations I might have as a potential witness in "Attieh v. UT."
>
> Here's how my schedule looks now. My UT classes will end on May 2. From May 5 through May 9, I have committed myself to conduct a Persian seminar at The University of Baltimore for a group of American government Persian specialists. I have a tentative invitation to conduct a similar workshop in Augusta (GA) from May 12 through May 16. The annual summer courses which I organize at University Towers here in town will begin on May 30 and end on July 11. The, from July 28 through August 1, I'll be back at The University of Baltimore for another Persian seminar.
>
> The non-academic language courses I conduct or administer take place with commitments which do not allow for rescheduling. Participants come from all over America, Europe, and The Middle East. Some plan their participation months ahead of time. The nature of my expertise in such courses is such that I cannot locate a substitute lecturer.
>
> All of this means that I'm committed to full-time activity on the dates cited above, which means that I would hope that my participation in "Attieh v. UT" could take place between May 19 and May 29 or from July 14 to

July 25. Also, the week of May 12 to May 16 is still negotiable for me. Let me know how my schedule fits with "Attieh v. UT."

P.S. Enclosed find my take on Robert Stofberg's deposition and his letter of 13 April 2000, as they relate to me.

As for Stofberg's letter, I wrote the following letter to Mary Jo Wilson, UT Associate Vice President and Director of the Office of Legal Affairs, on February 4.

You will recall my response of 17 May 2000 to your request of 3 May 2000 for documents pertaining to the lawsuit called "Aman Attieh vs. University of Texas at Austin" and my subsequent submission to your office of hundreds of pages from my files. Later, in response to a subpoena and a deposition of 9 September 2002, I found and submitted to Assistant Attorney General Judith B. Horowitz scores of other relevant documents. Subsequent to that deposition, I learned through a written communication dated 9 October 2002 from Professor Benjamin Loya, Chair of the Department of Middle Eastern Studies (successor department to the Department of Middle Eastern Languages and Cultures which was dissolved on 21 May 2002), that my departmental file contained a letter/memorandum dated 13 April 2000, which Professor Robert Stofberg, then Chair of the subsequently dissolved Department of Middle Eastern Languages and Cultures, put in my departmental file. Enclosed find a copy of "Robert Stofberg's Letter/Memorandum of 13 April 2000 from the DMES File of Michael Craig Hillmann."

On 6 November 2002, without knowing the contents of the cited letter/memorandum, I submitted a one-page rebuttal for inclusion in my departmental file next to the letter/memorandum. Then, after learning of the specific contents of Professor Stofberg's letter/memorandum, I requested in a letter addressed to Professor Loya and dated 17 December 2002 that he remove the cited letter from my file. In a note dated 12 January 2003, Professor Loya stated that: "This document [the letter/memorandum dated 13 April 2000] was written and put in the file by the former department chair and is a permanent part of your departmental file. I have no authority to remove it."

With the same request, I wrote three times to Professor Stofberg, most recently on 1 February 2003, and have not received a reply. I am writing to you because Professor Stofberg states in his letter/memorandum of 13 April 2000: "This document is being prepared at the direction of Legal Affairs at the University of Texas." I here repeat earlier requests made of Professors Loya and Stofberg that the cited letter/memorandum no longer remain in my file. The grounds for my request appear in the enclosure entitled "Michael Hillmann on Robert Stofberg's Letter/Memorandum of 13 April 2000."

An official at UT's Office of Legal Affairs answered the next day. I acknowledged the reply on February 10 as follows.

Thank you for your quick response to my request of 4 February 2002 that Robert Stofberg's *ad hominem* letter/memorandum dated 13 April 2000 be removed from my departmental file. You wrote in part: "That memo. . .was never meant to be included in your Departmental personnel file. For that reason, I have obtained the Department's only copy of the memo from Dr. Loya and have destroyed it. I have also asked Dr. Loya to make sure that no other copy of it. . .be placed in your Departmental personnel records."

Because I quoted pertinent items from the 13 April 2000 letter/memorandum in letters to four DMES colleagues whom Professor Stofberg cited and "quoted" therein and because I wrote multiple requests to Professors Stofberg and Loya to have the letter/memorandum removed from my DMES file, I am sending all six of those colleagues copies of this letter.

The matter of Stofberg's letter thus ended appropriately in personnel file terms, but not in other regards. The Office of Legal Affairs should not have "directed" Stofberg in April 2000 to gather negative hearsay against me from a select group of people without obliging him to check that hearsay with eyewitnesses and with me. The Office of Legal Affairs should not have allowed the letter to go or remain in my file.

More curiously, the letter did not appear in my file as submitted by the Office of Legal Affairs to attorneys in "Attieh v. UT." I say this with certainty because I spent two hours reviewing that file and searching for such letters. But the letter did appear in the departmental version of my file, as Loya verified in his correspondence with me. His verification, identifying a date for the letter, I communicated to Attieh's attorney Notzon, who made an immediate discovery request for it, which resulted in production of the letter by the Office of Legal Affairs. What all of this means legally I don't know. At the very least, however, the Office of Legal Affairs had exhibited unacademic and anti-intellectual behavior in the matter.

Almost as important to me personally, the chief legal officer of my university misspelled my surname in an official confidential letter, continuing a tradition in which the Liberal Arts Dean participated and which former MELC Chair Stofberg had initiated, although the latter was an equal opportunity misspeller and mispronouncer of colleagues' names in memos, letters, reports, and newsletters. In all three cases, it wouldn't surprise me if such spellings as "Thomas Man" and "Mann Ray" didn't register with them.

Two days before my letter to UT's Office of Legal Affairs, on the afternoon of February 8, Kamil Riyadh, my next-door neighbor at the south end of WMB's 5th floor corridor, with whom I had exchanged no more than 'hello's for more than three years, entered my office, sat down, and began talking as if we talked every day. He showed me a draft of a document he had prepared in answer to what he identified in the document were problems in his promotions file that Benjamin Loya, CMES Director and DMES Chair, had communicated in writing to him as the grounds for the unanimous DMES Promotions Committee decision in late October 2002 to recommend his dismissal from the UT faculty. Riyadh said he would be presenting the document to Provost Pederson on Tuesday, February 12, at a meeting which, according to Riyadh, Pederson had called to give Riyadh a last chance to defend himself before the former submitted his recommendation on the latter's tenure file to President Faulkner.

With Riyadh sitting across from me, I added editorial notes to the document's twenty or so pages as I read them. Afterwards, I told him that the charges as he represented them in the document seemed insubstantial. In response to questions on my part, Riyadh added that rumors that he had plagiarized parts of his just published monograph or that he had engaged in full-time outside employment while teaching Islamic Studies at UT were untrue. I asked him directly the question which I had put repeatedly to Esfahanpur who had reported to me the department's promotions committee's decision in November: Is there any page in the book for which one could find a passage or paragraph or page from another book and put next to the page in his book leading a reader to think that the latter text came from the former? Riyadh answered: "No." I asked a second question which I had asked Esfahanpur in November: Did you accept a full-time appointment at a nearby university while in the employ of UT? Riyadh answered: "No, I taught one three-hour course there one semester with MELC approval."

I had no reason to trust or suspect either Riyadh's word on things or Esfahanpur's earlier report. The latter was violating confidentiality in talking about Riyadh, while Riyadh had not dealt honestly with me during his first year at MELC and had behaved antagonistically toward me thereafter. At the very least, however, DMES had entangled itself in another personnel issue through a failure to consult with experts and through its penchant for unstraightforward deliberations. It also seemed inequitable that Riyadh deserved a special meeting with a departmental promotions committee and a special review meeting with the Provost when the complainant in "Attieh v. UT" could not even get an interview for a new teaching position which consisted of the very work she had done competently and energetically for years.

When Riyadh left my office, my brain was working on as many non-academic cylinders as it has. While one part of it mulled over what Riyadh's affidavit might mean for the "Attieh v. UT" litigation, another part of it felt relief at my ultimate vindication, regardless of the outcome of Riyadh's promotion case, vis-à-vis those earlier charges of racism and religious discrimination. Riyadh had turned to me, of all people, when he needed a sounding board right before his last chance to save his job.

Two days before Riyadh's visit, on the afternoon of February 6, Provost Pederson submitted to a three-hour deposition in "Attieh v. UT." Parts of its transcript read:

> Q. [Robert Notzon]. What year and month did you assume your role as provost?
> A. [Pederson]. November four years ago, whatever that is. . .I'm sorry. I don't remember.
> Q. Okay. When did you become dean?
> A. Oh, gosh, four plus five–about nine and a half years ago, so 1994, something like that.
> A. I'd have to see the charter. . .I'd have to go back and look. . .God, I don't know. Excuse me. I need to. . .Well, now, that would be reasonable. . .Oh. God. Fifteen, twenty people. . .Oh, God. I'd have to–I haven't thought about this for so long. I don't remember. . .I'm not sure what your question is. . .But, again, I don't–you know, my recollection there is faulty. So I don't want to be. . .Let me think. No. I'm–too fuzzy on it to respond clearly. . .Let's think. . .No, I don't–I mean, I'm not recalling the meeting exactly. So it's hard for me to give you a straight answer. . .I don't remember reprimanding Stofberg ever. . .Well, he [Stofberg] was–rocky. . .It doesn't look like my handwriting, but it could be. . .I don't know if it is my handwriting. . .I mean, I don't know. . .I don't know. . .I don't know. . .I don't know. . .I don't know at this moment. . .I don't know. . .I don't know. . .I don't know. . .I don't know. . .I don't know. . .Probably English, but I. . .you know, I'm guessing. . .I have no idea. . .Somewhere in the early '70s. . .My fuzzy recollection is. . .No, not that I remember. . .I have no idea. . .Oh, boy. . .Oh, gosh. . .I'm–well, let's see. Let me think. . .Oh, gosh. . .You now, I don't. . .I'm thinking–I'm trying. I apologize. It's been a while. . .I don't know if it was before or after. I mean, I don't

know. . .And I talked with the Dean, and he talked with the dean in—I mean, the—was it the Dean at that point?

In most instances where Pederson gave the sorts of answers here cited, those answers related to questions to which Horowitz and Notzon knew the answers. Even I knew the answers, because of documents which Pederson and the rest of us had produced or read. Those documents and deposition statements led me to surmises about Pederson's involvement with MELC. First, he made two personnel errors with respect to MELC: naming Palestinian Christian Arab Peter Abboud MELC Chair in 1994 and naming Orthodox Jewish rabbi Robert Stofberg MELC Chair in 1998. Unfamiliar with the dynamics of Arab-Israeli/Jewish interaction, unfamiliar with Abboud's Palestinian Christian culture, and unfamiliar with Stofberg's Orthodox Jewish culture, Pederson couldn't easily have avoided these two personnel errors. Second, Pederson also made a procedural error in naming a MELC Chair Review Committee after realizing that seven or eight MELC colleagues did not want Abboud renamed Chair for 1998–2002. At that point he need only have thanked Abboud for his four years of service as Chair and proceeded to name whomever he wished as Chair for 1998–2002. He likewise made a faculty development error in naming beginning assistant professor Riyadh to the MELC Chair Review Committee, which action contributed to special status and clique alignment for Riyadh at a time when he needed basic academic mentoring from the very senior faculty outside of, or anathema to, the clique in which he found himself.

The upshot of the Stofberg and Riyadh errors, which likely arose in part from Pederson's understandable wish to sail smoothly from Deanship to Provosthood without controversy in his wake and his likely preference for crew decisions rather than a skipper's command, charted part of the course which "Attieh v. UT" took. By the spring of 2000, "Attieh v. UT" having become a troublesome and time-consuming matter for the university, Pederson could no longer afford to talk and think like an academic or intellectual. As his court deposition shows, he had to protect the institution which he was serving as an administrator. Such customary in-class and academic orientations as candor, discursiveness, speculation, and the weighing of two sides of issues presumably would not, from his administrator's perspective, serve the best interests of the university administration. More interesting from an academic perspective is the possibility that he may have thought that serving the best interests of the university administration was tantamount to serving the best interests of the university.

In contrast to Provost Pederson, Dean Applegate had no qualms about proactive behavior on his own part and decision-taking on his own, for which he appeared ready to take consequent responsibility. Also unlike Pederson, who appeared not to allow emotions or *ad hominem* factors to figure significantly in his judgments, the Dean trusted his instincts and candidly asserted that his personal take on people and things played a part in his decision-making from classroom to courtroom in the Attieh case. The irritation and anger which the Dean exhibits in his court deposition in "Attieh v. UT" speaks both to his self-confidence in instinctive takes on things and an understandable obliviousness or lack of concern as to how his demeanor strikes other people.

The record shows that the Dean disliked Abboud before MELC came into being—one Asian Studies colleague has called Applegate's views on this score an obsession—and that his dislike continued when he became Dean and Abboud became both an initiator of a faculty grievance against MELC and a chief supporter of the complainant in "Attieh v. UT." The Dean arguably crossed a line then and later when he threatened Abboud in 2001, demanding that the latter teach a section of First-year Arabic or else face a reduction in salary or dismissal, while having no idea about what was good for Arabic. Of course, if the Dean had said the same to Levy or Stofberg in Hebrew Studies, that would have at least made him evenhanded in his intrusion into a language faculty person's bailiwick.

The Abboud issue aside, the Dean made erroneous public statements about Attieh and MELC's Arabic Studies program in the spring of 2000 partly on the basis of misinformation he received from MELC and CMES, partly owing to his own apparent ignorance of principles, methods, and issues in the learning of living foreign languages, and partly because he allowed himself the anti-intellectual prerogative of using whatever verbal means he thought necessary to control or win arguments and achieve administrative ends in specific interaction situations. On several occasions, he as much as told his audience, as the saying goes: What are you going to believe, my words or your lying eyes!"

In instances where the Dean was repeating what he had heard, he made an unanticipated error for an administrator by not checking facts before speaking or writing ex officio and not investigating both sides of pertinent issues. The Dean bears responsibility for the unfavorable public relations which visited UT Austin during the spring of 2000 in the form of a steady series of articles in *The Daily Texan* and a score of meetings of concerned students and university administrators. Again, like Pederson in the matter of the reappointment of Abboud to the MELC Chair position, Applegate made life for the College of Liberal Arts and MELC more difficult than necessary. For he could easily have informed Attieh in the fall of 1999 that he was discontinuing the Arabic lecturer position in MELC as of 2000–2001, giving her that year to seek employment elsewhere.

In the matter of the search in 1999–2000 for an Arabic Associate Professor, the Dean also exhibited administrative inexperience in communicating with faculty. The Dean's animosity toward Abboud appears to have clouded his judgment. The situation in the Arabic language and linguistics programs in DMES as of 2005–2006 verified that the confused and confusing process of choosing Mohammad Mohammad improved neither discipline in DMES. As of 2005–2006, students had fewer Arabic linguistics courses to choose from than in 1997–1998, while it took students an extra semester or two of Arabic to reach intermediate levels of proficiency they achieved after two years of Arabic before 2000–2001.

But, for and in my book, the Provost and the Dean are irrelevant because they are administrators at a non-faculty-run university. When they became administrators, even if they kept teaching their favorite courses, seated in a Dean's or Provost's office they no longer seemed to think or behave like humanist faculty. This is less a criticism than assertion of a fact of life at many second-tier public universities. Humanities faculty think primarily in academic and intellectual terms. Administrators at non-faculty-run universities run risks in doing that.

Their depositions in "Attieh v. UT" reveal the Provost and the Dean as non-academic and non-intellectual in some of their job behaviors. UT insiders and old-timers might simply observe that Arnold Pederson was no Chet Lieb, and Reginald Applegate no Stanley Werbow. But that's only part of their irrelevance in my book. The two of them just don't have good clues about how things work culturally in Southwest Asia or how things should work in Arabic, Hebrew, Persian, and Turkish language classes or what the stakes are for Israeli(-Americans) and Arab(-Americans) and orthodox Jews and Muslims and their secular-minded American-born colleagues in Middle Eastern Studies at some American universities. More importantly, neither of them exhibits the hybridity which Salman Rushdie argues in *The Satanic Verses* is a necessary characteristic for survival and success in today's world. Of course, they weren't alone in lacking such hybridity. Stofberg and Loya also seemed to lack it.

During Pederson's deposition on February 6, Assistant Attorney General Horowitz stated: "It [the trial] starts May 12, and it's probably going to be the last two weeks of May and maybe the first week of June." The defendants would later request and receive a year's postponement of the trial date.

✍ February 13, Journal entry, Perry Lane, Austin. In today's World Literature class, I introduced Islam in anticipation of our two-week discussion of the *Koran* starting next week and later three-week unit on Rushdie's *The Satanic Verses*. I talked about the five pillars of the faith, American misperceptions of the religion, and ideas about how to read the *Koran*. Many Americans think the population center of Islam is in the Middle East, that most Muslims are Arabs, that Islam is not an Abrahamic religion, that Arab Islam occupied such regions as the Iranian plateau primarily through bloody force of arms (the American comedian Bill Maher regularly impugns Islam for its bloody early days), and so on. After class, back at the office, I put the finishing touches on an exhibit of photographs of Sadeq Hedayat, Iran's most famous writer, the centenary of whose birth we're celebrating next week with a lecture, a movie, a reception, a library tour of Hedayat holdings, and this exhibit. This week I've organized teach-ins on Hedayat in Persian language courses. The gods deserve thanks for Krylon repositionable spray on adhesive and foam board. I got fifty photographs and blurbs mounted in two sessions, one over the weekend and the second between classes on Thursday. At 3:30 my Basic Tajiki class began. Written in Cyrillic script and the northern sister to Iran's Farsi and

Afghanistan's Dari Persian dialects, Tajiki is about as easy as foreign languages get for adult American learners, except for the vocabulary hurdle. We read a couple of contemporary poems, interesting not only because of their language but also because of the importance of poetry in Tajik culture, which speaks to oral culture and the memorability of verse, the role of the national language in national identity, and 1,100 years of literature in a language whose earliest poems are no more difficult to read and enjoy that a contemporary newspaper article. Tajiki class over, I didn't have to move from my desk in Batts Hall 217 because Second-year Persian meets there the next hour. February 13 was a Hedayat teach-in, a review of a biographical sketch and a short passage from *The Blind Owl*. A Persian-only class, students responded to questions about Hedayat's life and vocabulary in *The Blind Owl* passage. They took turns paraphrasing the texts and describing important events in their own lives. They got me to digress during the last half-hour about the use of deferential *ta'arof* expressions in Persian, which my second-generation Iranian-American and mostly American students find puzzling and sometimes hypocritical in the social lives of their parents. For Tuesday, I gave them a six-page lesson on the movie *Dash Akol* and a copy of an English translation of Hedayat's story. We'll watch the movie late Thursday afternoon at The Texas Union. Outside in a light drizzle on the walk back to WMB 5.146, I felt the special satisfaction and afterglow which reward teachers after energetic and energizing classes, regardless of how high up or down the totem pole of significance what they teach may be. In humanities, after all, we teach and research subjects because they exist and reflect the human condition and not because they figure significantly in the current or a prior scheme of things. Jean-Jacques Rousseau says of himself on the first page of his *Confessions*, he's a worthy subject for a book because he exists and because only one of him does or ever will. In WMB 5.146, I packed up my laptop computer, the almost final manuscript of *Basic Tajiki Word List*, and notes for a television program in the works on Omar Khayyam to take along on my weekend trip to Scottsdale, where Sorayya already is. Peter Abboud stuck his head in my door to ask if we were still on for a drink and maybe dinner. I said, "For sure," and we drove in separate cars to Romeo's on Barton Springs Road, his favorite restaurant. No courthouse images had come to mind yet during this classroom day. On the drive to Romeo's, I imagined that "Attieh v. UT" might dominate the conversation. But it didn't even come up until we had almost finished a bottle of a California Syrah. Peter had just heard that Georgetown University was considering reprinting his book on *Colloquial Egyptian Arabic*, written decades ago, in a series called "Classics of Arabic Books." Cambridge University Press had also just written to express interest in publishing a new edition of *Elementary Modern Standard Arabic*, the classic textbook he coauthored, much reprinted and revised by Cambridge in the twenty years since its first publication. Peter would be trying out new *EMSA* materials in his First-year Arabic course next fall. He spoke with enthusiasm about increased American government funding of Arabic language projects, especially at the advanced level, and specific projects at University of Maryland and San Diego State University. Courtrooms entered the conversation when I chuckled at the Dean's deposition allegations *à propos* Abboud's standing as an Arabic linguist. Arabist *confrères* around North America would not guess in a hundred guesses that the Dean et al. were describing Abboud in asserting lack of productivity and up-to-datedness in the case of a particular Arabic professor. Our talk then turned to the affidavit which Kamil Riyadh had submitted a week earlier to both parties in "Attieh v. UT." Although he had received a faxed copy of the affidavit several days earlier, Peter said over dinner that he had not had a chance to read it yet. If I were in Peter's shoes and had heard that a junior faculty person who had sullenly opposed me from the fall of 1998 through the spring of 2000 had now put in writing an opposite take on things, I'd have done everything short of canceling a class in mid-sentence to find or make time to read the four pages of the unanticipated and startling document. ✍

Riyadh's affidavit read in part:

> Sometime in the Spring 1998 Semester, then Dean Arnold Pederson asked me to be on an Interim Committee to review Professor Abboud's Chairmanship. . .Given the make-up of the Interim Committee and the information conveyed to me by Dean Pederson, it was clear to me that he wanted to remove Professor Abboud from the Chair. That is, everyone on the Committee appeared to have some complaint against Professor Abboud except me. . .There were no Arabs on the committee, but there were three Jews. . .I have attached a copy of the Report that the Committee produced. . .I am not aware of any effort being made to allow Professor Abboud to respond to the allegations leveled against him. There was a definite effort by the Committee to keep this Report confidential and not share

it outside of the Committee and the Dean. . .Professor Abboud was accused of playing favorites with salaries and other issues in MELC and that somehow Dr. Stofberg was free of such favoritism. From my perspective, it was abundantly clear that he played favorites and that these favorites were closely aligned with the Hebrew Program. . .Dr. Stofberg would also show a strange competitiveness when it came to enrollment numbers. That is, when Hebrew Studies had an enrollment greater than the Islamic Studies and Arabic Studies Programs, Dr. Stofberg would brag loudly at the faculty meeting of that fact. However, when Islamic Studies and Arabic Programs had higher enrollments than Hebrew Studies, Dr. Stofberg would not mention enrollments at all. I also vividly recall a letter that Dr. Stofberg wrote to the Dean where over 90% of the letter related to Hebrew Studies and possibly one sentence concerned Islamic Studies. It was also my observation that when Dr. Stofberg was present in his office, which was a rare occasion, he would be working on the Hebrew Studies Program to the exclusion of all else. . .There was also a very emotional and aggressive attack on Professor Abboud from Dr. Copeland during one of the [Arabic Associate Professorship] selection committee meetings. The Chair, Dr. Stofberg, made no effort to stop Dr. Copeland or to rebuke him for his outburst. This lack of action by Dr. Stofberg and the general knowledge within MELC of Dr. Stofberg's obvious dislike for Professor Abboud sent a clear message to me that Dr. Stofberg was not interested in what Professor Abboud had to say. No one else on the search committee discussed the needs of the Arabic Program or what role the new Associate Professor would play.

If Riyadh hadn't turned on me in mid-1998, I'd have helped him avoid the writing and research pitfalls which reportedly figured in the department's vote to recommend his dismissal from the university. If Riyadh hadn't specifically requested that I have nothing to do with his promotions file, he'd have had a chance to defend himself in semi-public. If Riyadh hadn't acquiesced to the anti-Abboud camp, Attieh would have received the votes to get an interview for the new Arabic position, and "Attieh v. UT" would not have happened.

✍ February 15, Journal entry, North Scottsdale. At twenty months of age, John Craig "Jack" Garrett, whose stay-at-home "Mommy" happens to be a psychologist and teacher, says these things: "airplane, airport, baby, baw [ball], bawk [bark], bed, bird, blanky [blanket], book, box, broom, bubbles, boogers [snot], button, cactus, car wagon, Casey [his dog], SiSi [Sorayya], cheers [with a drink and glass touching], chin, choclate, cold, Come on, Come on. . .SiSi, cookie(s), cracker, credi card [credit card + money], Daddy, Daddy work, doggy, dog, don't, door, door [shut the door], drop(ped), duck, dust, feet, flower(s), glasses, ha [hot], happy, hat, hat open, Have some. . ., hawn [on], hello, hi, horsey, horse, Jack [instead of "I"], jacket, juice, keys, kitty, knock, Mike [me as opposed to "Mikey," one of his best friends], milk, Mommy shopping [in contrast to "Daddy work!"], monkey, moon, nana [banana], nice dog, night night [I want to go to bed], no, no sit [get up], noise, outside, pants, peepee, picture on [take my picture], picture [camera], poopoo, purse, rice, shoe(s), shoot [spoon], shopping, shower, silly, Sit down, sock(s), sown [phone], stuck, sun, snack, toast, truck, wagon, wawa [water], What're you doin?, work, wow." The last word was what I thought of all of this. ✍

✍ February 25, Journal entry, Perry Lane, Austin. The Tuesday session of my World Literature course should be underway as I write, today's topic Hafez's Persian *ghazal* poems. But I'm home at the dining room table, an inch of ice and snow on a patio deck visible from where I sit. Sorayya is cooking soup for lunch, our lives momentarily having the flavor of fighting against winter nature in Austin's mini-version of the "Storm of 2003," which struck the East Coast last week. I called Jim in Baltimore to verify the worst, twenty-plus inches of snow everywhere, good news to unsympathetic me in my plans to ski in Maryland and Pennsylvania during Spring Break. Jim has found us a resort in West Virginia where we'll spend a couple of nights, not far from Whitetail Mountain Resort in Pennsylvania. We'll play it by ear the rest of the week. Fellow Austin Skiers will wonder how I can feel as excited about hills in Pennsylvania and Maryland as about our Thanksgiving and January trips to Breckenridge and Vail/Beaver Creek. It's all the same to me on the slope if the trails are white, steep, preferably groomed, and not bumpy. At night as well, it doesn't matter to me if the pillow I rest my head on belongs to Chateau Lake Louise or a Holiday Inn Express. Rain, sleet, and a little snow fell on Austin last night. Today the city is closed. In Belfast and Searsmont they would wonder what about weather they can have every day from early December to late March could cause a city to close down. UT is closed too. So I have ten unanticipated free hours in which either to try to finish the revised manuscript of *Basic Tajiki Word List* or to mull over MELC/DMES's imminent change of venue from classrooms to courtroom. Dunwoody Press will not be happy to hear which project I've chosen on my day of weathering Austin's great storm. Since early morning, I've been rereading nine volumes of my journals, dating from 1986 to this entry. ✍

✍ March 10, Journal entry, Bolton Hill, Baltimore. George M and I skied for five hours at Ski Liberty today. A clear sky and groomed crusty snow on the front side, also groomed but a little soft on the back, nearly empty runs, and great fun. I've rented a car for a return visit tomorrow, and may do the same thing on Wednesday. Jim picked me up at BWI Airport late Thursday afternoon. After dropping things off at his house, we walked to The Belvedere's Owl Bar for dinner, onion soup and a veggie quesadilla for me. Friday morning we drove to Whitetail, just across the Pennsylvania border after Clear Spring. Jim drew and read while I skied, until 3 pm. Then we drove to Berkeley Springs and Coolfont Resort. We walked in the snow around their pond and, after a drink at the bar, ate at the Coolfont Restaurant's seafood buffet, stuffed crab and wild rice the tastiest choices. Saturday morning I was on the slopes early, but fell and bruised a bone in my left leg just before lunch time. So, instead of lunch at Whitetail and an afternoon ski, we drove to Hagerstown for a lunch of meatloaf and gravy at a Bavarian restaurant. Before we sat down, the waitress told me to take off my hat. When I told the hostess that the restaurant's pay phone wasn't working, she shrugged her shoulders. After lunch we drove to Antietem, watched a movie about the battle, and drove around the battlefield areas. We climbed an observation tower from where we could see everything but the cemetery. In town, we visited the cemetery and looked at names of soldiers from Maine. Unimpressed with Hagerstown hospitality or shopping, we drove to Frederick. We shopped for owls at an antique mall, ate dinner at an Iranian-owned Italian restaurant, and returned to Jim's in Baltimore. Yesterday, we ate crab cake sandwiches at Phillips in the Inner Harbor and bought two books at Barnes and Noble: Eliot's poems for Jim and McPherson's book on Antietem for me. I rested my leg yesterday and read McPherson's surprisingly dull book last night. ✍

On the brink of the vernal equinox, the beginning of spring–Happy Central Asian and Iranian New Year!–, America launched a land invasion of Iraq on March 20. Air strikes began two days later.

✍ May 8, Journal entry, Bolton Hill, Baltimore. Jim took Cousin Ann and her Jim, and me to Helmand's tonight for another grand

Afghan dinner hosted by the brother of that country's president. I took Jim to Patrick's for Spanish fare last night. George S and I drank and ate and drank by the water at McCormick and Schmick's two nights ago. On Cinco de Mayo I ate a birthday dinner alone, pleasurably alone, people-watching at Dougherty's Pub. Sunday I attended a Loyola Blakefield reunion at George M and Cathie's, taking a light rail train to Timonium from Bolton Hill and enjoying a long walk in the country to The Meredith Farm before and after. Saturday night the reunion crowd met for dinner at Pierpoint's in Fells Point, where I talked more with Dick S than anyone else. I spent the day last Thursday in Manhattan, with walks up and down Broadway, before and after a dissertation committee meeting about Nietzsche and Hedayat at Columbia. Tomorrow another Persian Seminar at University of Baltimore will end with a class luncheon at House of Kabob on Harford Road. Then come tennis and dinner with George M and Tom B Saturday morning, I'll fly back to Austin and gear up for the 11th Annual Advanced Summer Persian Course at University Towers. Life is good! ✍

The October issue of *Texas Monthly* featured an article on UT Austin called "Greatness Visible." Writer Paul Burka begins the piece with a review of where UT started and where it was in the fall of 2003.

> In 1876, the state constitution called for the establishment of 'a university of the first class.' The University of Texas opened its doors in 1883, but here we are, 120 years later, the promise still unfulfilled. In the latest annual rankings by *U.S. News and World Report*, UT lost its spot among the nation's top fifty research universities, dropping from forty-ninth to fifty-third. Among the best public universities, it slipped from thirteenth to seventeenth. . .The other major ranking of universities. . .[,] Research Doctorate Programs in the U.S. . .is mainly concerned with graduate-level research and the reputation of a university in 41 individual fields of learning. . .High rankings beget an elite reputation, which perpetuates itself in more high rankings. This is the cycle that UT is trying to break—and it isn't succeeding. . ."

High student-teacher ratio, importance attached to fame of any sort and to athletics, inadequate scholarship and fellowship support for students, and other factors figure in UT's status. Almost everything which documentation in this book states, implies, and suggests contributes to the gravitational force of mediocrity and non-academic and non-intellectual orientations in UT Austin's quest to become "a university of the first class." Until even a small department like DMES achieves some distinction, UT will likely not achieve first-class status. Until departmental, college, and provost-level administrators behave toward DMES the way administrators behave toward non-Western language departments at faculty-run universities, UT will likely not achieve first-class status.

At the same time, the very existence of DMES speaks to a commitment on the part of UT to national research university status. As an academic needing that commitment, along with students and a library, the facts that UT is a major player in American academe and that nothing much goes on elsewhere that doesn't transpire also at UT, are sufficiently energizing. In a given semester in which I teach Tajiki, Hafezian *ghazal*s, and Zora Neale Hurston's fiction, things are happening that don't happen at that many American universities.

✍ October 28, Journal entry, Perry Lane, Austin. Catherine Grace "Gracie" Garrett entered our world yesterday morning. Sorayya, Ted, and Karen were in Scottsdale for her birth, while I waited here at home for the news. Last night I celebrated with two glasses of Rosemount Shiraz and a Mr. Gatti's veggie pizza. I probably won't see "Gracie" until Christmas Eve in Albuquerque. I'm waiting for a call from Sorayya now to hear about today's news and to get Eliza's hospital room telephone number. Jim flew to Austin today for a brief visit, arranged before Gracie's birth was moved to October 27 from the original Caesarean date of November 15. We shopped for another kayak at REI early this morning, kayaked on Lake Austin for several hours, and then ate chicken fajitas at Maudie Milagra's Tex-Mex Cantina at Davenport Ranch. ✍

✍ Thanksgiving Day, Journal entry, Keystone, Colorado. On Keystone's wide, sunny, and cold main mountain, the only one open this week, I skied on corduroy runs early this morning, devoured a cheeseburger and French fries for lunch, and flexed my improving ski muscles on one of the better blue runs this afternoon. At points during the day, inspired by surrounding peaks and Matisse-cut-out Lake Dillon, I thanked the universe for Sorayya, Eliza, Jack, Gracie, Jim, Jeff, good health, material comfort, warm and constant memories of Mother and Dad, good choices fortuitously made from earlier in life, The Cathedral School, The University of Chicago, skills that came into my world in my 6+ pound package, and much else. ✍

✍ December 13, Journal entry, Perry Lane, Austin. Last night twelve people came to dinner. Final editorial changes in *Basic Tajiki Word List* done, final grades for Fall 2003 courses submitted, and final arrangements for three days of skiing at Taos and a stay at the Taos Inn, our first long trip in my new ML 350, and then Christmas week in Albuquerque with Elizabeth and Jeff, and Jack and Gracie, at Jeff's parents' hacienda, I was in the mood for an evening of talk and wine. Before dinner, the Eagles sang their Greatest Hits in the Bose background. A Washington State Riesling and an Australian Shiraz joined the pre-prandial conversation. Pistachios, a creamed cheese and jalapeño marmalade dip, El Milagros Mexican Kitchen Style Totopos with Pace's Chunky Medium Salsa, and Sorayya's special guacamole dip, and crackers of all sorts whetted appetites. Then came a buffet supper of chicken kabob, ground beef kabob, Iranian steamed rice, spinach salad, and Iranian *taftun* bread. We sat at two tables. The conversation at Sorayya's, which Sylvia Sanders lit and stoked, argued for and against the proposition that Woodrow Wilson caused World War II by mistakenly involving America in World War I. Hollywood gossip kept things going at my table. For coffee, tea, and crème caramel, the two tables joined forces. By the time we got to postprandial stingers–the brandy and clear crème de menthe mix over ice which still smells and tastes like Cape May nights at Henri's to me–only five of us remained. One of us, Robert Notzon, brought up the subject of "Attieh v. UT." Actually, recalling the postponement of the trial date to May 2004, I brought the subject up by mentioning to Robert that I had commitments on the East Coast for the second half of May, with only May 2 to 13 open for me to testify, if things came to that. Robert then asked me what about the behavior of Stofberg, Loya, and the Dean in the 1998–2003 years had really gotten under my skin. In response, mentioning that the MELC years were my most productive as a Persianist, I likened their behavior to that of mosquitoes during summer river and lake bank fishing days in Maine, when I wear long pants and long sleeve shirts, spray a Deet product on exposed skin, and continue doing exactly I want to do. Robert persisted, and asked about any pay raises I had received during those years. I had to admit that I didn't know my salary, nor did I know if and when I had received merit salary increases for any of those years except one. I do not open any envelopes in the mail that look as if they surround correspondence about money. Sorayya, who manages all money matters for us, answered from the kitchen that I had received either insignificant or no pay raises during those years. Robert asked if I had taught and published more than MELC colleagues during the Stofberg years. Cold minty brandy taste in gullet, I smiled and shrugged my shoulders and said that I kept focused during those years by either ignoring *ad hominem* behavior around me or forgetting about specific attacks and accusations immediately after writing responses to them, and having Sorayya and a life to go home to. Robert perhaps wanted me to say that I thought administrative behavior toward me retaliatory. I didn't say that. But I agreed at the end of the evening to prepare a list of administrative actions toward me which no academic would expect at a university toward a colleague with twenty-five years of service and an energetic record of teaching and writing. By evening's end, I was feeling particularly noble, self-satisfied, and contented. ✍

On December 26, a massive earthquake struck southeastern Iran. It caused the deaths of over 40,000 people in and around the city of Bam. I dealt with my thoughts about the tragedy by designing a language lesson on examples of present perfect tense verbs in a newspaper report on the devastating effects which the earthquake had on Bam's famous medieval citadel. It would become Lesson 31 in *Persian Grammar and Verbs*.

Gracie at ballet class. Scottsdale, 2006.

Chapter 12

2004 and 2005

"His Majesty's Government views with favor the establishment
in Palestine of a national home for the Jewish people."
A.J. Balfour

"Every man has three characters: that which he exhibits,
that which he has, and that which he thinks he has."
Alphonse Kain

"I have come to regard the law courts not as a cathedral but rather as a casino."
Richard Ingrams

✍ January 1, Journal entry, Perry Lane, Austin. Leonard C took me to the UT–Wake Forest basketball game two nights ago. 8,000 other people also attended the exciting, energetic contest, full of three-point shots, hard play under the baskets, UT's platoon system matching up against Wake Forest's speed and quickness. UT's victory gave people, many of them burnt orange-clad, happy looks and bouncy steps as they strolled out of and away from the UT Erwin Center. Walking back to Leonard's car with our own happy looks and bouncy steps, we passed by a couple whom Leonard knew, a retired colleague of his and his wife. Leonard's former colleague had also served as Department Chair. During his tenure, Leonard recalled, not one Jewish candidate got hired. In each search, doubts which the Chair expressed about a potential (Jewish) colleague took the form of observations to the effect that the candidate in question was abrasive or aggressive enough so as not to promise to be compatible with other colleagues. Leonard also recalled a mid-1970s search at UT for the Law School deanship, which I hadn't remembered. According to Leonard, then President Loraine Rogers did not act on the Search Committee's recommendations concerning the four short-listed candidates. All of them happened to be Jewish. One of them was Marc Udoff, who later became President of University of Minnesota. On the way home, we stopped at Kerbey Lane Café to talk over his pancakes and my enchiladas. I did my best to describe the Stofberg–Attieh case without saying or implying that Stofberg's particular Jewishness was a chief ingredient in the volatile mix. Leonard understandably couldn't make heads or tails out of my description. But why did I, as a non-Jewish American, think I had to choose my words carefully in characterizing Stofberg's behavior to Leonard? While I was so choosing my words, I recalled an anecdote Leonard had recounted for me years ago. When he and Judy first came to Austin, they got homesick for things Jewish. One day they took their daughter Kay to Zilker Park to play and happened to meet another Jewish family there. Leonard said it brightened their day.

Except for African Americans, settlers in America mostly came with hopes for a better life and, in most cases, the chance to leave old world baggage behind. Some Jewish Americans seem different, for three reasons. First, the Holocaust perpetrated by the Third Reich wouldn't let Jewish Americans leave old baggage behind even if they wanted to. In fact, the Jewish and non-Jewish American world may perhaps never dispose of Holocaust baggage. Second, the establishment of the State of Israel created a sort of potentially permanent baggage claim center. Third, some Jewish Americans carry Jewish history like a back pack. In it they have stuffed myths and community records and memories of Israelite enslavement in Egypt, the exile and disappearance of the Ten Tribes, destruction of the First Temple and the Babylonian Captivity, destruction of the Second Temple and the beginning of the Diaspora, the fall of Masada, massacre of European Jews by Crusaders, persecution of Jews in Spain, expulsion of Jews from France, England, Spain, and Portugal, the first ghetto in Venice, and pogroms in Russia. I've sometimes thought that Reconstructionist Jewish Americans might have the most meaningful lives of all peoples not living in their ancestral lands: tribal identity and sensibility stretching back millennia, sensible cosmology and ontology, and comforting participation in a potential immortality, not just of the human race, but of their own tribe. In visualizing Jewish history and vicariously feeling some of its weight, I begin to sense how meeting another Jewish family could have brightened Leonard and Judy's day. I also wonder if even Reconstructionist Jewish Americans nurture hybridity in themselves, that combination of personalities or persons or perspectives that I think I need to make it in the 21st century. In any case, at DMES, six Israeli colleagues, an American rabbi, three or four Arabs, and three Iranian-Americans all have cultural baggage I don't have and can't appreciate. Moreover, they love America. ✍

On February 4, our first departmental meeting of the year took place. The single item on the agenda was faculty consideration of three candidates for the vacant position in Hebrew Literature and a faculty vote on any motions to hire and rank acceptable candidates. When the time to vote came, the department Chair of the moment asked colleagues to take out a piece of paper and write their choice on it. A Hebrew Studies colleague interrupted to suggest that a show of hands take the place of a written ballet so that everyone would know how everyone else had voted! The vote was unanimous in favor of Candidate #3. One candidate got bad marks in part because he didn't seem impressed with Austin. The candidate who didn't cotton to Austin, in front of people originally from the Middle East who want to or have to love Austin, could have been wondering where Austin's ocean and mountains were, where the city's museum was, where sidewalks along neighborhood streets were, where academic bookstores were, or even where downtown shopping and downtown were.

As for the winning candidate, who had a B.A. degree from UT, colleagues seemed confident that she would choose us over the other university from which she would likely get an offer: Hofstra. One Hebrew Studies colleague remarked that Hofstra was on Long Island, that fact alone enough to allay worries that the candidate might actually think about not choosing UT.

All three candidates were Jewish, as are all seven or eight Hebrew Studies colleagues in DMES. All Arabic Studies colleagues are Arabs, but not from the same Arab culture or the same religion. The two Islamic Studies colleagues are Iranian-American and Muslim in name, but not overtly Muslim in behavior. Contemporary Hebrew literature seems not to appeal to non-Jewish Americans in these parts, where, except for Christians of specific stripes, few non-Jewish Americans seem to take Hebrew courses.

✍ February 18, Journal entry, Perry Lane, Austin. Eliza, Little Jack, and Littler Gracie arrive tomorrow at noon for a week. In anticipation, I've tried to get everything about tomorrow done today, except for going to class. In my Advanced Persian Language class, we're still on the fifth section of Al-e Ahmad's *A Stone on a Grave*. Students have copies of the relevant reading lesson in *Advanced Persian Reader*, and a new glossary for the section. I'll probably spend most of the hour discussing characteristics of an "Iranian national character" as Iranian writers and other intellectuals define it, so that students can begin to decide how typical and/or representative Al-e Ahmad was as a post-World War II thinking man. In my Second-year Persian 2 class, I've announced a review test, which Behrad can administer. ✍

✍ March 19, Journal entry, Big Sky, Montana. In bed at ten last night, I am up now at seven and eating corn puffs, prunes, and mixed fruit for breakfast. My last day of skiing until next November awaits me outdoors. We arrived Sunday afternoon. The Bozeman Airport had a hunting lodge feel to it. The bus ride to Big Sky must have been beautiful, through Gallatin Valley and all. I slept the whole way. I'll enjoy it on the way back to the airport tomorrow. Six of us are in Powder Ridge Cabins #12, the best-appointed and most attractive lodgings yet on an Austin Skiers trip, the grandeur of Chateau Lake Louise aside. It's ski-in ski-out. Sunday and Monday I had okay days on the slopes, even risking the bowl off the top of one face of the mountain, albeit not without five or six rest stops on the way down. During the pauses, I looked back up the mountain as if admiring the upper mountain scenery, while letting the burn in my thighs and heavy breathing subside. I took the day off Tuesday and rented a car for a drive to Livingston where or near where, according to Mother, Grandfather Craig lived with Great-grandmother Craig from 1886 to 1905. I spent several hours on and near Main Street where his saloon could have stood. The trip will add five or six pages to *To and From A Village in Maine*. Wednesday I felt at home on the mountain, and discovered during the day that my favorite sort of run is a groomed, packed blue trail. The most pleasing run, after it's over, is a steep black which, from the bottom, I can marvel at having negotiated. I've also learned that four hours of skiing is my daily limit, not counting time on the lifts, my morning break for hot chocolate and a Snickers bar and a long lunch break for chili or a burger and Gatorade. In the club Nastar races yesterday morning, I finished the course with a time of 31.94 seconds, 14 seconds slower than the course's pace setter. I skied as fast as I was willing to let myself go, and enjoyed it. ✍

In April, in response to Defendants' submission of a Motion for Summary Judgment in "Attieh v. UT" and in anticipation of a May court date, Robert Notzon asked me to submit an affidavit corroborating "through personal observation, opinion or general reputation knowledge" a statement of "factual background." Two of its ten items read:

> Item 27. From 2000–2001 through 2003–2004, I did not see Mohammad Mohammad's name in any University Course Schedule next to the title of any course except for Arabic language courses. At the same time, Mohammad informed me early one evening during the 2003–2004 school year that he was teaching an extra Arabic language course in UT's Extension Division. Because of the fact that Mohammad was not teaching any course except for language courses, I no longer heard colleagues make the argument that Mohammad could teach more sorts of subjects than other candidates for the new Arabic position. I have observed that Mohammad, a hardworking language-teaching colleague, has taught nothing beyond what Attieh used to teach, albeit with a lesser quantity and variety of instructional activities and. . .with more mixed reviews from students.
>
> Item 28. Attieh's non-reappointment [as Senior Lecturer in Arabic for the 2001–2002 academic year] changed MELC/DMES's Arabic language program. In all but one section of 1st- and 2nd-year Arabic courses. . .students thereafter did not get exposure to a four-skills environment to achieve proficiency levels comparable to 2000–2001 and earlier. In addition, they subsequently had less contact with the[ir Arabic] instructor of record than in the 1994–2001 era. But classes remained and remain at least as oversubscribed, which is to say that DMES's Arabic language program still needs the full-time lecturer slot it eliminated as of 2001–2002.

On Cinco de Mayo, a date on which lots of things have happened to and around me over the years, including my birthday, Attieh attorney Notzon sent the following e-message to me, Roger Allen, Jack Tannous, Mehdi Alosh, et al. "I am very sorry to report that only five days before trial was to begin in Dr. Attieh's case, a judge (Republican, no less) has granted summary judgment against Dr. Attieh's case on behalf of UT. This means that she is precluded from going to trial, essentially saying that as a matter of law she has no case. This is of course absurd and we will be considering our options for appeal."

A dispassionate lay person reading everything but the documents produced by attorneys and judges would almost certainly find for the plaintiff in "Attieh v. UT," meaning that he or she would certainly use the terms discrimination, bias, and retaliation in describing behavior toward Attieh from August 1998 through January 2001. A dispassionate lay person who also read the documents produced by attorneys and judges would likely conclude that both sides had (or equally lacked) merit, but that the inexplicable behavior on the part of Stofberg et al. might tip the scales in favor of giving Attieh her day in court.

A dispassionate lay person who not only read the documents produced by attorneys and judges, but learned something about the law and legal precedents in the process, might conclude that whatever wrongdoing took place, it was debatable that the sorts of evidence needed to demonstrate it in legal terms had been offered to the court. In other words, the situation remained as the Equal Employment Opportunity Commission had concluded in 2000, that discrimination, bias, and retaliation may have taken place, and that some suggestive evidence appears in the files. But EEOC could say or do no more than say that; and, apparently, a court needed more to schedule a trial.

Attorney Notzon likely had his fingers crossed in hopes of getting his case past the Motion for Summary Judgment, because a jury of Aman Attieh's peers would have applied as much sympathetic common sense in response to testimony as legal principles. A jury trial would have meant placing a casino bet on red or black, a 50% chance. But, the crux of the issue was the more chancy and prior crap shoot as to which judge would get the case. A liberal Democrat would have meant a green light for a jury trial. A conservative Republican meant a red light, and no jury trial. Patrick Keel, who later lost a reelection bid for his seat on the bench, made for as red as a light could locally get. The successful Motion for Summary Judgment was bad luck of the draw for Attieh–Notzon in a judicial system which everyone knows going in is political and involves election to seats on the bench. If only legal appeals involved state reciprocity. Were that the case, Notzon would have jogged to California, his appeal motion in a backpack, smiling all the way. Or, if Notzon had Dick Deguerin's deep pockets and connections, he might at least have gotten another venue or judge.

A week after hearing the news about "Attieh v. UT," Sorayya and I made our late spring pilgrimage to Baltimore. As usual, we stayed at Jim's on Bolton Hill. Behrad Aghaei, who flew up from Austin, stayed with us, and helped me conduct a two-week Advanced Persian Seminar on Al-e Ahmad's *A Stone for a Grave* for government Persian specialists at The University of Baltimore.

From Baltimore, Sorayya and I flew to Miami Beach and a long weekend at the Hilton Fontainbleau and a talk there at the invitation of the Iranian American Medical Association. Actually, I didn't so much give a talk as set up group discussions among the 200 or so physicians in attendance to develop a list of what they considered chief features of Iranianness. After twenty minutes or so, group representatives reported twelve items as very important to them as Iranians: (1) family, (2) friendship, (3) their national Persian language, (4) hospitality and socializing, (5) Iranian cuisine and foods, (6) respect for elders, (7) politeness and courtesy, (8) special feelings about the spring season, (9) Iranian history and traditions, (10) love of poetry, (11) spirituality, and (12) personal reputation and good name.

More interesting were other categories of attitudes and stances in individual Iranians about which they also reported, some of them in a questioning intonation, apparently seeing a less appealing side to pairs of arguably culture-specific qualities and orientations in individual Iranians, among them: (13) culture-specific fatalism vis-à-vis a sense of culture-specific individual will; (14) pessimism and optimism; (15) humility versus putting on airs and showing off; (16) informality sometimes and ceremonialness on other occasions; (17) independence of speech often tempered by or perhaps overridden by a concern for what "(the) people" think; (18) trustingness hand in hand with skepticism and conspiratorialism; (19) the valuing of honesty and uprightness while recognizing the role of hypocrisy and duplicitousness in some Iranian lives; (20) appreciation of both openness and simplicity, on the one hand, and cleverness and deviousness, on the other; (21) coexistence of flexibility and one-track-mindedness in the same Iranian personality; (22) an Iranian-specific mix of modernity and faddism with traditionalism and antiquarianism; (23) an attraction to or infatuation with and an aversion from the West in equal doses–xenophilia hand in hand with xenophobia; (24) apparent comfort with a patriarchal order despite commitment to individualism and individuality; (25) adaptability and a feeling of familiarity in the face of a perennial sense of alienation; (26) a favoring of open-minded intellectualism in the face of recognized harboring of biases and prejudices; (27) a concomitant culture-specific sense of cultural superiority and a sense of cultural inferiority; (28) a cultural mix of audacity and pushiness with reticence and timidity; (29) conservatism and reactionarianism balanced by a willingness to change; and (30) ambiguousness, duality of views, and ambivalence, contrasting with a sense that successful Iranian-American lives may depend upon syntheses.

In summarizing their list of Iranian qualities or characteristics or traits, I told the audience that some of them gave me the impression that they think they face dilemmas as Iranians in today's world, that they are facing some sort of identity crisis, and that something negative inheres in the terms "dilemma" and "identity crisis." I added that, recognizing the facts of the survival of Persian Iranian culture throughout history and the success of Iranians throughout the world in today's world, one can arguably view ambivalences and dualities (or, if you will, dilemmas and identity concerns) in Iranian culture as tools and motivation for survival and progress. Such pairs of terms as past and present, religion and secularity, tradition and modernity, history and myth, group and individual values, and belonging and alienation in individual Iranians speak to the complexities of Persian Iranian identity. But, the culture as a whole would seem to derive energy and enrichment from its deep-rooted dualities, dipolarities, tensions, conflicts, and concerns. What some thinking Iranians have called an Iranian cultural identity crisis may constitute a perennial and paradoxically natural or salutary condition for Iranian life.

✍ August 29, Journal entry, Perry Lane, Austin. Sorayya and I returned Monday evening after four balmy days with Gracie, Jack, Eliza, and Jeff at their condo on Coronado Island. Jogging, swimming, tennis, delightful hours with Jack and Gracie, okay fare at restaurants, a perfect breakfast at Coronado Hotel just up the boardwalk, and the comforting realization that Eliza and Jeff have a good rhythm and already achieved prospects in their family's life made the days even more relaxing. Oceanside San Diego has a good feel to it. Unnoted in earlier entries were August trips to Georgia, Baltimore, and Maine where I hooked two big trout at a St. George River spot I'm keeping secret, and Sorayya's $600 slot machine winnings at Horizon Casino in Vicksburg on the drive home. Tomorrow night we're joining Jim and Elizabeth

George at their house for dinner and TV front seats for the first Bush–Kerry presidential debate. ✍

✍ October 25, Journal entry, Austin Airport. My flight from Baltimore landed an hour ago. Sorayya's from Phoenix will land shortly after five. I'll while away two hours here at the airport until she arrives. Her Tuesday-to-Monday trip to Scottsdale happened because a long weekend in Baltimore for my Cathedral School Reunion didn't interest her. The Cathedral reunion at The Meredith Farm last from 3 to 10 on Saturday. Cathie prepared a wonderful beef dinner. George set up a full bar on the patio, to which I added a case of French wine. After dinner, we sang Fats Domino songs and reminisced. Fourteen or fifteen of us, about half of the Class of 1954, were there, along with a handful of honorary class members who had left Cathedral before graduation, and nine or ten spouses and other significant others. No one at the Reunion had trouble returning to the 1950s and treating everyone else in the open, unsuspecting way we treated family, neighbors, and schoolmates in pre-high school years. The one bottle of wine remaining at evening's end George brought to Lynda and George S's last night. Lynda put on a chic dinner party with lively conversation among the seven of us. George Porter and Jim were the other guests. On Sunday, Dave Brune treated George S, George S's son-in-law Steve, and me to golf at Pine Ridge. Halfway through the front nine, it started to rain. So, we called it a day after nine holes and retired to Michael's for lunch. That turned out to be my one chance to have a crab cake on the trip, although I did have seafood Thursday night, when I took Jim out for his birthday dinner to Legal Seafood at the Inner Harbor. Jim's birthday, The Cathedral Reunion—the ever effervescent Charlotte Carozza stopped by late in the evening—dinner at Lynda and George's, and golf. Now that I'm writing it all down, the totality makes for a full weekend, and I've left out the big event. On Friday I drove to McNeil's Language Research Center in Hyattsville to discuss *Dictionary of Newer Persian Words*, a new, three-year Persepolis project. At lunch, I met two executives from McNeil Technologies corporate headquarters. The COO told me that they want to get me to join them in their language training business. The fact of such an option is exhilarating. Not many academics have a chance to start a new career with as much promise as their old one. Sorayya's plane is a half-hour away. In mid-December we're expecting a houseful of guests from Scottsdale, Baltimore, Göttingen, Houston, and Fort Lauderdale. We've hired a Santa Claus to surprise the children, read *A Christmas Story* to them, and give them presents on Christmas Eve. Jack will think it a treat to sleep on a mattress on the floor at the foot of our bed. O, I almost forgot the even better news at LRC. After the *Dictionary of Newer Persian Words* project, they want a book on Persian grammar and a guide to advanced Persian conversations. Those projects, my five-week University Towers course each summer, and my five or six weeks of seminars at Georgia Center for Language and University of Baltimore each year keep my juices flowing, the goals in non-academic proficiency language programs now as satisfying as achievement goals in university language courses. ✍

✍ November 23, Journal entry, Austin Airport. Our Austin Skiers United flight to Denver leaves at 6:05 pm. We'll probably get to our Hi Country Haus condos in Winter Park by 11 pm, after a grocery and liquor stop at Applejack's on our bus route just west of Denver. Twenty of us are making the trip, seventeen of us on the United flight and three others joining us at Winter Park. Rainer Vanoni, my sometimes condo-mate, is the trip leader. Lou Horwitz, our best skier, says the early season snow at Winter Park is fine. Sorayya will drive to Houston tomorrow to spend Thanksgiving at Pari's. We spent Saturday night there two weeks ago when we attended the *Encyclopaedia Iranica* 2004 Gala at River Oaks Country Club, a black-tie evening well worth the $350 per plate price tag. Sorayya looked great, and I always feel great in a tuxedo. We bid to $45,000 on a car being auctioned, but lost out to someone who bid $60,000, and then redonated the car for a second auction. CNN's Rudi Bakhtiar served as master of ceremonies. Ehsan Yarshater presided over the proceedings. When I left the house this morning, our new kitchen was nearing completion. By 8 o'clock, the granite guy, the carpenter and his assistant, and the plumber were already hard at work. The refrigerator should have gotten there early in the afternoon. Sorayya has yet to decide on a wall color. I just called Eliza whose voice almost didn't get to my ears with all of the Jack and Gracie noise around her. None of that tumult ever seems to fluster "Mom(my)." I've tried to reach Sorayya, but no luck. ✍

In early December, Sorayya cancelled our subscription to *Time Magazine* minutes after she heard whom *Time* had chosen as 2004

Man of the Year. Everyone had a grand time at Christmas on Perry Lane. Next year we'll spend Christmas in Santa Fe and Albuquerque. 2005 CE equaled Year 1425/6 AH in the Muslim calendar and Year 5765/6 in the Hebrew Calendar, and sixty-five in mine.

In early January 2005, news reached us that Leonardo Alishan, the brightest star in our Persian Studies program over the years, had died. Teary-eyed, I sat down to write a remembrance of him for DMES colleagues.

Leonardo Paul Alishan (1950–2004), the Armenian/Iranian/American poet, literary critic, short story writer, and academic, died at the age of 53 in a housefire at his Salt Lake City home in the early morning hours of January 9, 2005. His death received notice in *The Salt Lake City Tribune*, on Salt Lake City's ABC television affiliate news programs, and in the Armenian American press.

Born and raised in Tehran, Leonardo Alishan completed an undergraduate degree in English literature at The National University of Iran in Tehran and began graduate study at The University of Texas at Austin in 1973. Alishan completed M.A. and Ph.D. degrees in Comparative Literature, majoring in English and Persian literatures. He wrote his doctoral dissertation on "Major Trends in Modern Persian Poetry."

While at UT, Alishan also pursued an interest in writing poetry. He first published poems in Austin magazines and later in national magazines. He wrote poetry in Armenian, Persian, and English, more in English as time went on.

In 1978, Alishan joined the faculty of the Department of Foreign Languages at The University of Utah, where taught English and Comparative Literatures for twenty years, received several teaching awards during those years, and had a local and even national reputation as a dynamic public speaker.

Throughout the 1980s, Alishan contributed seminal critical articles on Mehdi Akhavan-e Sales, Jalal Al-e Ahmad, Forugh Farrokhzad, Ahmad Shamlu, Nader Naderpur, and Ahmad Shamlu to such UT-produced volumes as *Major Voices in Contemporary Persian Literature* (1980), *Iranian Society: An Anthology of Writings by Jalal Al-e Ahmad* (1982), *Literature and Society in Iran* (1982), *The Sociology of Persian Literature* (1985), *False Dawn: Persian Poems by Nader Naderpour* (1986), and *Forugh Farrokhzad A Quarter-Century Later* (1988). In addition, Alishan regularly presented papers at national conferences and at a series of poetry and Persian literature conferences at UT Austin. By the end of the 1980s, Alishan was arguably the best known Iranian-born critic of modernist Persian poetry in America.

In the 1990s, Alishan turned his attention more to poetry and published his poetry in many magazines. He also published two volumes of poetry: *Dancing Barefoot through Broken Glass* (1991) and *Through a Dewdrop: A Collection of Haiku, Tanka, and Senru* (2002). His poems dealt with love, romance, family, and the poet's Armenian heritage. He also published short stories.

The score of entries under his name at Google.com suggest the breadth and richness of his contributions to poetry and fiction, while those poems and stories themselves testify to the warmth, vitality, sensitivity, and distinctive artistic talent of their author. Alishan is survived by his ex-wife Neli, whom he married in Austin in 1976, and three children.

On February 9, in response to a request for a five-year review of the Office of the Dean of Liberal Arts under Reginald Applegate's stewardship, I wrote the following letter to the Committee for the Dean Evaluation of the College of Liberal Arts.

At your invitation, I am writing, first, to describe my perception of the administration by the Dean's Office of affairs in the Department of Middle Eastern Languages and Cultures/Middle Eastern Studies during the past five years and, second, to request that your Committee recommend to the Dean's Office specific actions to improve DMES.

As to my first aim in writing, this letter describes personal perceptions directly and indirectly, directly in this paragraph and the next several paragraphs and indirectly through implications behind requests in subsequent, numbered paragraphs. I have no information about, or view of, the Dean's overall performance as Dean of the College of Liberal Arts during the past five years and do not know how much responsibility his office bears for the what happened in the Department of Middle Eastern Languages and Cultures (= MELC) from 1999 to its dissolution in May 2002 and what has transpired in the Department of Middle Eastern Studies (= DMES) from the summer of 2002 to February 2005. For that matter, the Dean's handling of Aman Attieh's lectureship in Arabic, the hiring of Mohammad Mohammad, the promotion of one junior Islamic Studies colleague, the special support and voice given another junior Islamic Studies colleague, the public and humiliating dismissal of Robert Stofberg from his position as MELC Chair, and the private and presumably humiliating threats to Peter Abboud concerning the Dean's demand that Professor Abboud add First-year Arabic to his teaching load, among other situations and actions, are mostly a matter of public record, from articles and letters in *The Daily Texan* to departmental correspondence and depositions, including the Dean's, in the "Aman Attieh vs. The University of Texas" litigation. In cited regards, questions about judgment, timing, and tact arose. Had the Dean dismissed Professor Stofberg from his position as MELC Chair as soon as evidence of the latter's *ad hominem* administrative style and incompetence surfaced, MELC's history would have played out differently. MELC might not have witnessed the wholesale departure of graduate students and the effective end to its graduate degree programs. MELC faculty might not have resorted to routine submission of complaints to the College of Liberal Arts and other offices, with consequent souring of intradepartmental relations. MELC might have developed a departmental philosophy or departmental policies or, at least, passed some sort of baton to DMES so that its successor department might have felt it didn't have to keep looking over its shoulder.

Presumably lacking a charge from the College of Liberal Arts, the Department of Middle Eastern Studies has to date neither applied admissions standards for entering graduate students nor defined expectations in terms of degree requirements for degree-seeking graduate students (students receive degrees in a language area without competence in reading, listening, and/or speaking in that language and write dissertations acknowledged as lacking appropriate discipline-specific focus or rigor). DMES has no clear lines of communication or responsibility between and among faculty and staff, no written or institutionalized policies on any faculty or student matter (except for a recent decision, for which it offered no written rationale in response to at least one submitted position paper to the contrary, not to allow students to earn letter grades through the Credit by Examination procedure).

If a senior DMES faculty person talks about things other than course matters in class or teaches from notes from years past, DMES has no charge from the College of Liberal Arts which would result in a policy with which to respond. DMES does nothing to achieve relative equity in faculty teaching loads, some faculty members obliged to teach three courses each semester, others two (DMES has stated that College of Liberal Arts policy states that differing conditions have obtained in different cases at the time of appointment to positions). With College of Liberal Arts encouragement, DMES expects some, but not all, senior faculty members in all languages to teach lower-division language courses. Lacking guidance from the College of Liberal Arts, DMES does not have a consistent or formal policy with respect to salary merit increase recommendations, and had no criteria after its first two-and-a-half years of operation to guide faculty deliberations in this regard. DMES does not include all tenure-track or even all tenured faculty or even all senior tenured faculty in all departmental deliberations relevant to those faculty's areas of teaching and research. Decisions in DMES concerning specific language programs can take place without input on the part of faculty who know and teach languages in question.

DMES has two tenured faculty members hired to teach Arabic Linguistics, only one of whom teaches courses in the discipline, there being no mandate from the College of Liberal Arts that DMES offer a full range of courses in Arabic Linguistics. DMES has two different First-year Arabic courses, different in materials, methods, and instructional objectives. DMES's Arabic program has needed another full-time Arabic language faculty member since 2001. DMES has had no regularly offered mainstream Arabic literature offerings since 1998. DMES has two different First-year Persian courses, different in materials, methods, and instructional objectives, one of which courses does not lead directly to Second-year Persian. Islamic Studies in DMES has no overall core humanities or social science focus or scope, perhaps in part both because of a lack of academic Islamic Studies training in its faculty and because of the departure of three of its faculty since the early 1990s. Hebrew Studies in DMES has had no regularly offered mainstream Hebrew literature offerings since 2000, while some Hebrew Studies faculty appear to view Hebrew and Jewish Studies as coterminous.

The language and literature programs in DMES have no standing in their fields in North America. Among its fifteen core language, literature, and culture faculty, DMES has only three faculty members with any standing around the world in their specific fields or disciplines. It would arguably take substantial improvement in four or five arenas for DMES to evolve into a mediocre humanistic enterprise within four or five years. But such improvement could arguably come with such actions, policies, and encouragement on the part of the College of Liberal Arts as the following.

Because MELC/DMES has routinely exhibited wariness and invoked suppositions about the views of the College of Liberal Arts as a necessary consideration before reaching almost any policy decision of or on its own, in neither the foregoing description nor the following recommendations do distinctions appear between what might seem strictly departmental matters and joint DMES–Liberal Arts matters. Moreover, if the College of Liberal Arts has charged DMES to develop policy or to take action relating to foregoing matters or following recommendations, not all tenured DMES faculty know about it. The historical and arguably continuing timidity of MELC/DMES to present its own case to the College without prior fretting about the reaction at the College of Liberal Arts clouds faculty ability to discern which matters properly relate to DMES policy-making and decision-taking.

(1) If the College of Liberal Arts could allow DMES to undertake a search for an established, well-known senior teacher-scholar (but not another person with a graduate degree from UT Austin), that addition to the faculty would both give DMES immediate visibility and encourage DMES colleagues to strive for excellence, especially in the area of research activity and productivity.

(2) If DMES immediately updates its brochures and web site information (with the help of competent technical writers), that might constitute both a first step toward needed definition of departmental programs and philosophy and a first step in a desirable public relations campaign.

(3) If the College of Liberal Arts charges DMES to establish admissions standards for incoming, degree-seeking graduate students, ending its practice of accepting applicants into its graduate degree programs who lack undergraduate degrees in the discipline they wish to pursue and who receive scores of 275, 375, and the like on the Verbal Section of the Graduate Record Examination, both the quality of DMES students and their writing would improve and the incidence of problems with graduate degree students would diminish (e.g., complaints, appeals, changes in supervisory committee membership, and threatened litigation).

(4) If the College of Liberal Arts and DMES would immediately agree to expert outside evaluations of its Arabic, Hebrew, Persian, and Turkish language programs, such a review would likely lead to improved instruction and instructional materials development therein. At least two DMES language faculty have been requesting such a review in Arabic and Persian since the fall of 1998. MELC/DMES and CMES rejected the request then and declined to act on it thereafter.

(5) A similar review, by the College of Liberal Arts, of research facilities, at least in Persian, would reveal that DMES cannot support serious gradu-

ate faculty or student research in the areas of Persian language, lexicography, linguistics, literature translation, and the like, because University library holdings have not kept up with developments in relevant fields, especially secondary and tertiary sources. For example, in order for the most basic work on Persian language subjects involving dictionary use and translation to take place at DMES, PCL would have to acquire 20–30 dictionaries published in Iran during the past fifteen years, dictionaries recommended in Persian classes to students but currently unavailable to them at UT. DMES has apparently abandoned the OALL practice of faculty preparation of library acquisitions requests which the department would then submit to the library bibliographer in question.

(6) If DMES informs all language faculty in specific language areas about policies respecting that language. . ., language instruction and student awareness of expectations in languages courses would likely improve.

(7) If DMES could establish language program policies to the effect that its language faculty make use exclusively of instructional materials designed for the specific student population in their language courses, that its language faculty establish communicative environments in their language class settings, that its language faculty use proficiency- and performance-based methodology in their language classes, and that its language faculty not allow native speakers of their languages to register for lower-division language courses, immediate marked improvement in DMES language courses would likely occur.

(8) If the College of Liberal Arts and DMES could find a way to involve all senior DMES faculty in deliberations about economic constraints and options, Liberal Arts and Middle Eastern Studies might catch up with similar colleges and departments elsewhere in America who have improved their research, equipment, fellowship, and student-employment opportunities, at least in Arabic and Persian, through proposal submissions and institutional involvement in major government-sponsored projects, amounting to millions of dollars for universities aware of and pursuing possibilities.

In dealing with perhaps its smallest and likely its least visible or reputable department, the College of Liberal Arts has presumably acted in good faith in its recommendations, appointments, and decisions since the founding of MELC/DMES in 1994. The College has presumably reached conclusions in its dealings with MELC/DMES through counsel with specific departmental faculty members and through study of reports, data, evaluations, and the like submitted by specific departmental faculty members. Unfortunately, the process didn't work in MELC and doesn't appear to be working in DMES. Each of the names. . .[twelve names]. . .has a story of misjudgment behind it. MELC/DMES tenure files have had problems, among them incompetent and incomplete files, charges of faculty misconduct, questions about authorship of faculty writing, and recommendations written by non-experts or persons junior to a faculty person in question.

✍ March 15, Journal entry, Fairfield Inn, Fairfield, Pennsylvania. Bean and ham soup, a half-carafe of BdeR Cabernet, duck, and salad at dusk, after skiing a third day at Ski Liberty, in an 18th-century inn and former Confederate Army Hospital. Sorayya's absence notwith-standing, another perfect time. I experimented with blades on the slopes today and concluded that I don't like rollerblading on snow. I had to snowplow on the stubby things all the way down a green run. Ski Liberty's four or five, 5–minute blue runs, and few other skiers mid-week, couldn't suit me better. I rest on the lift up and waste no time on the runs down. I tried night skiing for the first time last night, but much prefer daytime visibility and scenery. Jim drove up from Baltimore on Sunday and drove straight to work in Timonium this morning. We had a good time driving in the country, looking at an-tiques, eating at old places, and relaxing. I've decided to return to Jim's tomorrow afternoon. I've got a meeting at Language Research Center in Hyattsville on Friday and will fly home to Austin on Saturday at the end of a ten-day trip. The high points have been a two-day Persian Dictionaries Seminar at University of Baltimore, a dinner with both Georges, and this spring-break ski trip. ✍

✍ March 27, Journal entry, Perry Lane, Austin. The Society of Iranian-American Women in Austin put on its Annual Norooz Celebration at the Park Plaza Hotel last night. About 700 cheerful people attended. Hamid Forugh and his Ava Music Group were a big hit. Ditto for the dancers from UT's Iranian Students Academic and Cultural Association. I missed the annual Wednesday-Eve-before-New Year party at Zilker Park, which also draws many hundreds of people. Over the years, our Austin social life has gravitated more and more to Iranian-American activities and friends to the point where a loosely knit group of about thirty people–and I'm part of it because of Sorayya–throw parties. Our turn comes once every two or three months. We have a dinner invitation most weekends: mostly Iranian food, lively conversation, guests of all ages, Iranian music in the background, then eventually in the foreground, some dancing, and some serious vodka drinking. An altogether relaxing respite from an American world in which some of our acquaintances sometimes don't feel at home, and a temporary simulation of "back home" for Sorayya. We usually stay un-til midnight, knowing that revelers will carry on until two or three or four in the morning. The occasion for these get-togethers is usually the best possible occasion, just to get together and share time and its plea-surable passing. Between parties, Sorayya has almost daily Starbucks or Russell's or lunch dates with the other Sorayya, Touran, Sheila, et al. . . .And she'll get or make six or seven calls from the same people most days. We've often wondered if we could find such easy companionship and Iranian-American social life if we moved to Scottsdale or Baltimore. ✍

✍ April 22, Journal entry, Arcadia, Scottsdale. The Pahlavi monarchy didn't survive, despite American support. The Islamic Republic survived despite American opposition. The Pahlavi monarchy began in power politics. The Islamic Republic began with a plebiscite in the streets of Tehran on December 10 and 11, 1978. For me 1965–1967 and 1969–1973 had the same surprises in Mashhad and Tehran as Tehran had in the 1980s, not counting the war, for Azar Nafisi in *Reading Lolita in Tehran*. It's a good read. Academic Iranian(-American)s in The States find lots wrong with it, which its bestseller status may have something to do with. If Azar had had the experience of living as a single adult on her work income alone, she'd have found the surprising life in Tehran more surprising. ✍

The long requested external evaluation of Middle Eastern language programs, which Loya and Stofberg had persuaded a Liberal Arts Dean not to call for in December 1998, took place at the end of April. But it did not involve requested language class visits or a review of language course syllabi. Part of the June report by the external committee read:

> The language programs at UT are mostly academically oriented [i.e., achievement]. Increasingly, however, students study languages, and especially Middle Eastern languages, for professional purposes [i.e., proficiency skills]. . .[which call for] content-based and task-based instruction. . .faculty members in the Arabic Program and in the Persian Program do not frequently communicate with one another within each program [e.g., Esfahanpur does not communicate with Hillmann] and between the two programs. Nor does it appear that they often make major decisions via consensus in each program [e.g., decisions in Arabic take place without consulting Abboud]. The students are aware of this since they are the people who usually suffer most from this lack of communication.

✍ May 23, Journal entry, Bolton Hill, Baltimore. In my first experience with a mini-van, a Chrysler Town and Country, Sorayya and I drove from Baltimore to celebrate a Cape May birthday weekend with both Georges, Cathie, and Lynda. We guys played golf at the Cape May National Golf Course, and George M and I played tennis on Har-Tru at the Cape May Tennis Center. We dined at the Lafayette

Hotel, The Chalfonte Hotel grandly visible from the second floor foyer and walked on the beach at Cape May Point. Lynda and George S had brought Happy Hour fixings from Baltimore, which we much enjoyed in their room, the middle room in our three third-floor oceanfront rooms at The Stockton Motor Inn. The weather cooperated the whole weekend. We lost our way for a half-hour in New Jersey on the drive back and stopped for a late lunch at an old fashioned diner called Ye Olde Oak Diner across from a big old oak tree in Millville. In Baltimore, we've enjoyed Cirque du Soleil's *Varekai* show, the patio at 'b' on Bolton Hill three times, Tapas Teatro, Paul's at Inner Harbor, the movie *Crash*, walks around Bolton Hill, George M's birthday party at the farm, Nordstrom's, Helmand, UBaltimore and Pine Ridge golf driving ranges, and a Persian Fiction Seminar at University of Baltimore, Behrad teaching half the sessions. There are fun plans for the rest of the week, and home to Austin on Saturday after three weeks at Jim's. Sorayya agrees with me that life is good. ✍

On June 16, in the matter of Cause Number GN1–04059, "Aman Attieh, Plaintiff, v. University of Texas at Austin, Robert Stofberg, and Benjamin Loya, in their official and individual capacities, Defendants," The Third Court of Appeals at Austin, Travis County, Texas, produced their opinion, stating: "Because we agree with the University, we affirm the trial court's judgment." In response, Robert Notzon and Tony Dìaz filed an Appellant's Motion for Rehearing.

This ended the "Attieh v. UT" litigation. Because only the orchestration of things so that Aman Attieh couldn't interview for the new Arabic language position in the spring of 2000 had seemed demonstrably discriminative or retaliatory to me in legal terms, Attieh's failure to get a trial hadn't surprised me. At the same time, that failure didn't mean that she wasn't on target in her suspicions and allegations.

Moreover, Attieh's grievance submittal to EEOC and her law suit were themselves salutary events. They obliged Middle Eastern Studies faculty and administrators and College and University administrators to reflect on their own roles in the affair and to revisit behavior that some observers thought sexist, biased, discriminatory, or retaliatory. In practical terms, they had to spend hours and hours of their time reviewing and accounting for their own behavior. Attieh had forced them to take notice, likely leading them to make changes, if not in their thinking, at least in their official or public conduct toward women faculty in positions like hers, a colleague whom The University, behaving in non-academic and anti-intellectual ways, strove to denigrate in the process of defending itself.

At the end of the 2004–2005 academic year, Attieh did not reapply for her Senior Lecturer position at Rice University. She had never warmed to Houston and thought that her Arabic students at Rice didn't have the commitment to Arabic that her UT students had had. Over the summer, further review of Attieh's UT personnel dossier led to a recalculation of her employment, resulting in her qualifying for a 20–year retirement package. In September 2005, Attieh began teaching Arabic at Texas State University at San Marcos and at St. Edward's University in Austin.

Her bright enough academic future not withstanding, no legal or other action could return her to the classroom at her beloved University of Texas. No legal or other action could take back the words used to attack her from September 1998 through early 2003. Nothing could un-print the unwanted reports on her life and work in the local press. How unfeeling the faculty and administrative community had shown itself to be toward one of their own graduates, a woman who had dedicated twenty years of her professional life to their university.

As a single parent, whose husband had left her and her small daughter in Austin to fend for themselves, Attieh had a sometimes difficult life beyond the work place. During the First Gulf War, her daughter Angela, whose father's surname is Takriti, had to face anti-Arab sentiments at high school. Attieh also has had to help an ailing mother back in Lebanon. Attieh herself faced health issues. Among other travails, Attieh had to live for almost a year in an apartment because her house had developed mold. For her whole career at UT, Attieh never brought personal problems to work. Moreover, on the job she was as solicitous as anyone could be. She would help a colleague pack up and move. She visited colleagues at the hospital. She ran errands for colleagues. She kept in touch with everyone. She hosted dinner parties. Personal connections and relationships with students mattered to her. She put in long days at the office and taught long hours. She exuded commitment to Arabic language learning, to the approaches and methods and materials she used in her classes. Despite all of her energy and caring and commitment, six or seven colleagues had developed strong negative feelings about her and proved unfeeling in their deliberations about her future at UT.

That reaction of colleagues to her had much to do with Peter Abboud, whom some of those same faculty wished simply to bring down. According to her antagonists themselves, it also had to do with "principle." First, they argued that, as an untenured lecturer, Attieh should not serve as departmental Undergraduate Adviser. But both Yildiray Erdener, a lecturer at the time, and Monica Yaniv, a lecturer without a graduate degree, later served as Undergraduate Adviser. Second, at least one former Arabic Teaching Assistant filed a complaint of harassment and/or intimidation about Attieh. A similar complaint against Stofberg had counted for nothing in his career progress. Third, Attieh was demanding in some interactions with some departmental staff. Stofberg had demanded, without repercussion, the dismissal of a staff person at a faculty meeting, the while knowing that the staff person in question would be transcribing the audio recording of the meeting. Jacob Levy browbeat staff member Trudie Redding in my presence one afternoon. I intervened and told Levy that, if he didn't dare talk that way to me, he shouldn't talk that way to a staff person. Fourth, it was alleged that Attieh browbeat students, chief among them a graduate student whose allegations faculty opposed to Attieh accepted without question. Those same faculty members, after the student in question switched from Arabic to Hebrew Studies, voted to dismiss that same student from its Hebrew Studies program in large measure because of his allegedly objectionable behavior toward a female Hebrew Studies colleague. Fifth, colleagues who didn't know Arabic or Applied Linguistics alleged that Attieh's teaching materials and methods were out-of-date. Those same colleagues voiced no criticism of other language faculty colleagues who, unlike Attieh, weren't developing communicative environments in their classrooms (i.e., they were using English instead of the target language in class) and, unlike Attieh, were employing grammar-translation and audio-lingual methods and materials (instead of proficiency and performance materials and methods). Moreover, no one proposed censuring or penalizing one senior language faculty colleague famous since the mid-1970s for not preparing for class and for rarely staying on message once in class. Sixth, anti-Attieh colleagues observed that she had not published much. At the same time, at least two senior colleagues had published little since the late 1970s without facing criticism or consequences. Seventh, Attieh had refused to certify for credit Arabic study on the part of two CMES students who had taken a summer course at a program at a fellow Western Consortium of Middle Eastern Centers university. Attieh had recommended that those students not advance to the next level of Arabic at UT as a result of their inadequate performance on proficiency tests. Several years later, the summer language programs of the Western Consortium of Centers of Middle Eastern Studies, which just hadn't gotten results, grew moribund. The Consortium sponsored no single summer program in 2005 and announced no single program for 2006. Eighth, some colleagues accused Attieh of having an aggressive and sometimes abrasive personality. But, any aggressiveness or abrasiveness colleagues may have felt they observed in Attieh's behavior paled in comparison with the reputation of a senior colleague whose name was synonymous with abrasiveness, stubbornness, self-centeredness, and self-serving behavior for everyone in the Department from 1975 until 2000.

The facts are that Attieh was demanding and territorial as Coordinator of the Arabic Language Program, that she was demanding in her dealings with departmental staff, that she was authoritarian in chairing the departmental Course Committee, and that she presumed to advise or monitor Arabic literature specialist Walid Hamarneh and Islamic Studies specialist Khaled Abou El Fadl.

When given administrative responsibility, Attieh often behaved in ways that an outside observer might see as "Middle Eastern," natural in hierarchical environments in which individuals in authority behave as if they have authority. The firmness of her convictions about teaching methodology, for example, the importance of a communicative environment and exclusive focus on Modern Standard Arabic as the register of instruction, and her sense that the Arabic language should serve as an umbrella over such fields as Arabic Literature and Islamic Studies led her to involve herself verbally in discipline-specific and faculty-freedom arenas in which she didn't have requisite academic training or expertise.

With strong feelings about Arabic-related matters, Attieh often displayed impatience with others who held different views. She would often raise her voice. In such situations, I'd be remembering her good and indispensable work in Arabic and ease out of any confrontation to which a conversation might lead. Walid Hamarneh did the same thing.

In short, Aman Attieh was, as the saying goes, high maintenance. If she had understood how things operate in American business and that only people who can protect their own interests can afford to be high maintenance or aggressive, she might have chosen her battles judiciously or published more. Without tenure, she said what she thought, which those academics willing to do so usually start doing only after they have tenure. The fact that she was a woman perhaps made what wouldn't have seemed particular noteworthy or aggressive to other Middle Easterners and an Orthodox Jewish rabbi in a male faculty person's demeanor seem overly aggressive in Attieh's.

A home remodeling specialist who did work for Sorayya and me thinks Lebanese and Palestinian Arabs face with Israel the situation which Native Americans in America have vis-à-vis The United States of America. America and Israel have happened. Native Americans and Palestinians have no choice but to adjust and try to succeed in the new situation. Now, I don't share this view. But it reminds me of a potentially culture-specific issue with respect to responses by Attieh and Abboud to untoward and unfair things that have happened to them. Does the fact that they can't seem to put the past behind them relate to an arguably Arab cultural unwillingness to move beyond a past they couldn't control and embrace a present in which they can't rectify that past?

My view of the whole Attieh package was that she was worth the price. Our Department paid a stiff price between August 2001 and August 2006 by not having thought she was worth it. Our Arabic Language Program lost the place it once had on the national and international map. Moreover, nothing in Attieh's personal way of doing things offered a rationalization or justification for the behavior of Stofberg, Loya, Applegate, Fernea, Esfahanpur, and Copeland toward her. Three of the cited individuals are, in turn, in their own ways, much more high maintenance than Attieh. In two of those cases, the maintenance fee was arguably not worth the price.

The June 16, 2005 Appeals Court Opinion (posted online at pc07. com), closed the book on the Attieh versus Stofberg et al. matter in legal terms, but not in cultural terms. At the end of Chapter 11, I suggested arguably culture-specific dimensions to Ali Akbar Esfahanpur's actions and reactions to people and events in the story. Of course, Esfahanpur's Iranian(-American) role was only a voice in the chorus–which included two other Iranian-Americans–of a MELC/CMES anti-Arab drama, in which CMES Director Loya and MELC Chair Stofberg played the chief roles as representatives of an arguably specific and culture-specific Israeli(-American) or American Israeli-wanna-be orientation.

Benjamin Loya's role as CMES Director from 1995 to 2003 in what began happening to MELC's Arabic Studies program in September 1998 had a mostly private paper trail until his September 2002 deposition in "Attieh v. UT." In that deposition, Loya made arguably untrue statements with respect to documented actions on his part vis-à-vis Arab colleagues. He also revealed therein that he had apparently applied different standards in writing about Arab colleagues than about colleagues in other areas.

Loya had arrived at UT Austin particularly sensitive to questions about his ability as a Jewish Israeli-American to function adequately as an Ottoman or Arab World historian. As my guest at lunch during his first days at Texas, he expressed bitter feelings about Paul English, whose questions about his appointment had reached the pages of *The New York Times*. We never had lunch again. First, having hosted that first lunch–hospitality, as my mother-in-law used to say, is a two-way street–, I would have lunched with Loya again only if he reciprocated. Second, I took umbrage at Loya's comments about Paul English, whose concerns about a Syrian Jewish Israeli-American serving as an Arab historian at The University of Texas proved incorrect only politically. Third, Loya told me early in his tenure as CMES Director that he found it almost impossible to work with Peter Abboud. To that statement I replied: "You're from the Arab Middle East. You speak Arabic. Peter Abboud is from the Arab Middle East. He speaks Arabic. Peter Abboud is older than you and senior to you in academe. You don't need a degree in rocket science to choose the verbiage and style which can make things work between CMES and DMES." Loya chose to do it by working around Abboud, talking behind the latter's back, communicat-

201

ing constantly with the College of Liberal Arts, consulting with members of MELC's Hebrew Studies faculty, and making MELC language program concerns issues in the context of the Western Consortium of Middle East Centers. Having no authority over any MELC faculty or programs, Loya's retaliatory actions smacked more of atmosphere poisoning and weaseling than legally reprehensible behavior. But, then, as I have just said, his paper trail didn't often cross my desk until I saw his December 1998 letter to the Dean. In that letter, he accuses two people of wrongdoing in 1997 and 1998 with whom he had no contact in 1997 and 1998. The chief bases for his groundless accusations in that letter were statements by Stofberg.

The documentary record of Robert Stofberg's behavior and actions from September 1998 through mid-May 2002 cannot have failed to cause concern on the part of the UT Office of Legal Affairs and the Attorney General's staff representing UT Austin. From my first review of the 1998–2002 years to the final stages of putting this book together, I, who know little about the law as a result of following heart instead of head in the mid-1960s, wonder why UT Austin couldn't have said that Stofberg's actions, contrary in a score of situations to University policy and regulations, constituted behavior for which the University should not bear responsibility. In other words, if Stofberg violated his contract with the University as MELC Chair, he could or should have answered on his own for such actions. But, as one Middle Eastern Studies faculty member opined, Stofberg's yarmulke may have given him a free pass. Parenthetically, some sort of free pass may make sense for Native Americans, African Americans, and Jewish Americans for various and obvious reasons, but not at the expense of innocent parties.

Stofberg's multifaceted answer should have consisted of: (1) a written apology to Aman Attieh for any actions on his part which she construed as harassment, discrimination, and/or retaliation; (2) voluntary enrollment in a gender-sensitivity course; (3) participation in lower-division Hebrew language teaching and encouragement of Hebrew Studies colleague Jacob Levy to do the same; (4) a written apology to Peter Abboud for any negative comments which Stofberg made to MELC colleagues behind Abboud's back; and (5) completion of a reading list on Arab cultures and the religion of Islam.

Stofberg made at least twenty demonstrably false statements in his deposition in "Attieh v. UT" and made multiple accusations of misbehavior on the part of MELC colleagues while knowing he had no evidence to support those accusations. It bears repeating that at a departmental Executive Committee meeting in April 2001, Stofberg dismissed the application of a female candidate for the position of Assistant Professor of Arabic Literature because he thought her behavior too assertive and aggressive for a woman. It bears repeating that Stofberg made untrue statements in his deposition about his research writing productivity between late 1974 and 2003.

Growing up in what I'm guessing was likely a culturally monolithic environment in New York City and seeing the world first through the prism of undergraduate education at Yeshiva College, Stofberg presumably had either a chip on his shoulder with respect to the world beyond his or suspicion about that world. In light of this, one wonders what could have possessed him to choose Texas as his life-time home, a place where he might naturally behave toward goyim as he has and where he might often talk about suing people. Ironically, he faced the only lawsuit which MELC/DMES brought on itself. Moreover, he could easily have faced other law suits brought by Abboud, Zilla Goodman, the unnamed female candidate for the Arabic literature position, Walid Hamarneh, Seth Wolitz, and me.

Litigation, however, never tempted me. You can't sue a male mosquito for biting! Moreover, litigation involves an arena in which parties to it have no real control, and doesn't suit what I do when I want things my way: write and talk freely. As long as I can get words like these in *From Classroom to Courtroom* to the people I want to hear or read them, I need no other forum.

But a question about litigation remains: How did Middle Eastern Studies at The University of Texas get embroiled in it? To my mind, the Arab-Israeli conflict brought us from classrooms to a courtroom. Stofberg didn't take particular offense at what Annie Menzel alleged he had said. He took offense at her analysis of life in Israel. Stofberg didn't know enough to think that methodological or other academic problems existed or didn't exist in the Arabic language program or that Walid Hamarneh had or had not developed a viable Arabic literature program. But he did know that Abboud, Attieh, and Hamarneh presumably disapproved of the Jewish State of Israel and believed that Palestinians had a right to live not only in the West Bank and the Gaza strip, but also in an Israel neither exclusively nor primarily Jewish. Stofberg and Loya had shown unmitigated approval of Kamil Riyadh until word reached MELC and CMES that, behind closed classroom doors, Riyadh, when asked, was telling students of his support for Muslims in Israel and around it. Loya and Stofberg thereafter changed their minds and voted for Riyadh's dismissal from the department. It would further appear that university administrators at Texas cannot include pro-Arab or pro-Palestinian opinions in their idea portfolios, likely and partly out of wariness about possible charges of anti-Semitism.

The Israeli-Arab conflict had now, albeit thirty or forty years late, become part of Middle East faculty discourse at Texas. Students should hope that the Arab-Israeli conflict and debate remain center-stage in Middle Eastern Studies at Texas and lead Middle East academics to argue their cases with one another instead of trying to win their battles behind the scenes and behaving in public as if no conflict exists.

Of course, as the saying goes, I don't have a horse in this race. Having a horse in this race can lead to the pluses and minuses readers like me sense on almost every page in Thomas Friedman's *From Beirut to Jerusalem*, who spent years in Lebanon, Israel, and Palestine. As for me, I've never studied Judaism or the history of territory where Israel now exists. I've never studied any of the Hebrew Bible except for The Book of Genesis and Psalms, which I teach in world literature courses. Any study I've done of the Arabic language, Arabic literature, the *Koran*, and Islam, I've done in order to increase my familiarity with the Persian language, Persian literature, and Iranian art and culture.

In my view, the Arab-Israeli conflict does not rage in Israel and neighboring lands because Israelis are oppressors or because Palestinians are terrorists. Things have happened with the result that many Palestinians have lost property, homes, wealth, and dignity. Identifiable oppressors didn't cause the desperate situations of many Palestinians. The situation caused the situation. Jews who settled in the region wanting to become citizens of a Jewish Israel pursued dreams in good faith. Their success meant failure for many Arabs. Annie Menzel thinks of Christian European settlers vis-à-vis Native Americans when she thinks about Jewish Israelis vis-à-vis Christian and Muslim Palestinians. The good-faith settling of North America by those European settlers brought great harm to an indigenous population, just as the settling of Palestine by Jewish European settlers brought great harm to the indigenous population. Those Europeans obviously can't and shouldn't leave either place. But they have to make things right for displaced, dispossessed indigenous peoples. Making things right means, first of all, establishing an inclusive society with equal rights for all citizens.

Common sense should tell even literal-minded religious people that The Hebrew Bible does not give any people a special deed to a specific land. Judaism and Islam are both Abrahamic religions, Ishmael entering the world before Israel. For that matter, if Judaism did not have the precept that a person is Jewish by virtue of having a Jewish mother, rather than by virtue of having a Jewish father, Ishmael, son of a Jewish father and an Egyptian mother, and all of Ishmael's descendants would presumably qualify as Israeli citizens according to the Law of Return.

For a believer in the twenty-first century, the Holy Land, to which no one has a Biblical or Koranic birthright, has to be a place where believers can go whenever they want and live if they can, but not a place where they have special rights all year round. Similarly, the Saudi Arabians will eventually have to allow an international coalition to maintain the hajj sites in that country. Jerusalem should have a similar administration.

The land south of Lebanon and west of Syria and Jordan and northeast of Egypt, including the Sinai Peninsula, could comprise one country, with all of the people now living there having equal citizenship and attendant rights in that country. People who used to live there and who want to return there would have the right to do so. The new country, a secular republic, would have two national languages, Arabic and Hebrew. The country would strive to create an atmosphere for visitors and citizens like that in Beirut in the years before June 1967. The new country would welcome all sorts of personal religiosity in its people. But no religious group would have such control over any communities as to oblige other people to change their behavior because of a particular religious majority.

Let's suppose two hypothetical happenstances. First, the American government ceases all aid and support to Israel and the people in the territory south of Lebanon, west of Syria and Jordan, and northeast of Egypt, including the Sinai Peninsula. Second, the people in this defined region have to reach an accommodation without warfare or other coercive force. Let's suppose that America and other governments resume aid and support to the resulting political entity.

If I had a horse in this race, I'd likely not think or write the preceding naive paragraphs. But that's what humanistic academics do some of the time, behave toward texts and ideas as if, in the classroom or in print, they don't have a horse in the race or that they have two or three or all of the horses in the race. Or they have no qualms about criticizing one or more or all of the horses in the race or about criticizing the race itself.

Because UT's Arabic language program would have improved from 2001 through 2005 if it had one more full-time instructor, the Arab-Israeli and related conflicts shortchanged Arabic students at Texas during those years. Texas's Arabic language program would have improved if it had had the same standards in 2005 as it had in the 1990s. But Arab-Israeli and other politics wouldn't allow that. UT's Arabic Studies program would improve if its tenured faculty members had the same opportunities to teach their specialties as do the two most senior faculty in Hebrew Studies. If some people at the departmental and college level would stop thinking that they have only one horse in the race, these improvements could happen almost overnight.

On October 6 (2005), during a brief conversation in the DMES photocopy room, Mohammad Mohammad mentioned that "Judith" had told him that Notzon and Attieh were planning to "go after" him before the Appeals Court turned down their appeal. I replied that I hadn't heard that and didn't think it made sense. After all, Mohammad hadn't done anything to Attieh. Mohammad added that it didn't matter now since it was all over. As he said this, I was removing printouts of a draft of *From Classroom to Courtroom* from the office printer. The pages in hand, I said to Mohammad that I didn't think it was over yet.

On October 17, I received the following undated and unsigned memo from the Center for Middle Eastern Studies.

> Enclosed please find your invoice for personal copying during AY 04–05. Charges: 6¢ per copy, 3¢ if using your own paper. Next year (AY 05–06) we will be charging 8¢ per copy. Thanks!
> Personal Copies made in AY 04–05: 1/26/04–9/20/05. . .Michael Hillman Michael Hillman Michael Hillman Michael Hillman Michael

Hillman Michael Hillman. . .[name cited 55 times in columns with dates and numbers of photocopies]. . .Totals 9668 pages. . .$579.84.

The next day, I sent a check to DMES/CMES, along with the bill and a note requesting that DMES/CMES check computer files and elsewhere to make certain my surname, misspelled fifty-five times in the photocopying bill, appears correctly spelled everywhere!

On October 26, Peter Abboud paid a visit to WMB 5.146. Every week or two we have a chat, which invariably includes rehashing on his part of departmental history, which has unfortunately, yet understandably, stayed on his mind. He has said more than once that it stays on his mind, and that he thinks about it incessantly outside of class, in part because he lives alone, which means he takes work home mentally. At home another life doesn't await him. His trips to Dallas to visit his daughter and her family–Peter has three grandchildren–and his long drives north to Ann Arbor to consult with colleagues on Arabic grammar and to Rochester (MN) to see his brother, and his trips to the Arab Middle East, are likely the only times he leaves the department behind. He loves driving.

During this visit, we got talking about Peter's acquiescence to the demand in 2001 that he add a First-year Arabic language course to his teaching load. He told me that, in retrospect, his acquiescence was likely cultural in origin, extending back to a morning in late April 1948. On that day, the young teenager Peter Abboud set out with his three brothers, mother, and father, an uncle, and two aunts, along with one aunt's husband and the latter's two brothers and a sister, in a three-car caravan from Jaffa for a new exilic life in Cairo. What happened to orchards and land belonging to his mother and her family, Peter doesn't know. Peter's father, who spoke four or five languages, had served as a customs official in the Mandate State of Palestine. Peter recalls that they fled in fear that the fate of Deir Yassin would visit them if they stayed in Jaffa.

✍ October 31, Journal entry, On Southwest Flight 315, over West Texas. Five exhilarating days with Elizabeth *et famille*. I left Austin at 7 am on Thursday and reached 6412 East Calle Rosa, only a fifteen-minute taxi ride from Sky Harbor Airport, by 8:30 am Arizona time. I then met one-week-old James Maxmilian "Max" Garrett, as peaceful and agreeable a newborn as ever made. Jack attends Camelback Desert

Ridge School five mornings a week. Last week's letter for learning was "I." Gracie attends Temple Solel Pre-School three mornings a week. When Sorayya and I picked her up on Thursday, she insisted on carrying the tote bag of everyday stuff for school which parents bring, almost as tall as she is, from the school door to the car. Invariably up at dawn and usually without much sleep, Elizabeth fixes breakfast for Jack and Gracie, and then gets them ready for school. In the background, a washing machine or drier whirrs or hums, all day it seems. Then, she gives Max his morning feeding. He graciously falls asleep again. Sorayya, who arrived to help the day before Max arrived, did the driving to and from school most days during her two weeks with Elizabeth, and grocery shopping once a day. Eliza often orders groceries online. They arrive within a couple of hours at no extra charge. Sorayya and I had three hours alone together during my five days there, which we spent mostly apart shopping at Fashion Square Mall on Saturday. We also sneaked in a breakfast on Friday at Le Grand Orange after dropping Jack off at school. Once or twice a day, I walked to Old Town along the canal, the morning walk to buy newspapers. Friday night Jeff took me to a Phoenix Suns basketball game. Gracie's birthday party took place yesterday. We were twelve or so grownups and eight or nine, well-behaved, happy children. Eliza served not so good delivery pizza, a light and not too sweet store-bought white cake with pink frosting, balloons, assorted snacks, and party favors. The children sat at a long children's table on a patio out back. I talked sports with Ron and this and that with Bret and Allyson, and children with Robin. In the afternoon before the party, Lisa Hines called. I answered, there being no one else home except for Max and his babysitter, and we had a good chat. Gracie hugged me, ran to me, and talked to me all the time the last two days. On Friday, we took her to a park to swing, ride a train, and take a ride on a Merry Go Round. Jack was his usual articulate self. He and I went to the movies together yesterday, a clay cartoon *Wallace & Gromit: Curse of the Were-Rabbit* film for kids. Jack liked it, although the puns, allusions to other movies, and some scary violence seemed a bit much for a four-year-old. We shared a big bag of popcorn and a sipped a large cup of lemonade. We are at ease with one another. Jack likes and gets jokes. "Mike, are you being serious?" He listens to explanations and definitions of new words. He goes to bed willingly, and much enjoys the "book party" which Eliza or Jeff host on Gracie's bed every night. Gracie can add information at book-page-turning, sometimes before Jack predicts what the next page will hold. I hosted the book party one night. One of the books they chose was a serious bird book, and I didn't know enough just to read the first sentence in each paragraph. Halfway through the book, both of them started laughing and slid off the bed and ran to the family room to say goodnight to everybody. Sorayya and I can't figure out how we'll orchestrate things to be nearer to Elizabeth, Jeff, and our three hopes for the future. We have free Southwest Airlines tickets most of the time and a Companion Pass for Sorayya. But I'm selfishly hesitant to spend time in Scottsdale when mountains elsewhere have snow on them. Both of us have a difficult time outdoors in the long Arizona summer. ✍

✍ November 26, Journal entry, Keystone Village, Keystone, Colorado. The sunny first day here I didn't feel coordinated or confident. The just as sunny second day I was tired by lunchtime. Yesterday, I felt as sunny as the sky, but still stopped at noon. My NASTAR race time was 35.5 seconds, not quite twice as slow as the pacesetter's. Today, cloudy and with snow flurries, I felt good and am looking forward to Santa Fe in December. Stillness. Grandeur. Expanse. Fresh air. Whiteness. Solitude. Friendly gravity. Self-indulgent risk and fear. Accomplishment. Look back up the mountain. Endorphins. Appetite. No mosquitoes. ✍

On December 19, we began a familiar journey, Austin to Coleman, Post, Lubbock, Santa Rosa, and Santa Fe. Four days at El Dorado Hotel on the square in Santa Fe, two days of skiing on the one blue run open at Santa Fe Ski Area, and then three days at Hacienda Garrett in Albuquerque with Karen and Ted, and Jack, Gracie, and Max, and their parents. Jim flew from Baltimore to Albuquerque to join us there for three days. On the 28th, no good snow nearby, we drove back to Austin.

I brought the manuscript of *From Classroom to Courtroom* on the trip to look it over if I found time. I didn't.

Chapter 13

2006–2007

"The UT administration has a duty to ask,
outside the context of a courtroom,
whether it did something wrong."
DailyTexanOnline.com, 2 June 2004

Everything that has happened and happens in our Department of
Middle Eastern Languages/Studies has taken place and takes place in
multiple contexts, the most important the Middle East, almost the
only region in the world with a name that relates a region to Western
empires. The area is presumably "Middle" or "Near" in relation to
London. People talk these days about East Asia, Southeast Asia, South
Asia, Central Asia, but not "West Asia" or "Southwest Asia." Some
Middle East observers, perhaps taking a cue from the Hebrew Bible,
may consider naming a sign of control or ownership. Moreover, such
terms as South Asia and Central Asia do not bring to mind a social
or cultural monolith. No one talks about a Southeast Asian culture.
But, people talk about the Middle East as if it constituted an entity, as
if Iranians and Egyptians shared something, as if Iraqi Sunnite Kurds
and Shi'ite Muslim Iranians shared something, as if peoples speaking
Arabic shared much more than New Zealanders and Americans do.

Our department, whose name speaks to Western bias, studies peoples who speak Arabic, Hebrew, Persian, and Turkish. But we don't
study what people have written in Arabic about the Summer 2006
War in South Lebanon. We don't read or talk about what the Kurds in
Turkey say about their lives. We don't mourn the scores of Iraqi civilians who die in the streets of Iraq most days these days, or American
military men and women who lose their lives there some days as well. In
early February 2006, a funeral in Pflugerville for an Iranian-American
soldier who had died in Iraq attracted a thousand Iranian-American
mourners who didn't know him or his family. More Americans have lost
their lives in Afghanistan and Iraq than lost their lives on September

11, 2001. Three hundred times more innocent Iraqis have lost their lives in Iraq than innocent people lost their lives on September 11. In our department, we don't ponder the fact that retaliation against Al-Qa'eda has proven more deadly to people in countries which America has invaded than Al-Qa'eda's day of attacks in America. Texts on life in Tajikistan or the return of the Taliban to power in parts of Afghanistan don't turn into language lessons in our department. In our department, foreign-born colleagues, nursemaids more loving than mothers, mostly don't criticize American foreign policy out loud. In our department, people don't talk about official Iran as if it had a story with two sides.

Hebrew Studies colleague Avraham Zilkha, echoing Benjamin Netanyahu and Simon Peres, calls Iranian president Mahmoud Ahmadinezhad a "clown" and cites "Jewish community paranoia" in the same breath. By the latter he says he means Jewish expectation of a Hitler in every generation, Ahmadinezhad today's Hitler.

From some Iranian perspectives–not including Ruhollah Khomeini's–, a distinction may exist between Jewish Israelis and Jewish Iranians (and other Jews). Some Iranians say they aren't anti-Jewish. Most educated Iranians in Iran, who may or may not know any Jews, are anti-Israel. They say that their anti-Israel sentiments aren't anti-Semitic. The American celebrity attorney Alan Dershowitz allows that criticism of Israel per se is not anti-Semitic, but that disapproval of the existence of the Jewish State of Israel is anti-Semitic. If the same Jewish population lived in the country of Israel and if as many non-Jewish Palestinians also lived there and if the nation's constitution privileged no Jewish, Muslim, or Christian group and no Indo-European, Turkic, or Semitic group, no Iranian government, some Iranians say, would have anti-Israeli sentiments. The Iranian government would then presumably exhibit anti-Jewish sentiments no different from the senseless anti-Jewish sentiments part of life in France and America. In any case, even anti-Islamic Republic Iranians point out that American investigative reporter Mike Wallace got outdone by so-called "clown" Ahmadinezhad in August 2006, just as Ruhollah Khomeini had outdone Wallace in Paris in 1978.

As for the Hitler comparison, some Iranians point out that a Muslim Iran never has assaulted the West, as Germany did before and after Hitler came to power. Iran has no expansionist agenda, as Hitler's

Germany did. Some Iranians may pride themselves on putative Indo-European ethnicity, but nothing in the agenda of the Islamic Republic of Iran cites that view as significant. American military forces killed more innocent Iranians in one missile strike against one Iranian airliner in June 1988 than Iran has ever killed Americans. America and Israel supported Saddam Hussein's Iraq in its 1980–1988 war against Iran, a war which resulted in the loss of hundreds of thousands of Iranian lives.

The President of the Islamic Republic of Iran notes that America and Israel assert a right to a nuclear arsenal and assert that Iran does not have such a right. Ahmadinezhad rejects America's right to legislate Iran's nuclear program. Official Americans think Ahmadinezhad's controversial speeches on the Holocaust and Israel simple-minded. He–who questions the fact of the Holocaust merely to push people's buttons–asks why he can't question a piece of history. He asks why this piece of history is sacred and not other pieces. He then wonders, if the Holocaust is as important as Europeans and Americans say they think it is, shouldn't they assuage their guilt by giving Israelis a home? He wonders what the Muslim Middle East did to have to house Israel? (He seems not to know that, long planned and in development before World War II, Israel would have come into existence without the Holocaust, but may have otherwise lacked the intensity of European emigration and the intensity of British and American support.)

But little talk of Iran, Lebanon, Palestine, Iraq, or Afghanistan emanates from DMES's offices or echoes up and down its two corridors. Almost everyone behaves there as if the Arab-Israeli conflict didn't exist there. Failure to acknowledge and deal academically with that conflict may hinder the Department's efforts to reach mediocrity as a group–only its Arabic program has always had above-mediocre status–and then beyond in the foreseeable future.

In addition, effects of Middle Eastern Studies versus Arabs Attieh and Abboud won't dissipate until the department's Arabic program, our largest, has more faculty members than does Hebrew Studies. In the meantime, most departmental colleagues behave as if the Middle Eastern Studies conflict years never happened. If they hadn't happened or if we forgot them, we wouldn't have to ponder our behavior in them. If anyone in DMES should happen to read *From Classroom to*

Courtroom, it won't facilitate letting bygones be bygones. More significantly, bygones can't be bygones because the fallout from the Middle Eastern Languages Studies conflict years has taken a toll.

Upon Larry Faulkner's retirement announcement as UT President, both Reginald Applegate and Arnold Pederson put their hats in the UT presidential ring. The Middle Eastern Studies conflict contributed, perhaps decisively, to their failed campaigns for that office. Applegate thereupon left Texas for Nebraska! Removed from his Provost position, Pederson returned to teaching in Economics. Benjamin Loya, CMES Director and first DMES Chair and an anti-Abboud/Attieh co-ring-leader, returned to the History Department in 2004 where, at the earliest he'll have spent twenty years in academe before promotion to Full Professor. CMES faculty member and minor anti-Abboud/Attieh figure Jonathan Copeland left UT for Boise! Illness forced retired CMES faculty member and behind-the-scenes anti-Attieh/Abboud voice Elizabeth Fernea to faraway sidelines. The dismissal of anti-Attieh/Abboud co-ringleader Robert Stofberg from the departmental Chair position in mid-2002 took away his pulpit and returned him to windowless "Life in Ancient Israel."

Peter Abboud, who might have become a casualty in the Middle Eastern Languages/Studies conflict, survived, in part because his enemies and detractors limped from the battlefield. If and when he can let the unpleasant past go, he'll stand as a victorious survivor, his national reputation, teaching career and popularity intact, and his forthcoming *Advanced Modern Standard Arabic* and recasting of *Elementary Modern Standard Arabic*, both under contract with Cambridge University Press, crowning achievements. At dinner together in late October 2006, over ribs and a bottle of Australian Shiraz at Artz Ribs on South Lamar Boulevard, Peter expressed pleasant surprise at his new teaching schedule of two courses each semester, two courses of his own choosing. He also admitted that what happened to Applegate, Loya, Stofberg, and Copeland was a relief to him. Ever gracious, Peter had included in his guest list for a birthday party his daughter Ruth had thrown for him at Green Pastures in July 2006 even those Middle Eastern Languages colleagues who did not stand up to Applegate/Loya/Stofberg from 1998 onward. But the Middle Eastern Studies conflict did have its casualties.

Arabic Literature specialist Walid Hamarneh, the first, has emerged as a victor among departmental casualties. Hamarneh left UT for the University of Western Ontario and later left UWO for a position as Arabic Section Head at Swarthmore College, responsible for a consortium Arabic program at Swarthmore, Haverford, and Bryn Mawr. He also directed a successful intensive summer Levantine Arabic Course at University Towers in Austin for Persepolis Institute from 2002 through 2006.

A second casualty, Hebrew Literature specialist Zilla Goodman left UT for a private Jewish secondary school in North Carolina and then reportedly moved to Colorado. She understandably chose not to keep communicating with former UT colleagues, a loss for me.

Turkish Studies colleague Yildiray Erdener stands as a third casualty. He had passively supported Loya and Stofberg in their anti-Abboud/Attieh campaign, only to discover that his acquiescence counted for nothing at promotion time, when he did not get effective DMES/CMES support.

A fourth casualty, whose support of CMES/DMES against Abboud and Attieh gained him their support for two years and then rejection, Kamil Riyadh left UT in 2003 reportedly for a state university in New Mexico. As of 2006–2007, Riyadh's name reportedly appeared in a faculty list at a historically black university in Louisiana.

A fifth casualty, more for the Arabic language program than for him, was former Arabic Assistant Instructor Chaouki Moussa, a successful businessmen alongside his academic employment during the 1994–2000 years. After discovering that his support of Abboud and Attieh and the latter's bid for the new Arabic position in 2000 meant that Mohammad Mohammad, who got that position, wouldn't have a reason to invite him to continue as an Assistant Instructor, Moussa subsequently concentrated on his business career. Along with Moussa, other first-rate graduate students of Persian and Arabic whose student careers suffered as a result of actions by Applegate, Stofberg, and Loya, likely count as a sixth sort of casualty, again a loss for DMES, if not for the students, who have moved on to good careers.

The seventh and chief casualty, Aman Attieh continues to teach. From 2004 to mid-2007, she taught Arabic language courses at Texas State University in San Marcos and an occasional Arabic or Arab

Culture course at St. Edward's University in Austin. In the summer of 2007, she joined Hamarneh in the Swarthmore College Arabic program. Nine current DMES faculty members attended the November 20, 1998 emergency faculty at which Stofberg and Esfahanpur attacked and berated Attieh. For as long as the six of those nine who did not object to those groundless and meanspirited attacks which ended in shouting and tears remain in DMES, the Department cannot likely put the Middle Eastern Languages conflict behind itself or contribute with integrity to DMES as a home to academic debate and intellectual discourse.

Another casualty of the conflict, not unrelated to the silence of those six DMES colleagues and the attacks of those two colleagues at the November 1998 meeting, was academic debate and intellectual discourse. Audible at least peripherally when the likes of Eisig Silberschlag, Irving Mandelbaum, Richard Williams, Esther Fuchs, Fedwa Malti-Douglas, Yair Mazor, Walid Hamarneh, and Zilla Goodman officed at our Department, only a whisper remains there of academic debate and intellectual discourse, e.g., Yaron Shemer and Karen Grumberg. At a Fall 2006 faculty meeting, several DMES faculty participated in ridiculing banter about a registered graduate student, as if the faculty meeting were a gathering of bazaar merchants around a coffee shop table.

For a variety of reasons our department has never encouraged or had high-level shoptalk. First, its faculty really have less in common, as Arabic, Hebrew, Persian, and Turkish language experts, than do Middle East area studies specialists. Second, the Department has never seriously discussed issues of standards or had standards of any sort.

In December 1990, in response to a departmental request for faculty views on the future of our department, I penned a long memo to the Departmental Review Committee. In it I stated that our department had not succeeded because we hadn't seen to it that all faculty learn to teach effectively, teach sufficient numbers of courses to make degree programs viable, and to produce scholarly research. I also noted that the Liberal Arts Dean of the day had earlier implied in a letter to our Chair that some of the department's problems might relate to the number of UT graduates on its faculty. I opined that, although the proportion might not be much greater than at a majority of North

American research universities with Middle Eastern languages programs, which means that the number of UT Austin graduates per se on its faculty may not be an issue, these faculty colleagues received degrees mostly in departments other than Middle Eastern Languages/Studies. In other words, the issue relates to the nature of UT graduate training in Arabic, Hebrew, Persian, and Turkish. In addition, tenured departmental faculty trained in non-Middle Eastern Languages departments might attach less importance to research and critical writing in their own careers. The design of graduate degree programs by UT-trained faculty in Middle Eastern Languages has proved flawed and lacking in appropriate discipline and area studies components. Some UT-trained Middle Eastern Languages faculty members have often seemed oblivious to ongoing debates in their areas at major programs, e.g., discipline versus area studies or foreign language teaching methods.

Of course, much of the strife in Middle Eastern Studies may have came with the territory and unbridgeability of gaps between Persian and Hebrew, Turkish and Arabic, Jewish Studies and Islamic Studies, or Palestinian archaeology as "Biblical" Archaeology. I had to remind myself during the 1990s that I was an American-born minority of one in a department of Middle-East born faculty members, not counting the special case of Rabbi Stofberg.

Suspiciousness, defensiveness, and behind-the-scenes machinations of a handful of colleagues contributed to our collective failure as a department. And untenured faculty in Hebrew and Islamic Studies, wary of the presumed power of their peers, acquiesced and participated in anti-Attieh/Abboud actions, at least through votes and silence.

At the same time, Attieh and Abboud held firm views about foreign language teaching and exhibited little willingness to compromise, especially when pointed questions about their program revealed ignorance about Arabic and foreign language education on the part of questioners and critics. They perhaps asked themselves why they should have had to answer to colleagues who either didn't know Arabic or didn't know anything about foreign language teaching. Moreover, as university academics administering a language program which got good results and rave reviews from its best students, they literally had the academic right to do things behind closed classroom doors as they saw fit. Yet, events showed that their determination to design and administer our Arabic

Language program as they saw fit without a willingness to debate issues (which they had a right not to do) did not ultimately get the results they wanted. For that reason only, even in a department which singled out Arabic unfairly, Abboud and Attieh should have thought of ways to insulate themselves from anticipated attacks through less aggressive interaction with antagonists.

As for my role in this Middle Eastern Studies conflict, it is an open book, this book, in which as an autobiographical narrator I doubtless unknowingly and unintentionally communicate to readers aspects of my own person and personality perhaps unadmitted to myself. At the same time, I took the advice I would have given Abboud and Attieh in mid-1998 if I had known what lay ahead in the fall of 1998 and after, and insulated myself in academic ways. I taught more and wrote more than potential adversaries. I answered every one-paragraph message with two paragraphs and every one-page letter with a two-page letter. I avoided initiating contact with College administrators. Most importantly, I didn't take my work and talk about mosquitoes home.

With the Fall 2006 Semester, a new chapter in the story of UT's Middle Eastern Studies began. For the first-time ever, Arabic Studies, its largest program, was not seriously understaffed. DMES had hired a new Arabic lecturer in August 2005. A year later, Emory University's Mahmoud Al-Batal and his wife Kristen Brustad joined our Arabic faculty. Their participation in our department's language teaching programs means that scales therein will tilt toward current methodology. It might also mean that our department could, for the first time, develop a culture or identity. If it does, Al-Batal and Brustad could tip scales there too, toward a culture of foreign language teaching expertise and the culture of intensive language learning settings. Even if foreign language acquisition may not seem an intellectual enterprise on its own, a philosophy about its teaching and its learning can give a university language department academic and intellectual underpinnings, and a shared culture. Of course, those three DMES colleagues untrained in what they teach and those two colleagues who don't stay up to date or on target in their teaching may impede progress, at least slightly, or they may respond to the now mainstream new ways and get their acts together.

If DMES develops a new identity, it could emerge as a leading American university environment for teaching and learning Middle Eastern languages and training future university language teachers, at least in Arabic. Peter Abboud can continue to play a role in Modern Standard Arabic pedagogy and the teaching of Arabic grammar and syntax. Al-Batal and Brustad can foster an environment in which they can train and otherwise influence a next generation of Arabic pedagogues committed to teaching students to acquire speaking skills in a middle register of Arabic. Mohammad Mohammad can develop a program in Palestinian Arabic and perhaps teach Arabic Linguistics, which he was hired to do, but didn't because of understaffing in Arabic language during his first six years with us. DMES's Hebrew language faculty can continue to enrich the lives of their American Jewish students. Also, in a changed arena and atmosphere, my books, syllabi, and ideas on intermediate and advanced Persian language training may play a more visible role in academic Persian courses. If DMES supports its implementation, my new, multi-volume *Persian for America(ns)* Syllabus could help put our DMES Persian language program at the forefront of such university programs. Departmental scuttlebutt has it that the College of Liberal Arts does not plan to support a tenure-track position in Turkish in the future. If that's the case, second-tier represents the upper limit of departmental aspirations in the world of university Middle Eastern Languages enterprises.

In October each year, a representative from every department in Liberal Arts serves on a College Promotion Committee which reviews files of colleagues applying or recommended for promotion and passes along their recommendations to the Dean of the College. My second stint as a member of this committee began in October 2006. After twenty hours of reviewing more nearly forty files, I participated in ten or so hours of deliberations and votes. The experience provided exhilaration and verification of various sorts that UT is a player in the larger university scheme of things. The other eighteen departmental representatives had done as much, if not more, homework than I. They spoke from rich perspectives and with impressive knowledge. The files were equally exhilarating and spoke to the dedication which academics have to finding, marshalling, and explaining data, testing theories and hypotheses with data, and adding a brick or two to the edifice of the world of knowledge. With only two days to review the files, I had to keep looking at my watch to make certain I wasn't spending more than thirty minutes on each. In several cases, I started a book in a file and, forty minutes later, had to force myself to put it aside at the end of its second chapter.

The candidates had these books in their files: *The Tangled Roots of Feminism, Environmentalism, and Appalachian Literature*; *Learning for the Left: Children's Literature, Cold War, and Radical Politics in the United States*; *Non-Gaussian Merton-Black-Scholes Theory*; *Becoming African in America: Race and Nation in the English Black Atlantic, 1760–1830*; *Trust and Power: Consumers, The Modern Corporation, and the Making of the US Auto Market*; *Level of Empire: The International Gold Standard and the Crisis of Liberalism in Prewar Japan*; *The Smell of Smoke and Roses: Inhaling Modernity in 20th Century Bulgaria*; *The Orient Within: Muslim Minorities and the Westernization of Nationhood in Modern Bulgaria*; *Hooliganism: Crime, Culture, and Power in St. Petersburg, 1900–1914*; *African Intimacies: Race, Homosexuality, and Globalization*; *Reliving Karbala: Martyrdom in South Asian Memory*; *The Life and Death of Texas German: A Study in New-Dialect Formation, Language Contact, Language Change, and Language Death*; *The Labor of Identity: Nation and Narrative in Polish Fin de Siècle*; and *The Unity of Plato's Georgias: Rhetoric, Justice and the Philosophical Life*.

For weeks after Committee sessions, I peppered conversations with tidbits from cited files as if the knowledge in those tidbits related to my everyday appreciation of the world. For weeks also, I felt some discouragement in imagining how DMES monographs would look on a shelf alongside cited books. My Promotions Committee experience also had me thinking more about the religions of my colleagues, which seems a more significant factor in DMES life than in other Humanities departments.

Now, personal religiosity, if it relates more to spirituality than to dogma, can offer much to individuals and enrich families, groups, and societies. But, Religions? Those Religions in which females do not serve in the priestly caste or cannot achieve the highest clerical ranks set bad examples for humankind. Those Religions in which 'God' chooses a special people or speaks a specific human language or has offspring through human birth operate in the realms of Greek, Roman, Persian, and Egyptian mythology. Those Religions which count male circumcision as significant for reasons other than health or which hold female virginity as a religious ideal or which require celibacy of its priestly class belong to a realm other than the world in which many thinking 21st-century people live. Those Religions which declare procreation as the chief function of sexual intercourse or which call masturbation a sin or which forbid birth control fail to take into sensible account the real world in which real people live. Religions which enjoin doing good and forbidding evil-doing, which, in other words, ask their adherents to see to it that others do good and avoid evil, wrongly challenge individual freedoms and posit a wrong-minded authoritarian social force. Religions which do not see homosexuality as a natural, if minority, genetic disposition and, therefore, condemn it seem woefully backward. Religions which think that any of its prophets or representatives cannot err when speaking as prophets or leaders are alien to thoughtful experience of history and life.

I couldn't explain to Jack, Gracie, and Max now or ever how a Religion which sees adherents of other Religions as likely headed to damnation can serve humankind. Of course, for that matter, I couldn't explain damnation or salvation or hell or heaven to them either, even at their "Once upon a Time" bedtime book-party sessions. As I told Elizabeth when she was small, I can tell them only that some people believe in God and talk to, or pray to, or think about God, and some people don't.

After twenty-four days in Tehran and Mashhad, Sorayya returned home on November 17 (2006). She reported that life is good there for visitors with family and friends there and for people there who have a home of their own and are apolitical. Traffic, she says, impedes everything in Tehran to the point where you resign yourself to the fact that you can get only one thing or errand done in the morning and one in the afternoon. At the same time, she thinks that talk by Iranians outside of Iran about how bad things are in Iran and about impending upheaval in Iran is wishful thinking. About reaction in Iran to the American elections in early November, she says that people like us there watch CNN News, but that politics, domestic and international, don't figure in the lives of people like us there. People are busy living and trying to enjoy living.

As for the reaction to the November 2006 American elections at 3404 Perry Lane, in Sorayya's absence, I opened a celebratory bottle of Amusant 2001 Cabernet for dinner and sipped wine blissfully until hearing the projected senatorial race result in Virginia which put a ribbon on America's gift to people like me. And, leading the new day in politics—although I'm not forgetting the artificiality of America's two-party system and the lack of forthrightness and enunciation of philosophy on the part of politicians in both parties—is a woman from Baltimore! I went to bed that night reveling in another facet of life's symmetry.

In early December, I prepared copies of a final draft of *From Classroom to Courtroom* to pass around for feedback. I gave copies to Peter Abboud, Aman Attieh, Avraham Zilkha, and Yaron Shemer. I sent a copy to Frank Sheeran for professional editing. I had earlier made copies of a partial draft manuscript available to DMES full professors and offered a copy to DMES administrators. I also sent a copy to Mary Jo Wilson at UT's Office of Legal Affairs with this note:

> You may recall the "Attieh v. UT" litigation several years back, my submission to your office of documents in anticipation of a possible court trial, my deposition in September 2002, and our exchange of communications concerning a letter mistakenly put in my personnel file around that time. I've written a book about the whole affair. Enclosed find an almost final draft manuscript of the book. "A Note to Reviewers" on the page facing the first page of text in the manuscript states why I'm sending you a copy before I make final revisions and send the manuscript to the publisher. The gist of the narrative doesn't hinge on any specific asserted fact or piece of information or document. That means that I'll be comfortable deleting or changing specific statements in the book which your office thinks are problematic in legal terms.

Addressing me as "Dr. Hillman" [sic], Wilson responded thusly:

> I am returning the manuscript you have written concerning the Aman Attieh litigation to you unread. I do so because The University does not assert any interests in scholarly or literary works authored by its faculty. . . Neither I nor any attorney in the University's Office of Legal Affairs can advise you as to whether specific statements in your book might be problematic in legal terms. Fact-checking or otherwise vetting your manuscript for statements that could be considered libelous are tasks that your publisher, or your personal attorney, will need to undertake on your behalf.

It didn't surprise me that the Office of Legal Affairs wouldn't join the conversation in *From Classroom to Courtroom*, although I'd treat its Director to dinner at Fonda San Miguel to hear their reaction to my characterization of their initiation of that behind-the-scenes investigation of me in 2000 and their apparent failure to include a relevant letter in materials made available to Attieh's attorney.

On March 9 (2007), Sorayya and I drove to Houston for the annual dinner and scholarship presentation of the Society of Iranian-American Women for Education. SIAWE had announced it as "black tie optional," but only the Junior League's bartenders, waiters, and I showed up in tuxedos! SIAWE had asked me to give a short talk on higher education after dinner. Part of it went as follows.

> Since the 1980s, more than half of the students in my classes at The University of Texas have been Iranian and Iranian-American. None of these students has majored in Persian. They've majored in Biology, Business, Chemistry, Engineering, Mathematics, Political Science, Psychology, Sociology, and the like. I generally hold my Persian courses late in the day when those students will not have any scheduling conflicts with more important courses. Parenthetically, among such Iranian-American students from the 1980s and 1990s are enough attorneys in Texas today to get me out of any problem which my talking and writing might get me into and enough sorts of health professionals to take care of whatever sorts of infirmity older age might have in store for me and, of course, enough financial advisers to advise me, albeit more than 30 years late, against a career in teaching Persian!
>
> Why these Iranian-American students take my classes has to do with what gives true meaning to the word 'education' in the phrase 'higher education'. For we all have met lots of people with college, university, and professional degrees who seemed lacking in education. But not most of my Iranian-American students, upwards of 200 of them since the early 1980s, who add Persian language and literature to already full schedules and the stress of impending LSAT, GRE, MDCAT, or other examinations, or interviews with companies.
>
> These students, mostly encouraged and sometimes bribed or threatened by their parents, know that education doesn't end with subject matter expertise, that the educated adult American in today's world needs a foreign language, needs to appreciate more than one culture, needs to have a taste for the arts, and especially needs a sense of his or her cultural heritage in our multicultural world.
>
> Now, it may be that Iranian-American parents, who arguably make up the best-educated group of immigrants to this country ever, would naturally have such a view about this sort of education as part of higher education. But there's more to it than that. They grew up recognizing that their Iranian history, their national language and the literature in that Persian language, and their cultural traditions defined them as individuals as much as the

town or city they were from or the formal academic training they had. After they came to this country, they realized that their cultural heritage was helping them adjust to life here and that the best sort of life here was a multicultural life in which American and Iranian values thrive together, except of course in the area of cuisine, where American food obviously can't compare with Iranian food!

Whether or not these Iranian-American parents have thought about their culture self-consciously in terms such as mine, their paternal and maternal instincts have led them to encourage their children to have the same exciting and perhaps necessary duality of perspectives in our twenty-first century world.

For those of you unfamiliar with Iranian culture, let me add an observation that may suggest how special it is for people part of it. In Iranian life today, poetry, lyric poetry, has greater significance as entertainment than sports or music. Turn to any Iranian-American at your table and ask him or her to name five or ten Persian poets who lived between the 10th and 14th centuries. You'll get answers. Ask that person to recite part of his or her favorite poem. You'll hear a poem. You can also likely hear a poem or two which the person you ask has composed.

One of the words in Persian denoting 'education' is *farháng*, which also denotes 'culture'. The educated individual, the person with *farháng*, is *bafarháng* or, as that word also denotes, 'cultured' or 'civilized'. Another Persian word *farhikhté* significantly denotes both 'university-educated' and 'cultured'.

Iranian-American students come to my classes knowing that Persian poetry and the Persian language have special importance for their parents and in their parents' culture. I hope they leave those classes thinking that they'll visit Persian poems, short stories, and novels in the future, that they'll preserve their Persian language heritage, and that they'll maintain Iranian cultural traditions as part of their American identity. When they do that, they guarantee that they'll have the most important sort of education in their higher education.

Tonight, we're celebrating the awarding of scholarships to students ready to begin another year of higher education with SIAWE scholarship support. Congratulations to those students. The celebration is taking place in the middle of March, just eleven days before the vernal equinox, the exact beginning of spring, which occasion is not unrelated to the 'education' part of higher education.

In Iran, over 2,500 years ago, construction began on a monumental complex of platformed buildings at Persepolis, a half-hour's drive north of today's city of Shiraz. The most important remains today from the Achaemenid Empire, this site, called Tákht-e Jamshíd in Persian, was not a political capital and wasn't even open all year round. It was a Persian memorial to the season of spring, when nature on the Iranian plateau approaches the ideal. People from all over the Persian Empire visited it at the beginning of spring every year to pay their respects to spring and its promise and beauty and the spiritual force behind spring.

Iranians have been doing the same thing ever since, here in Houston and around the world. Again, I ask any among us without an Iranian heritage to imagine what it must be like for a group of people to have cultural traditions 2,500 years old. As most of us know, this coming Tuesday evening, Iranian-Americans will gather in small and larger groups wherever they are in the world–in Austin hundreds of people will gather at Zilker Park Clubhouse–to say goodbye to winter and say hello to spring. They'll light small fires and jump over them, asking the fire to take winter's yellow sallowness from them and instill in them spring's redness. Before that evening, spring housecleaning will have taken place, and perhaps new clothes bought. At the moment of the vernal equinox, for which people usually stay up if it occurs in the middle of the night, family members will embrace one another and exchange New Year's greetings. The dishes served at the New Year's Eve dinner have traditions behind them older than American Thanksgiving dinner fare.

During the first days of the new year, people visit family and friends. On the 13th day of the new year, people leave their homes for an excursion in the country or a picnic, taking with them greens they've grown in their homes from before the new year, greens which have absorbed the old year's stale air. They throw those greens away. They return home with the fresh air and mood of spring, ready to face the future with fresh enthusiasm.

Tonight's SIAWE scholarship recipients signal the promise of the Iranian New Year, as they prepare to embark on new spring years in their lives in higher education. And if they appreciate the cultural heritage which the Iranian New Year presents and represents, respect for nature and its rhythms, the dedication to fresh starts and renewal–would not America be the better for it if these values permeated life everywhere in this country?–, and if these students perpetuate the Iranian cultural heritage through their own participation in it, and if they follow in the footsteps of students named Azimpoor, Bagherpour, Geranmayeh, Jafarnia, and Raja'i, among many others, the Society of Iranian-American Women for Education can rest assured that their 2007 scholarship recipients will emerge years hence from higher education with real education.

✍ Journal Entry, March 20, BWI Airport, Baltimore. Saturday evening, a Friday snowstorm blanketing the Gettysburg–Fairfield–Carroll Valley area with eight luxurious inches of snow, Jim and I ate Irish stew, apple pie, and such at Fairfield Inn–I was wearing my green German beer-mug tie–and listened to Irish music. The previous week, UT's Spring Break, found me back at University of Baltimore for a seminar on Religion in Iran, to which I had brought Navid Hayeri from Austin to team-teach (and give me afternoons off). After class on Monday, I drove to Liberty Mountain an hour north of Baltimore, just across the border in Pennsylvania, for four hours of spring skiing, hard work in the soft snow. Then, the March snowstorm hit on Friday, which made the weekend Jim and I spent in Gettysburg perfect for skiing.

My weekday meetings at Dunwoody were exhilarating. The press has given me a green light on *Persian Conversation(s)*, *Persian Grammar and Verbs*, and the already finished and about-to-go-to-press *Persian Listening*. That will realize my dream of a comprehensive four-skills Persian syllabus, which I first envisioned at the Peace Corps office in Tehran more than thirty years ago. ✍

Elizabeth, Jack, Gracie, and Max arrived in Austin on March 20, several hours before I did. When I walked into the house, the whirl-wind they usually bring to furniture and things had taken place. We played every day in "Jack's Woods" above the cliff behind the house. We ate at every restaurant in town with a playscape. Even Max loved the road company production of *The Lion King* which we saw a day before they ended their one-week visit. Elizabeth much enjoyed the Iranian New Year celebration at the Radisson on the 24th, an event which Sorayya and her Society for Iranian-American Women in Austin associates host every year. This time the featured attraction for the five hundred or more guests was Kia, formally with The Boyz, one of whose songs is the subject of a lesson in *Persian Listening*.

Sorayya and I drove to Dallas on April 9 for a Forough Farrokhzad commemoration at a local Iranian cultural society's monthly meeting at the Southfork Hotel. Sorayya criticizes my presentations at such gatherings, which I usually write out ahead of time, as being academic and incomprehensible. So this time I prepared nothing beyond photo-copies of texts of five or six poems by Hafez, Nima Yushij, and Forugh Farrokhzad. In the middle of the presentation, in which I was showing that Farrokhzad's modernity and individuality made it unnecessary for her to make use of analogues or correlatives in communicating personal experience, I compared her very realistic and apparently or potentially autobiographical descriptive lyrics to Nima Yushij's apparently auto-biographical lyrics in which he often chooses an object or phenomenon in nature rather than realistic autobiographic and personal detail to communicate his poetic speaker's state of mind to readers. I compared Farrokhzad as well to Hafez. I had chosen Nima Yushij and Hafez as foils because Farrokhzad often stated that those two poets had inspired her more than any other poets. In explicating the Hafezian ghazal I had chosen for this purpose, I tried to demonstrate that his objective correlatives were literary and linguistic, which is to say he chooses images, metaphors, allusions, and subjects and language register from a set repertoire particular to medieval Persian royal courts. At this point in my talk, although I didn't say as much to the audience, something came to me that would never have come to me had I prepared a lecture for the occasion. It dawned on me that a key to the critical appreciation of Hedayat's *The Blind Owl* lay in the appreciation of the narrator's use of cultural artifacts: a vase, a miniature painting, other objects, and two scenes, as objective correlatives which make possible reader experience of the points to Hedayat's lyrical narrative despite its unreliable narrator and the arguable absence of definable thematic meaning. Now, after years of looking at my manuscript of '*The Blind Owl' as Narrative* and not knowing why I hesitated to send it to a publisher, I had the final piece of what had been a puzzle with respect to its *sui generis* lyrical narrative. After rewriting the book's last chapter, I sent the manuscript to a publisher on the same day I sent Form 4868 to IRS to get an extension for filing 2006 taxes.

Sorayya flew to Phoenix on April 11 for a two-week visit with Elizabeth *et famille*. I joined her on April 20 for three days. Then back to Austin to wrap up second-year Persian and Omar Khayyam classes and prepare for another seminar at University of Baltimore, this time on Iranian Culture.

Sorayya and I left Austin on Cinco de Mayo for ten days on the East Coast. First came a birthday seafood dinner with Jim and George M and Cathie at Inner Harbor in Baltimore. Then five days of seminar presentations, I in the morning and Ramin Sarraf in the afternoon. Most afternoons, I practiced golf at Pine Ridge and UBaltimore's Mount Washington driving ranges. We had good meals at 'b' on Bolton Hill and Helmand and The Belvedere Owl Bar in Mt. Vernon. We hosted the Iranian Culture Seminar participants to House of Kabob for a buffet lunch. Early Friday afternoon, Sorayya and I took a train to New York City, deposited our bags at Hotel Pennsylvania, and hit the streets. We walked to Soho, dined at Balthazar's, and walked leisurely back to the hotel. On Saturday, we walked to and from the Metropolitan Museum of Art, where we spent a couple of hours looking at the Venice and Islam exhibit and paying respects to old favorites in the Modern Painting wing. Afterwards, I bought six owl figurines crafted by Theo Ronan, who has to get to MMA by 4:30 am to find a good spot nearby to display his animal figurines. Saturday evening, we again chose to walk to dinner, this time to Gotham Bar and Grill in Greenwich Village. Because it was raining when we emerged from the restaurant near midnight, we then took our one and only taxicab ride of the weekend. On Sunday, we shopped at Bloomingdale's, another invigorating walk from our hotel, and then walked to Seventh Avenue to have Mother's Day lunch at Redeye Grill. From there, we walked down to August Wilson Theatre to see a matinee performance of *Jersey Boys*, a show as good as its hype. We hummed tunes from it on the train late Sunday evening back to Baltimore.

Before the end of the Spring 2007 semester and our May trip East, DMES decided on two new tenure-track faculty positions: a Hebrew linguist and a second Arabic literature specialist. DMES faculty at large would not learn about the new positions until reading postings about them months later. Both job announcements featured this sentence which memory of departmental history likely inspired: "The Department places a high premium on collegiality and maintaining a diverse and hospitable working environment."

Language faculty would also later learn that DMES had decided that senior faculty in Arabic and Persian should no longer teach lower-division language courses, henceforth the responsibility of lecturers assisted by graduate student teaching assistants. In the light of the rationalizations by the College of Liberal Arts in the 1998–2002 years for its actions against Attieh and Abboud, new DMES policies raised several sets of DMES faculty eyebrows.

A departmental Persian Search Committee met on May 8, three days after Sorayya and I flew East, to choose someone to join DMES as a Persian Lecturer for 2007–2008. At the Committee's request, I submitted a ranking of seven of eleven applicants. I didn't rank four applicants whose files didn't fulfill advertised requirements for the position. The Committee voted to short-list one of those four and not to include two of the most qualified and most experienced candidates.

On May 23, the DMES Chair, a language specialist in Hebrew, sent me an e-message, which included these statements:

> I would like to outline in this message my plans for the near future as far as the Persian program is concerned. . . . The dynamics within the Persian program will change dramatically with the addition of a lecturer next fall, and with what I hope to see as a greater role for . . . [two Persian-speaking

Islamic Studies colleagues] in the program. During the summer of 2007, I would like to achieve the following: (1) A thorough review of the goals of the undergraduate program and the way in which it serves majors and non-majors alike. In particular I would like us to focus on the role of proficiency-based instruction in first-, second-, and third-year Persian classes and the instructional materials used in these classes. (2) A discussion on broader course offerings at the upper-division and graduate levels. (3) A review of TA/AI training and supervision practices. (4) A review of the graduate degree plans and their implementation in the training of current and future students. (5) A discussion on the role of Tajiki in our program. . . .I have asked. . . .[an Arabic Studies colleague]. . .to spearhead the evaluation and planning efforts, and he has graciously agreed to do so. . . . I request, then, that you stay in touch with him during the summer, and respond to his questions and requests in a timely and efficient manner.

In late May, I flew East again for a college reunion, the now annual Persepolis Golf Tournament with George M and George S, a dinner at House of Kabob after, and a weekend at Cape May with Hammie, back from China. On June 22, Sorayya and I celebrated our 40 years together, while Jack was celebrating his sixth birthday in Scottsdale. On July 5, we flew to San Diego for a week at the beach with Jack, Gracie, and Max on Coronado Island. Five days later, I tore a calf muscle playing tennis with Elizabeth and a friend and began a month of hobbling with a cane. We flew to Baltimore again on July 23, Sorayya off to Göttingen and Prague for three weeks and I to Maine.

✍ Journal entry, August 12, Holiday Inn Express, Frackville, Pennsylvania. Heading north, when I pull into the Maine Information Center at Kittery, I feel a sudden calm, not unlike what I feel when I drive across the canal bridge into Cape May and like I feel in early July crossing the bridge from San Diego into Coronado Island. At Kittery, I got my new fishing license, two new maps, and listened to the Maine accents of the information booth people. A woman asked a staff person: "Do you know if there's an ATM around here?" With a pleasant smile on her face, the Mainer answered: "Yes, I do. And, no, there isn't!" Actually, my Maine doesn't begin at Kittery or anywhere on the Maine Turnpike until Augusta, when I turn off onto Route 202. Even then, I'm still waiting for my Maine, as I drive past businesses that could be anywhere and through two traffic circles, and across Kennebec River bridge. The sign that then reads Route 3 and Route 202 says to me, "You're home." At midday on July 25, that's where I was. Two hundred years ago, my Bartlett ancesters and then my Craig ancestors took basically the same route, from Winthrop, Readfield, and Mt. Vernon, on the west side of Augusta, to Searsmont, for them a trail of spotted trees, for me a comfortable winding ribbon of asphalt through and around green hills and past Togus Pond, Threemile Pond, China Lake, Sheepscot Pond, and then Lake St. George and the Route 173 turn-off to Liberty Village. I had wanted on this trip to walk from Readfield and Mt. Vernon to Searsmont as part of my getting into the ancient history part of *To and From a Village in Maine*. But my bad left leg wouldn't let me do that. In fact, for the first week in Waldo County, I couldn't negotiate river banks at two of my favorite fishing holes. The road wound down through Liberty Village and around and down and past South Montville, and straightened out for the last miles down Woodmans Mill Road to Searsmont Villege and two weeks of living simultaneously in 2007 and, to pick a childhood summer, 1952. I fished in Searsmont's Anderson Stream and St. George's River, as I've done off and on for more than half a century. I paid almost daily visits to Riverside and Oak Grove Cemeteries there and had one-sided conversations with seven generations of forebears there. Every day that the Searsmont Historical Society was open, I visited with Joyce Withee there and finished the footnotes for *Gold Rush Letters from Maine, 1853–1867*, a little book of fifty pages and the texts of eighteen letters which my great granduncle Charles Augustus Craig wrote home to Searsmont from California where he went to make his big "pile" and from where he never came home again.

From my room at Duckrap Motel on Route 1 near Lincolnville Beach, I set out on country roads most days in my aptly named Jeep Liberty SUV, without a destination, stopping at village general stores for a coffee-flavored milk or a veggie submarine sandwich. I visited Readfield three times, the second time with Jim, who drove up from Baltimore to join me for a week.

To and From a Village in Maine needs another summer to get finished, and the walk from Readfield to Searsmont. But I've learned its lessons already, mostly from this trip which will end in Baltimore tomorrow after another two hours of driving the scenic route south. What I know about the difficult lives of most of the Craigs, Bartletts, Keatings, and others in Readfield and Searsmont over the past two hundred and fifty years makes what I spend time writing about, in this journal and in academic articles and books and in *From Classroom to Courtroom*, self-indulgent. Ditto for almost all of the events and statements in *From Classroom to Courtroom*, which has suddenly come to mind for the first time after a summer of travel and thoughts about travel and family. ✍

Sorayya and I flew back to Austin on August 20. Nothing had come of those firm DMES plans for summer work on the Persian language program. Because two prospective Persian lecturers turned down DMES offers, DMES will open another search for a lecturer to join us in 2008–2009. Proficiency-based instruction will likely take longer than that to begin playing a role in our First-year Persian course. And if late Spring 2007 departmental words and deeds accurately reflect DMES's style of doing business, old MELC/DMES administrative ways are alive and well in our department.

Nevertheless, tomorrow (August 30), I'll return to WMB 5.146 and to—I think this, want to think this, at the beginning of every academic year—a better Department of Middle Eastern Studies, a department with at least a strong minority group commitment to good language teaching. If it isn't, no matter, the stakes remain as low as ever outside of classrooms. Moreover, nothing can diminish the feeling I get the first day of school every term, from Cathedral School in Baltimore in the late 1940s to Texas State in the mid-1990s. The same will doubtless hold true for The University of Texas at Austin tomorrow.

I'll back out of the driveway, turn down Perry Lane, see The Tower in the distance, and smilingly visualize the first session of Sa'di's *Golestan*, for which nearly twenty students have registered. Little that people call work can better that feeling, except for how it feels when a class that has gone well has just ended. What takes place between the beginning and end of classes sometimes finds me in a state of absorption, aware of what I'm doing but unaware that time is keeping score.

Even without the drive to and from my building almost in the shadows of The Tower and without what transpires in classrooms nearby, similar feelings color life at 3404 Perry Lane, where Sorayya, who was born in Mashhad and whose mother hailed from Ashkabad (Turkmenistan), has spent more than half of her life. We dance there to unspoken lyrics and silent rhythms, and looking up from books at each other with sudden smiles. A road bicycle and a hybrid bicycle used to particular Austin roads and paths hang at the ready in the garage. A yellow kayak and a green kayak used to particular Town Lake and Lake Austin shores and coves hang dry and thirsty from hooks on the garage's outside back wall. My running shoes and cross-trainers, used to the Murchison Junior High School track and Town Lake's hike and bike trail, are itching for feet. My hiking boots and poles point to new adventures. Then, there are tennis shoes and rackets used to courts all over town. And tents and coolers, and fishing poles, and golf clubs. Skis, ski boots and ski poles take the edge off hot, humid days with their memories of ski seasons past and the promise of runs to come. A dozen back packs. A dozen baseball caps. Books too numerous to read again and some never read. Partial manuscripts of books too numerous ever to finish writing. Thousands of pictures, images, and memories of Eliza's years with us before she left for college and her own life. The day we bought the house, she and I brought sleeping bags to it and spent the night, as if we worried that, otherwise, a thief might come and take the house away.

When we first arrived in Austin, I described it for friends in Baltimore and Chicago as a lotus-eater land, comfort zones everywhere. That description then had criticism in it. Travel elsewhere since has me more appreciative of Austin's easy life, almost to the point of forgetting its chief drawback: its distance from many things (oceans, mountains, urban[e] culture, Broadway, museums, and academic bookstores). There is no necessarily inviting far away when one joins in the rhythm of daily life. In Austin we have our Iranian-American social life, six or seven restaurants we go back to, shopping for everything within a ten-minute drive, the privacy of our Perry Lane nook with its deer and raccoons, two families of cardinals, hummingbirds which dive toward the feeders under eaves unannounced in May and return every day for months, lizards that somehow occasionally find their way into the house, and a solitary owl we hear at night but can't find in the daylight. Owls haven't taken up residence in the two owl shacks I nailed onto trees out back this past winter. The morning bird serenade has its music still, thirty years later. There is also Sorayya's grand kitchen, and my owl collection. Mother's watercolor paintings line both walls in our hall gallery leading to the Hillmann Realty/Persepolis Institute office. Books there are waiting to get written. Journal volumes have still blank pages. A Sony Vaio laptop computer in the kitchen, an e-MAC desktop and MAC PowerBook G4 Laptop computer in the second living room, and MacBook laptop and HP desktop computers in the office offer instantaneous connections to wherever and whatever we momentarily are curious about and are ready to produce letters and memos and e-messages. I can fill up two pages of a letter as quickly as my fingers can keyboard the words, and enjoy the writing, whatever the subject, as much as anything. From the second living room and its Martha Stewart furniture bought partly in unspoken response to the System's attempted scarlet lettering of her, we can see our three levels of decks, for different moments, moods, and meals, and beyond the uppermost, Jack's Woods.

Life is better than good. If only it could stay that way. Or, if only we could find a 'Little Gidding' to "to arrive where we started / And know the place for the first time," and move beyond sensible Khayyamic truth, as Eliot did. Of course, Khayyam's truth may have to do: "Darling–Let's sit with flowers, and drink our wine / Where blooms will bloom from your dust and mine."

Jack and Max at the beach. Coronado Island, July 2007

About the Author

Michael Craig Hillmann has published more than a hundred articles on literature and culture and over twenty books, among them *Persian Carpets* (1984), *A Lonely Woman: Forugh Farrokhzad and Her Poetry* (1987), *Iranian Culture: A Persianist View* (1990, 1992), *From Durham to Tehran* (1991), *Reading Iran Reading Iranians: Second Edition Revised* (2002), *Tajiki Textbook and Reader: Second Edition* (2003), and *From Classroom to Courtroom* (2007).

In the early 1970s, Hillmann served as Language and Cultural Affairs Officer for the American Peace Corps in Tehran. In 1974, he joined the faculty at The University of Texas, where he teaches Persian language and literature and the occasional English literature course. In 1977 he founded Persepolis Institute, an Austin-based group of Persian specialists offering non-academic language services to government and business. In 1989 and 1991, Hillmann conducted research in Tehran. In 1993-1994 he served as Durant Chair of Humanities at St. Peter's College in Jersey City. In 1996, Hillmann was the only American Persian Studies academic to participate in the First International Congress of Persian Professors at Tehran University. In the fall of 1997 Hillmann was Visiting Scholar at Institut d'études Iraniennes de l'Université de la Sorbonne Nouvelle in Paris. In 2004, Hillmann and a group of Persepolis Institute colleagues began work on a Persian-English *Dictionary of Newer Persian Words* and a series of Persian textbooks, among them *Persian Listening, Persian Grammar and Verbs*, and *Persian Conversation(s)*.

From Classroom to Courtroom is the second volume in an autobiographical trilogy. The first was *From Durham to Tehran*, on the subject of research trips to Durham (UK) and Tehran, and Persian Studies. The third is *To and From a Village in Maine* (2009), on the subject of forebears of the author who settled in Readfield, Maine, before the American Revolution.

Michael Hillmann and his wife Sorayya live in Austin. Their only child, Elizabeth Craig Hillmann Garrett, lives with her husband Jeff(rey) Garrett and their three children, John Craig, Catherine Grace, and James Maximilian, in Scottsdale, Arizona.

Printed in the United States
103993LV00004B/178-189/A

9 781434 350640